WILDLIFE AND THE PUBLIC INTEREST

WILDLIFE AND THE PUBLIC INTEREST

Nonprofit Organizations and Federal Wildlife Policy

JAMES A. TOBER

PRAEGER

New York
Westport, Connecticut
London

Library of Congress Cataloging-in-Publication Data

Tober, James A., 1947–
  Wildlife and the public interest : nonprofit organizations and
  federal wildlife policy / James A. Tober.
    p. cm.
    Bibliography: p.
    Includes index.
    ISBN 0-275-92581-1 (alk. paper)
      1. Wildlife conservation—Government policy—United States.
    2. Wildlife conservation—United States—Societies, etc.
    3. Environmental policy—United States. 4. Environmental policy—
United States—Societies, etc. I. Title.
QL84.2.T62 1989
333.95'16'0973—dc19   88–19045

Library of Congress Catalog Card Number: 88–19045
ISBN: 0-275-92581-1

First published in 1989

Praeger Publishers, One Madison Avenue, New York, NY 10010
A division of Greenwood Press, Inc.

Printed in the United States of America

The paper used in this book complies with the Permanent
Paper Standard issued by the National Information Standards
Organization (Z39.48—1984).

10 9 8 7 6 5 4 3 2 1

Contents

Tables

Preface

Of the millions of species with which we share this earth, we have named only a small portion. Most of us are familiar with only the most minute fraction of these, and we care deeply about many fewer still. Yet the policies that affect the well-being of species, even those unnamed, occupy significant space in our collective decision-making structure. Some species or groups of species, such as the white-tailed deer or whales, occupy rather permanent places on the agenda; others, such as the snail darter or Furbish lousewort, have occupied transitory ones. This book is a study of collective decision making as it concerns wildlife, primarily in the United States. Its major perspectives delineate its purposes more clearly.

First, this is very much an industry study; it examines the structure, conduct, and performance of the wildlife industry, by which I mean the constellation of organizations and individuals that institutionalize the relationships between humans and wild animals. This is a complex industry; the organizations within it, as well as the objects of their attention, are diverse and numerous. It is an industry substantially influenced by the interests, passions, and deeply held beliefs of millions of people—of elected and appointed officials, of political activists, sport hunters and birdwatchers, scientists, and philosophers. Yet despite this diversity there is a fundamental coherence that recommends a comprehensive approach. A primary purpose of this inquiry is to explore the nature of this industry with a view toward understanding existing patterns of interaction with wildlife and some of the policy choices that face us.

Cross-cutting this perspective is a special focus on the nonprofit organization. This is particularly appropriate for wildlife since, historically and presently, nonprofit organizations have dominated large segments of the industry; it is appropriate as well because of the growing interest in this "third" sector as an important complement to the more thoroughly studied governmental and proprietary sectors. A second purpose, then, is to highlight the role of the nonprofit sector within a particular industry. The contention here is that this can be accomplished only through an industry study. Recitation of nonprofit organization accomplishments in isolation cannot account for alternative uses of the resources employed therein nor for the organizational spillovers beyond the nonprofit realm. Cooperative ventures among organizations of different types are common. Competition among them may promote efficiency and innovation but risks redundancy. These interorganizational features are critical to an understanding of nonprofit organizations, and they are commonly overlooked in third-sector studies.

The initial research for this book was conducted in the spring of 1980, while I was on leave from Marlboro College and in residence at the Program on Non-Profit Organizations of the Institution for Social and Policy Studies at Yale University. Supplementary research was conducted in the fall of 1986, during which time I enjoyed a Marlboro sabbatical and had the good fortune to renew my affiliation with the program. I am grateful for this support from Marlboro and from the program and its directors John G. Simon (1980) and Paul J. DiMaggio (1986). I benefited enormously throughout the development of this work and from discussions with and comments from Marlboro colleagues, program participants, and others, including Richard Cole, Paul DiMaggio, Robert Engel, David Forsythe, Charles H. W. Foster, Castle Freeman, Mary-Michelle Hirschoff, Michael Krashinsky, Richard Murnane, and Nancy Shestack. I owe special appreciation to Stephen R. Kellert, Yale School of Forestry and Environmental Studies, and Robert Cameron Mitchell, Resources for the Future, who generously shared with me their work in progress and directed me to the pertinent work of others.

Among the important research materials gathered is a set of interviews, conducted in the spring of 1980 and fall of 1986, with individuals representing a wide range of nonprofit organizations and government offices. These individuals were, without exception, generous in sharing their time and knowledge. The dedication and enthusiasm with which they pursue their work accounts in large measure for the vitality of the wildlife issue area described herein. Upon reading portions of earlier drafts, several of these individuals supplied additional information and comment, and they were hugely tolerant of my persistent follow-up questions. The reader may assume that unattributed remarks throughout are drawn from these interviews and subsequent conversations.

A sketch of the central ideas of this book was presented to Independent Sector's National Conference on Philanthropy, October 1980. A midterm version appeared in January 1984 as a working paper of the Program on Non-Profit Organizations. The present version was in large measure made possible by the unflagging support of my wife, Felicia, who read and commented on several drafts, and of our children, Joanna and Daniel, who excused my absence on too many occasions and who are at least as pleased as I that it is complete at last.

WILDLIFE AND THE PUBLIC INTEREST

1

Dimensions of Wildlife Policy

We are now in the midst of a second great debate over the allocation of property rights in wildlife. The first debate, entered into with the creation of Colonial deer seasons and wolf bounties, was not fully engaged until the final third of the nineteenth century, when sportsmen, naturalists, and humanitarians organized to challenge the free reign of frontiersmen and market hunters. This debate was resolved in part with the recognition that wildlife was the property of the several states, held in trust for their citizens. By the early twentieth century this broad notion had been institutionalized in state fish and game agencies, staffed by scientific managers and funded by fishing and hunting license fees and, later, by taxes on sporting arms and ammunition. While in theory state property rights applied to all wildlife, from the "mighty" bull elk to the "lowly" spiny river snail, in fact concern was limited almost entirely to game and fur bearers, managed to encourage a sustained harvest, and to predators and pests, managed to minimize their impact on the human economy. Other animals species, and all wild plants, remained essentially free goods, except as landowners, both public and private, restricted entry to trespassers.

The second debate, entered into with the rise of wildlife protection groups in the late nineteenth century but not fully engaged until the midtwentieth century, questions this limited coverage and considers the merits of expanding the range of species for which property rights might be recognized. These groups assert that nonconsumptive users of wildlife derive benefits equally legitimate to those derived by consumptive users, but that even consumptive users, given more sophisticated ecological understanding, ultimately would be better served by a more restrictive assignment of property rights. For instance, "insignificant" species may lead the way to important advances in the treatment of human disease or may serve as the "canary in the miner's cage," warning self-interested humans of impending ecological disaster.

The first debate was not characterized by any significant attempt to weigh wildlife benefits against benefits derived from other uses of the resources on which wildlife might depend. Indeed, implicit in this debate was the subservience of wildlife to other resource demands— for farm and ranch lands, timber, mining, and cities and towns. The fate of the millions of bison migrating across the Great Plains or of the billions of passenger pigeons flocking throughout the eastern hardwood forests was more or less irrelevant to the individual quests for private income in an era of resource abundance and rapid economic growth. A feature of the second debate is the threat to other resource claims that the exercise of property rights in wildlife might entail. Thus, property rights in coyote may threaten property rights in sheep, and property rights in snail darters may threaten rights to flood control or recreation. The first debate established the science of wildlife management and the role of technical expertise in wildlife policy; the second debate questions the dominance of that perspective and advocates broader notions of citizen participation and collective decision making.

The first debate led to the establishment of state-level management and to the development of expertise and vested interests in the fish and game commissions. Participants in the second debate have sought to create a countervailing power base at the federal level. Federal access also offers, through the treaty-making power, the opportunity to extend property claims beyond national boundaries. Just as residents of one state have an interest in the management of migratory waterfowl temporarily residing in another state, so it is between nations. International agreements may confer upon the federal government management authority that otherwise would remain with the states. Many current policy controversies focus precisely on the boundaries that separate state from federal jurisdiction. Although this dispute finds ample fuel within the wildlife policy arena, the "sagebrush rebellion," challenging federal control over huge expanses of western lands, reminds us that its scope extends far beyond.

Several strands of the second debate suggest third and subsequent debates. One strand reexamines Native American claims to wildlife and is related to a growing interest, worldwide, in the preservation of traditional cultures and their natural environments, both of which are threatened by economic growth and development. Another addresses property rights in new forms of life created in the laboratory through genetic engineering. A third challenges the very notion of assigning property rights in animals, wild or domestic, and asserts the principle of animal rights. Each of these strands, given the current strength of organizational interests, is likely to direct the evolution of the debate in a significant way.

Throughout these debates, the nonprofit, voluntary organization has been the dominant organizational form for seeking adjustment in the structure of property rights in wildlife. Nineteenth-century sportsmen's clubs worked for the passage of protective legislation, and they enforced that legislation until they could prevail upon the states to issue licenses and fund public wardens.[1] These organizations and their successors have continued to speak for sport hunters and other consumptive users of wildlife. A host of other groups, many of which predate by decades the environmental movement of the 1960s and 1970s, now prevail upon state and federal governments to move in new regulatory directions. These organizations and their constituencies lobby, testify, sue, and demonstrate, but they are not limited to actions so overtly political. They may engage in broad educational and scientific activities that inform the debate and contribute to the setting of agendas, and they may seek opportunities, within the existing structure of property rights, to advance organizational goals for wildlife, as through the breeding of endangered species or the acquisition of critical habitat.

This book examines the contemporary role of nonprofit, nongovernmental organizations (NGOs)[2] in the development of wildlife policy in the United States. A succinct statement of its central concern is, What difference do NGOs make? The general, and usually unsupported, observation is that such groups make a great deal of difference. Thus, "since private conservation organizations are the voice of the conservation-minded citizenry of the nation, nearly all favorable government actions are attributable to their activity."[3] It may be wise to add to this, "as long as nobody else cares." One NGO spokesman, upon learning of the present inquiry, volunteered that he wasn't sure how he wanted it to turn out. "I wouldn't want to find out that conservation groups have no influence, but I wouldn't want some people on the hill to find out that they have been unduly influenced by a bunch of crazies." He, and others who might share his apprehension, may rest assured that the answers herein are nowhere stated so unequivocally. Indeed, the first approach to an answer to the above question might run as follows:

Every advocacy group can tell stories that confirm its influence in the wildlife policy arena. In the short term, in the absence of such groups, legislation would go unsuggested, laws unenforced, and proposed rules uncontested. In the longer term, these groups, plus other NGOs with primary emphases that are educational or scientific, clearly are integrated into a dynamic process that, together with changes in public opinion, maturation of the economy, and patterns of resource use, have created a place on the national agenda for wildlife resources. At the same time, many policy debates occur primarily within the NGO community, as groups favor different strategies for responding to the plight of the California condor, for preserving the integrity of the Endangered Species Act, or for influencing the development of U.S. positions in international negotiations. Furthermore, because of the uncertain effects on wildlife that result from the implementation of specific policies, even a demonstration of political influence does not necessarily show a desired impact on wildlife itself. Finally, even should the desired impact on wildlife be achieved, its social consequences must be assessed.

It is not enough, therefore, to ask whether NGOs make a difference. We must ask whether they make an important difference—that is, do these organizations systematically affect the efficiency with which society's resources are allocated and/or the fairness with which society's rewards and burdens are distributed? Do they protect or promote cherished social values? It is commonly observed, for example, that the proliferation of voluntary organizations increases the costs of collective decision-making, at least in the short run, by raising issues that would otherwise not require resolution and by increasing the number of parties with claims to be heard. Decision making is slowed as legislators are caught among competing and powerful interests that increasingly make single-issue demands and reject the politics of compromise. Edmund Muskie remarked, just prior to his departure from the Senate, that "people are unhappy with Congress because it represents them too well."[4] The administrative agencies face similar demands. Federal land managers who, in years past, might easily have shot feral goats and burros destroying the habitats of indigenous species, now face demands that these populations be protected in their adopted environments or at least be humanely removed.[5] The Carter administration's ill-fated Energy Mobilization Board, seeking to short-circuit public participation in energy policy making, spoke to the perceived difficulties in achieving desired legislation in the face of "obstructionist" environmentalists and the groups that represent them.

On the other hand, it is argued that within the greater plurality of perspectives and ideas there may lie better solutions. The delays occasioned by conflict may permit more careful consideration of alternatives and therefore choice with a smaller probability of regret. Benefits may lie not in the decision itself but in the legitimacy that the process confers on the decision. Thus, even if from the planner's perspective it absorbs more resources than it justifies in improved solutions, broad participation survives on its own merits.

This concern for the efficiency of decision making arises out of a narrow view of the policy process, holding that clearly stated problems are somehow presented for resolution and that policy making consists of identifying solutions, detailing the consequences of each, and choosing the correct one. But the policy process is more convoluted than that. Participants in the process not only influence the choice of solutions, they also articulate the very problems to be resolved and the kinds of evidence acceptable in their resolution. Nonprofit organizations, in seeking to legitimize new participants and styles of participation (or, alternatively, in seeking to preserve and protect the legitimacy of existing ones) contribute to the evolution of the policy process itself and, more generally, to the orderly transition of social values.[6]

Beyond issues relating to the proliferation of ideas and constituencies are issues relating to the nonprofit form that these organizations assume. For example, while the contributions of voluntary organizations would not be entirely lost to the wildlife issue-area were the nonprofit form unavailable, this organizational form may provide niches for entrepreneurial energies and other resources more congenial than those available within the proprietary and governmental sectors. New resources may thus be drawn into the issue area, and the productivity of resources that would otherwise be employed else-where may be increased. Voluntary organizations, in command of whatever of these resources they can muster, often are able to act in ways that governments could but choose not to or that governments would like to but are not permitted to or cannot afford. They direct agency agendas within broad legislative mandates, and they monitor performance. In recognition of this symbiosis, implicit and explicit cooperation between the voluntary and government sectors is com-mon and important. Finally, wildlife and environmental policy are frequently concerned with issues that have costs and benefits that accrue over the very long term and that are measured imperfectly or not at all in the marketplace. The irreversibilities associated with extinction are an obvious example. The voluntary sector is perhaps able to focus on costs and benefits ignored by the proprietary sector and assess their importance over a longer time horizon than appears optimal to a government constrained by bureaucratic cycles and electoral politics. But let us not make too much of these unique claims on behalf of NGOs, for as is argued below, it is more useful on balance to examine not a single organizational form but an issue area as it is molded by a constellation of organizations and the people and resources that move among them.

The exploration of these and related issues invites a somewhat dis-cursive journey. Chapter 2 outlines the wildlife industry, describing the wildlife policy issue area and the organizations that inhabit it. Chapters 3 and 4 offer two case studies that demonstrate the com-plexity of policy issues and suggest the range of NGO actions and influence. These cases concern (1) the management of the California condor and the evolution of a controversial captive breeding program for the endangered bird and (2) the management of the bobcat and its relationship to U.S. participation in the Convention on Interna-tional Trade in Endangered Species of Wild Fauna and Flora (CITES). Chapter 5 examines the activities of individual organizations in the policy arena. These activities range from conventional lobbying by advocacy organizations to cooperation in the creation of hybrid decision-making structures and to market transactions that further organizational goals without political action. Chapter 6 explores the community of NGOs and the relationships of NGOs with the organi-zational environment of the wildlife issue area. A brief conclusion draws together some observations on wildlife policy making and on the role of nonprofit organizations.

NOTES

1. James A. Tober, *Who Owns the Wildlife? The Political Economy of Conservation in Nineteenth-Century America* (Westport, Conn.: Greenwood, 1981), and John F. Reiger, *American Sportsmen and the Origins of Conservation* (New York: Winchester, 1975).

2. The usage of "nongovernmental organizations" (NGOs) follows the convention in the international policy arena. The literature on nonprofit organizations also identifies private, voluntary organizations (PVOs) and nonprofit organizations (NPOs), which are generally interchangeable with NGOs. The term is, however, necessarily more inclusive than "public interest group" or "citizen interest group," since NGOs may represent narrow economic interests as well as broad public interests, and they may produce goods and services as well as information and advocacy.

3. Robert E. Jenkins, "Habitat Preservation by Private Organizations," in Council on Environmental Quality, *Wildlife and America: Contributions to an Understanding of American Wildlife and Its Conservation*, edited by Howard P. Brokaw (Washington, D.C.: Government Printing Office, 1978), p. 416.

4. Quoted in Steven V. Roberts, "Slow Pace of Congress," New York *Times*, October 5, 1979, p. A20.

5. See, for example, Susan M. Schectman, "The 'Bambi Syndrome': How NEPA's Public Participation in Wildlife Management Is Hurting the Environment," *Environmental Law* 8 (1979): 611–43.

6. See Hazel Henderson, *Creating Alternative Futures: The End of Economics* (New York: Berkley, 1978), pp. 277-96; Bill Devall, "The Deep Ecology Movement," *Natural Resources Journal* 20 (April 1980): 299-322; and Lester W. Milbrath, *Environmentalists: Vanguard for a New Society* (Albany: State University of New York Press, 1984). The fundamental transition addressed here is, in Milbrath's terms, from the dominant social paradigm (DSP) to the new environmental paradigm (NEP). Transitions need not be so grand, nor of course need they move in this particular direction. The Moral Majority would surely point to a very different transition that it hopes to facilitate.

2

The Wildlife Industry

The term "industry" conjures up images of raw materials, smoke-stacks, and assembly lines; "wildlife industry" may therefore suggest a limited range of activities in which wild animals, as raw materials, are transformed into useful objects for human consumption. This narrow focus on extractive processes is of course inappropriate for a resource that speaks to such a broad range of human values—from utilitarian to aesthetic to spiritual—as does wildlife. The dimensions of the wildlife industry must therefore be drawn broadly so as to encompass the rich and varied activities related to the creation and preservation of wildlife values.

The wildlife industry includes individuals, organizations, and institutions that, through private action or public participation, demonstrate their interest in wild plants and animals. As between private and public expressions of interest in wildlife, the present inquiry focuses on public expressions. It takes less interest in the motivations and behavior of the deer hunter than in the efforts of hunters to preserve access to the hunt or of antihunters to constrain that access; less interest in the manufacture and sale of lizardskin handbags than in the politics of trade regulation; and less interest in understanding the motivations of individual interest-group members than in the place of these groups in the policy process. Its focus, in short, is on wildlife policy, here defined as that set of laws, implementing regulations, and underlying values that give structure to the interactions of human beings with all other nondomesticated life-forms.[1] The breadth of the inquiry is generally limited, first, by the exclusion of marine fisheries (except insofar as species such as the Atlantic salmon are of interest because of their scarcity) and, second, by the focus on national policy-making. In the latter regard, however, the critical importance of the shared jurisdiction between the states and the federal government requires that the states and their interests figure prominently in the analysis.

As the range of protected species increases, as the complexities of the natural world become better understood, and as the threats to wildlife shift from those that are visible and immediate, such as over-hunting and habitat change, to those that are invisible, uncertain, and delayed, such as persistent pesticides and acid rain, all environmental policies and all development policies become wildlife policies. Indeed, wildlife NGOs have addressed nuclear disarmament and global climate change and have forged alliances with antinuclear groups, labor unions, and world religious leaders. This raises important problems for voluntary organizations, the identities of which are threatened by their expansion into new policy areas and which come to resemble one another to an increasing degree. It also raises problems for the scope of this inquiry. The present inquiry is limited to those policies that focus primarily on wildlife. However, examples from other issue areas, especially from the broader realm of environmental politics, will frequently illustrate processes of interest here.

Insofar as the present work constitutes an industry study, it is useful to note that in the field of industrial organization, inquiry is customarily divided into structure, conduct, and performance.[2] By structure is meant the descriptive characteristics of size, numbers, and institutional matrix binding together the players; by conduct is meant the behavior of individuals and organizations within the industry as they seek to achieve their goals, implied or explicit; and by performance is meant an assessment of the industry against standards such as efficiency or equity. This book progresses more or less through these three levels of inquiry, always moderated, however, by the special focus on nonprofit organizations. The present chapter, then, sketches the structure of the wildlife industry. It briefly explores the diversity and abundance of wildlife itself and the patterns of interaction between human and nonhuman populations. It turns then to profile the organized interests in the wildlife arena—their numbers, their origins, and the resources at their command.

THE INTEREST GROUP ENVIRONMENT

Wildlife Abundance and Diversity

The abundance and diversity of life on earth is truly remarkable. Recent evidence suggests that as many as 30 million species presently exist, most of them tropical insects and marine invertebrates, and most of them not yet identified. Indeed, a "mere" 1.6 million species, perhaps as few as 5 percent of the total, have been named.[3] Over half (55 percent) of these species are insects. The others are flowering plants (14 percent), ferns, fungi, and algae (9 percent), noninsect arthropods (8 percent), other invertebrates (8 percent), protozoa and bacteria (2 percent), and vertebrates (3 percent).[4] Among the vertebrates there are approximately 20,000 species of fish, 2,600 amphibians, 6,500 reptiles, 8,600 birds, and 4,100 mammals.[5] The numbers of species that naturally occur in North America are a great deal smaller—about 380 species of mammals, 650 species of breeding birds, 865 species of trees, and 88,600 species of insects.[6]

The millions of species that today inhabit the earth are but the smallest fraction of the species that have lived at some time in the earth's history, indeed probably less than 1 percent of as many as 4 billion. To what extent species disappear as the result of Darwinian selection and to what extent as the result of rare environmental stresses (sea level changes, meteor collisions) that strike groups of species, irrespective of their "suitability," is now being intensively studied and debated, but there is no doubt that extinction is the common fate of life on earth.[7] These numbers would suggest a mean rate of extinction of approximately one per year over the history of life on the planet, although the distribution, as described by the fossil record, has been anything but uniform. The most recent of the periodic extinctions, at the end of the Pleistocene some 11,000 years ago, has been associated with the action of the human population. Although human complicity remains uncertain for that event, it is increasingly easier, as one moves toward the present, to associate changes in abundance and distribution of wildlife, and extinction itself, with human behavior toward wildlife and modifications of the environment.

For the period between 1600 and 1980, some 194 vertebrate extinctions have been documented, most of them island species and over half of them birds. Only seven, including the passenger pigeon and the Carolina parakeet, were native to mainland United States and Canada.[8] But since 1980 these numbers have rapidly been made obsolete. Several U.S. vertebrate species have been added to this list as they awaited protection under the Endangered Species Act, and several others have been removed from protected status subsequent to their declared extinction.[9] The vast majority of these extinctions can be associated with habitat destruction, exotic species introduction, hunting, or some other human activity.[10] Vertebrate extinctions are but the tip of the iceberg. Recent estimates suggest a rate of extinction of perhaps 1,000 species per year, the bulk of them in the tropics.[11] This pattern of tropical impoverishment is likely to continue, because that is where most species are located and where habitats are being dismantled most rapidly. Estimates prepared for the *Global 2000 Report to the President*, assuming a reasonable distribution of species across habitat types and projecting rates of tropical deforestation, suggest that .5–.6 million species extinctions might occur by the year 2000. More recent estimates raise that number as high as 2 million.[12]

The interest in rates of extinction reflects not merely scientific curiosity but important policy concerns. The genetic diversity risked by current global patterns of resource use has great, if not always well defined, value. It cannot, of course, be assumed that this value everywhere exceeds the alternate value created through the reduction of diversity, but this is certain to be true for some species. A number of recent studies have catalogued utilitarian and nonutilitarian values— conventional and unconventional, existing and speculative, important and obscure—that society might wish to ascribe to particular species, species groups, or to wildlife generally.[13] A widely reported illustration is the 1978 chance discovery of a small patch of *Zea diploperennis*, a perennial relative of domestic corn that may offer significant economic benefits should its perennial nature be incorporated into commercial seed. Another illustration is found in the newly devised strategy of the National Cancer Institute to search more aggressively for anticancer agents in nature by screening thousands of tropical plant species (drawing on the expertise of tribal healers), marine invertebrates, algae, and fungi. The risk is that the species collected and later found to be effective anticancer agents may, meanwhile, have been extinguished.[14]

But wildlife policy, and therefore this inquiry, does not focus only, or even primarily, on choices concerning the extinction or survival of known or unknown species, but rather on choices concerning the modes of interaction with species that survive and even thrive: whether and under what conditions may the bobcat be harvested for export; what concern must the tuna industry demonstrate for the porpoise; how should the Bureau of Land Management regard wild mustangs on the range? Furthermore, although it is increasingly difficult to isolate national from international management concerns, this inquiry is focused primarily on U.S. policy and U.S. species. The variety and abundance of wildlife were among the more notable features of the North American environment as described by the first European settlers. In the intervening centuries, much of this wildlife has been consumed or destroyed. The decimation of the huge bison herds that roamed the Great Plains and the catastrophic decline and final extinction of the passenger pigeon are but two of the more dramatic consequences of our interactions with wildlife, but the same drama was played out and continues to be played out, different in detail and on a smaller scale, over the centuries and across the land.[15]

Despite a history of what may justifiably be called exploitation of wildlife resources in the United States, there is today a great diversity and abundance of wildlife, albeit very different wildlife from that of 400 years ago. This is due in part to the fact that the huge expanse of habitat and abundance of wildlife allowed significant regions to escape exploitation, while increasing incomes and changing preferences generated an effective demand for protection of species and habitats. It is also partly due to the importation, planned or otherwise, of exotic species; to the success of specific management programs implemented to rebuild, often for controlled harvest, certain populations; and to the capacity of many native species for rebuilding their own populations, in the absence of human intervention, once noxious impacts are removed.

Abundance is known with greatest certainty for species that have been the object of past public policy. When species are endangered and populations small, accurate or even exact counts are available. Thus it can be said with some certainty that as of this writing there are 28 California condors, 1,200–1,800 adult Kemp's ridley sea turtles, and in Alaska, 3,000–5,000 polar bears. The white-tailed deer, an object of management from earliest colonial times, are estimated to number 12–14 million, about half of the estimated population prior to European settlement, but 30 times more than the estimated low population in 1900. There are 2–3 million turkeys trotting the

American woodlands; the average annual mallard breeding population over 25 years is estimated at 8,493,000, and for ten species of duck it is 36,328,000.[16] Marine and insect species, however, may be represented by hundreds of millions or by billions of individuals. At its height, the Peruvian anchovy fishery harvested an estimated 320 billion fish per year from what must have been a larger population. There are certainly trillions of Antarctic krill, a major food source of baleen whales. Some insect populations may have 10^{18} individuals. The most significant species of all, in terms of its impact on other species, is the human species. At 5 billion, we are probably the most numerous of the world's mammals,[17] and our "success" as a species accounts in large measure for the changing fortunes of other species with which we share this earth.

Patterns of Interaction

Wildlife holds a particular fascination for North Americans, as for all peoples in all times. Millions of U.S. residents hunt, fish, feed wild birds, visit zoos, and follow tour guides through exotic habitats around the world. The late Marlin Perkins, host of "Zoo Parade" for 8 years and of "Wild Kingdom" for 23 more, and Jacques Cousteau, television's undersea adventurer, are household names. The press follows the plights of California's condors, Canada's harp seals, and the Grand Canyon's burros. Animal welfare, sporting, and wildlife organizations are among the oldest and most successful public interest groups in the nation.

Interactions with wildlife are customarily divided into consumptive and nonconsumptive, distinguished according to whether the plants and animals are themselves harmed. Consumptive uses include primarily hunting, fishing, trapping, and collecting; nonconsumptive uses include bird watching, wildlife photography, and zoo visits, among a wide variety of other activities. In practice this distinction is not always clear. Whale watching, for example, generally regarded as nonconsumptive, may be sufficiently intrusive to include a consumptive component.

The broadest base of knowledge about patterns of interaction has been provided by Stephen R. Kellert's detailed national survey of attitudes, knowledge, and behaviors toward wildlife. Kellert found, for example, that 44.4 percent of respondents reported having fished within two years. This is three times the participation rate for hunting, but dedicated hunters (those who engaged in the activity more than 35 days in two years) are proportionately more numerous than dedicated fishers. The largest proportion of hunters (42.7 percent) and fishers (28.4 percent) participate primarily to consume the harvest, but social and aesthetic motives are important as well.[18]

There are, of course, numerous other ways in which wildlife is consumed as a result of human activity. Species regarded as pests are routinely exterminated. Insects, rodents, and birds that threaten agricultural and forest crops have long been subject to systematic control; public health resources are devoted to organized attacks on viral, bacterial, and protozoan pathogens and their insect and rodent carriers. Consumer demand for food, fashion, and pets generates extensive harvest of wildlife, mostly abroad. Some 200 million bullfrogs enter into commercial trade each year, 8.2 million pounds of which found markets in the United States in 1984; about .5 million birds are legally imported into the United States for the pet trade. Foreign demand for U.S. wildlife accounts for the harvest of 50 tons of wild ginseng per year, requiring 30 million plants.[19] Cacti are dug, legally and illegally, to satisfy domestic and foreign markets. Butterflies and other insects gather dust in amateur collections around the country.

Wildlife is also consumed incidental to other activities. Thousands of porpoises drown each year in the nets of tuna boats; millions of birds collide with power lines and picture windows; and like numbers of animals are dispatched on the nation's highways. Pesticide residues, especially of DDT, have accumulated in the food chain, with well known, catastrophic impacts on predatory birds. The most important impact on abundance and distribution is land use change, which may be regarded as a consumptive use, not so much in that it threatens individual animals but in that it alters the prospects for whole populations, species, and communities.

Nonconsumptive interactions with wildlife are undertaken by significantly greater numbers of participants than are direct consumptive interactions. Kellert reports that two-thirds of his respondents had fed wild birds within two years of the survey, while one-fourth had engaged in bird-watching. Although only a very small portion of bird-watchers might be judged to be serious birders (indicated by their use of a field guide), over half claimed an ability to identify 20 or more species. Over three-quarters of the respondents watched "Wild Kingdom" sometimes or frequently. Nearly half had visited a zoo, a third had read a book about wild animals, and just under one-fourth read *National Geographic* frequently.[20]

Participation in wildlife-related activities both determines and is determined by knowledge, attitudes, and opinions regarding wildlife; these, in turn, provide a basis for public policy involvement. Knowledge of wildlife is limited, with highest levels shown concerning domestic and threatening animals. For example, 26 percent of the respondents in Kellert's survey knew that the manatee is not an insect (it is an endangered marine mammal), whereas 80 percent knew that a mule is a cross between a donkey and a horse and 84 percent knew that the copperhead, cottonmouth, coral, and rattlesnake are poisonous snakes.[21] Self-rated knowledge is relatively high for issues such as killing baby seals for their fur (43 percent rate themselves as very or moderately knowledgeable) and the effects of pesticides such as DDT on birds (42 percent). But knowledge is relatively low for such issues as the Tellico Dam/Snail Darter conflict, which at the time of the survey was attracting extensive press coverage (17 percent), or steel shot versus lead shot in waterfowl hunting (14 percent).[22] In general, knowledge levels are highly correlated with education and with membership in animal-related activity groups, both consumptive and nonconsumptive.[23] A similarly low level of knowledge was found for a broader range of environmental concerns by Robert Cameron Mitchell in his 1980 survey conducted for the Council on Environmental Quality.[24] These findings, in turn, are consistent with low knowledge levels detected in other policy areas, which may be seen to threaten the classical view of participatory democracy, in which informed citizens actively and knowledgeably participate in their own governance.[25]

With or without knowledge, however, there is no shortage of opinion on wildlife issues, much of which is based on relative preferences for various species. Some species clearly have more public appeal than other species, whatever their "contributions" to ecological stability or human well-being. Kellert observed that "the public appeared to be far more aware and, in all likelihood, concerned about relatively emotional issues involving specific, attractive, large and phylogenetically "higher" animals, than issues involving indirect impacts on wildlife and dealing with biologically unfamiliar and 'lower' animals."[26] For example, in response to a question posing a trade-off between lower energy costs and endangered species protection, 89 percent of respondents said they would protect a bird, such as the bald eagle; 73 percent the eastern mountain lion; 71 percent a fish, such as the Agassiz trout; 70 percent the American crocodile; 64 percent a butterfly, such as the silverspot; 48 percent a plant, such as the Furbish lousewort; 43 percent a snake, such as the eastern indigo snake; and 34 percent a spider, such as the Kauai wolf spider.[27] For a given species, preferences also depend on the proposed use that would threaten it. Whereas 87 percent of respondents would endanger a species of fish for drinking water, 83 percent would endanger it for crop irrigation, 72 percent for hydropower, 48 percent for industrial purposes, and 39 percent for recreation.[28] Similarly, support for hunting varies dramatically with the proposed justification for the hunt. Whereas 85 percent of respondents support hunting for meat, 37 percent support hunting game mammals for recreation and sport (40 percent for waterfowl), and 18 percent support hunting for trophies.[29]

Participation in wildlife policy making is based on preferences that may or may not be informed by knowledge. Whether this state of affairs contributes to good policy is debated. Robin Hansbury-Tenison, chairman of Survival International, an NGO concerned with the welfare of the world's tribal peoples, remarked with great distress that the probable downfall of certain Indian tribes in South America "doesn't have the same emotional appeal that clubbing young seals on the head has."[30] Whether the attractiveness of certain species derives from a cultural heritage (the eagle), a general aesthetic appeal (the butterfly), or perceived human qualities (baby seals), the preferences are nonetheless real and are incorporated into the policy debate. Furthermore, wildlife and animal welfare groups might reasonably take strategic advantage of these preferences in the selection of causes and the design of fund-raising solicitations. As one well-known figure in wildlife conservation observed at a conference on animal rights, "If you want to hook people, don't try to do it with a clam." The public relations downfall of the Endangered Species Act in 1978 might be said to have resulted in part from "doing it with a snail darter." That a three-inch fish could stop the multi-million-dollar Tellico Dam, by its fortuitous discovery nowhere else but in the Little Tennessee River below the dam site, seemed to some to indicate environmentalism out of control. Ultimately the act was amended and the dam was completed. One might imagine a different outcome had the dam threatened not the snail darter but, for example, the bald eagle.[31]

Interest Groups and the Environment

The growth in the number, size, and visibility of interest groups is well known and widely reported.[32] This growth has occurred in a society that has historically featured organized interests as important actors under constitutional freedoms of assembly and expression. The group basis of American life has been encouraged by decentralized decision making, diverse racial and ethnic groupings, extensive physical resources, and weak political party discipline. The period beginning about 1970 may represent the most dramatic growth of groups, but it has not been the only period of concentrated growth; nor is it interest groups alone, but organizations generally, that show increases. The concurrent growth of groups in a number of issue areas suggests that the substantive issues alone cannot explain the dramatic rise. To a certain extent the process is self-sustaining. Groups beget groups in a competitive battle for influence, and the prevalence of groups contributes to a framework that accords legitimacy to group involvement in political life. But there are certain recent changes that explain, or are at least roughly correlated with, the recent rapid growth of interest groups and, in particular, the emergence of the relatively new public interest group. These changes, selectively discussed at greater length in subsequent chapters, fall into four categories: changes in the size and prominence of government; changes in governmental process; changes in public policy; and changes in technology.[33]

Governments have grown in size and complexity at all levels. More important than increases in government employment and spending, however, is the growth in the impact of government on the daily lives of individuals and organizations. Indicative is the growth in the bulk of the *Federal Register*, the daily record of the federal government's regulatory agenda, which increased ninefold, from 9,562 to 87,012 pages per year between 1950 and 1980. Although by 1984 the number of pages had declined substantially (to 50,997), at least in part through a concerted effort to achieve such a reduction, the compendium remained 2.5 times the size of its 1970 counterpart. A related indicator is the growing concentration of interest groups, lobbyists, and attorneys in the nation's capital. The number of Washington-based lawyers more than tripled, to 37,000, in the decade ending in 1983, and 30 percent of national nonprofit trade and professional associations are headquartered there.[34] A recent count of Washington representatives, those persons who work to influence government policy and actions in their own or their clients' interests, produced about 10,000 names.[35] In the environmental arena, most national groups are based in Washington or maintain a major staff presence there. Mitchell, examining 12 major environmental NGOs, found that their collective Washington lobbying strength grew from two in 1969 to about 40 in 1975 to 88 in 1985.[36]

Although one might hypothesize that government programs supplant those of nonprofit organizations in response to interest group advocacy, thereby reducing the size and prominence of the nonprofit sector, it is more likely that the growth in government has been a cause of group proliferation. Not only do regulatory programs invite, and occasionally fund, public participation, which then becomes institutionalized through interest groups, but the programs create property rights, which groups seek to garner and protect. Furthermore, bureaus seek constituency support in their own struggles to survive and grow. The major environmental legislation of the late 1960s and early 1970s predated, for the most part, the well organized and articulate environmental movement that has since emerged.[37]

Another dimension of change at the federal level is congressional reform and the decline of party discipline, leading to a distribution of power among a growing number of committees and subcommittees, all with staffs growing to cope with increasingly complex issues and often with overlapping jurisdictions. A similar proliferation is characteristic of administrative agencies, which through expansions of established missions, gain jurisdiction in new policy arenas. An example of the resulting administrative overlap may be found in the regulation of foreign trade in wildlife and wildlife products, shared among the Public Health Service of the Department of Health and Human Services, the Animal and Plant Health Inspection Service (APHIS) of the Department of Agriculture, the Customs Service of the Department of the Treasury, the National Marine Fisheries Service of the Department of Commerce, the Fish and Wildlife Service, and the Wildlife Enforcement Program of the Department of Justice. Multiple points of access and influence may require that interest groups concerned with these issues maintain a division of labor not otherwise merited by the logical structure of the issues, but such divided jurisdictions also invite interest group participation in coordinating the work of overlapping agencies and committees.

Established interests have a way of persisting even if, by some logical analysis, they have been largely superseded by new perceptions, knowledge, or reality. As Hugh Heclo has observed, since "very few policies ever seem to drop off the public agenda as more are added, congestion among those interested in various issues grows, the chances for accidental collisions increase, and the interaction tends to take on a distinctive group-life of its own in the Washington community," leading to the "development of specialized subcultures composed of highly knowledgeable policy-watchers" who constitute fuzzy-boundaried "issue networks."[38] This characterization is particularly apt for the wildlife issue area.

Additional support for the growth of groups is offered by specific legislative provisions subsidizing the nonprofit sector through favorable postal rates and tax exemptions. Finally, technological change, especially advances in computerization and mass mailing techniques, have permitted groups to solicit support from millions of prospective donors and to communicate regularly, and on a selective basis, with members and contributors.

Cross-cutting these changes, which alter the climate for groups in all issue areas, is the particular growth of concern for wildlife and environment, broadly expressed in the complex set of phenomena known as the environmental movement.[39] The public celebration of Earth Day (1970) and the passage of landmark federal wildlife legislation, such as the Wild Free-Roaming Horses and Burros Act (1971), the Marine Mammal Protection Act (1972), and the Endangered Species Act (1973), rode the high crest of the movement. The fervor has calmed; environmentalism has been institutionalized in school curricula, in corporate planning offices, in electoral politics, and in Congress; during the Carter administration, many of the movement's leaders found employment in government. But economic and energy fears urged caution in implementing costly controls and in forgoing public works projects. At the same time, public opinion polls continued to show strong support for movement goals.[40]

The second environmental decade differs substantially from the first. The discussions of future strategy occasioned by the tenth anniversary of Earth Day featured increased attention to the courts and agencies, new coalitions with other social movements, retrenchment and compromise, negotiation, and a global perspective.[41] These changes, conditioned by events to date, were the result of new knowledge, new perceptions of problems and solutions, and the practical politics of environmentalism. Practical politics were to change dramatically, however, with the 1980 election of Ronald Reagan, a reminder that, to whatever extent NGOs shape the environmental and wildlife issue area, larger political forces dominate.

THE STRUCTURE OF INTERESTS

The organizations that constitute the wildlife industry are large and small, wealthy and impoverished, old and young. They number in the hundreds, employ thousands of people, derive support and legitimacy from millions of members and donors, and spend hundreds of millions of dollars annually. All seek to capture economic and political resources for strategic dispersal in pursuit of organizational goals. These goals may speak to the interests of group members alone, as in the case of trade associations, or they may speak to a broad conception of the public interest, distributing benefits to supporters and nonsupporters alike. Table 2.1, offering a typology of wildlife NGOs, suggests the rich fabric of organizational life.[42]

Origins

The community of wildlife organizations can count among its members a few quite venerable organizations, the origins of which coincide with the late-nineteenth-century awakening of environmentalism and the assertion of federal interest in wildlife and other natural resources. These include scientific organizations, such as the American Ornithologists' Union (1883); sporting organizations, such as the Boone and Crockett Club (1887); zoo organizations, such as the New York Zoological Society (NYZS, 1895); organizations seeking humane treatment of animals, such as the American Society for the Prevention of Cruelty to Animals (ASPCA, 1866); and conservation organizations, such as the National Audubon Society (NAS, 1905), which traces its actual roots to a 1886 club founded by George Bird Grinnell through his weekly sporting journal, *Forest and Stream*. Many other organizations created during this period have fallen by the wayside or have been absorbed by others. The National Sportsmen's Association (1874), the National Association for the Protection of Game, Birds and Fish (1885), the National Game, Bird and Fish Protective Association (1893), and the League of American Sportsmen (1898) were among the short-lived national groups orga-

Table 2.1
The Wildlife Industry—A Typology of Nongovernmental Organizations (NGOs)

Type	Characteristics or Interests	Examples
I. Representing Proprietary Concerns	A. Compete with wildlife/sustain patterns of resource use threatened by changing protection for wildlife	National Cattlemen's Assn. National Forest Products Assn.
	B. Harvest or exchange animals or animal products	Pet Industry Joint Advisory Council North American Falconers' Assn.
II. Representing State Governments	Monitor boundary between state and federal jurisdictions over wildlife	International Assn. of Fish and Wildlife Agencies (IAFWA) Western States Water Council
III. Non-Membership Foundations and Research Insts.	Grantmaking, research, education	National Geographic Society (NGS) Wildlife Management Institute (WMI) African Wildlife Foundation (AWF)
IV. Representing NGOs	A. Associations	American Assn. of Zoological Parks and Aquariums (AAZPA)
	B. Permanent Coalitions	Natural Resources Council of America Monitor Consortium Wildlife Coalition International (WCI)
	C. Temporary Coalitions	Alaska Coalition Endangered Species Reauthorization Coalition Marine Entanglement Coalition
V. Representing Individuals	A. Professional associations serving as repositories of scientific expertise	Wildlife Society American Ornithologists' Union (AOU)
	B. NGOs acquiring habitat, often for transfer to governments	The Nature Conservancy (TNC) Ducks Unlimited (DU)

C. Scientific and educational NGOs, including zoos, aquariums, botanical gardens, and museums

American Museum of Natural History
New York Zoological Society (NYZS)
San Diego Wild Animal Park (SDWAP)

D. Environmental law organizations

Environmental Defense Fund (EDF)
Natural Resources Defense Council (NRDC)
Mountain States Legal Foundation

E. Political action committees

League of Conservation Voters (LCV)
Animal Political Action Committee

F. Sporting organizations, seeking to protect traditional and legal rights of hunters and trappers

National Rifle Assn (NRA)
Boone and Crockett Club
Wildlife Legislative Fund of America (WLFA)

G. Broad-based NGOs with origins and primary interest in wildlife

National Audubon Society (NAS)
National Wildlife Federation (NWF)
World Wildlife Fund—U.S. (WWF-US)

H. Broad-based NGOs with limited interest in wildlife

Sierra Club
Friends of the Earth (FOE)
Wilderness Society

I. Wildlife NGOs with roots in the humane movement

Humane Society of the U.S. (HSUS)
Animal Welfare Institute (AWI)
Defenders of Wildlife
Greenpeace
Fund for Animals

J. Animal rights groups

People for the Ethical Treatment of Animals (PETA)
Committee to Abolish Sport Hunting (CASH)

K. Specialized wildlife groups with interests in single species or species groups, both to promote management for harvest and to protect

American Horse Protection Assn. (AHPA)
Whitetails Unlimited
American Cetacean Society
Desert Bighorn Council

23

nized to promote uniformity in state game laws and restrictions on market hunting. Only the Boone and Crockett Club, founded by Theodore Roosevelt and Grinnell and including such persons of prominence as Henry Cabot Lodge, Owen Wister, Francis Parkman, Albert Bierstadt, Gifford Pinchot, and J. Pierpont Morgan, has survived, although it is now more likely to be called on to defend sport hunting than to take the offensive against those who threaten the viability of sport hunting by extensive slaughter of game for the market.[43]

The early beginnings and persistence of a few organizations notwithstanding, the vast majority of wildlife organizations, as of other types, are of much more recent origin. The recent and rapid growth of nonprofits, especially of public interest groups, has been noted. However, while the total number of nonprofit organizations increased 17 percent in the decade ending in 1984, this increase was not sufficient to maintain the proportional importance of nonprofits among all organizational types. Only the narrower set of educational, charitable, and scientific 501(c)(3) NGOs, increasing by 32.3 percent during the same period, outpaced the general growth in all organizations.[44]

A narrower focus on environmental groups can be gained by examining the number of groups listed in the *Conservation Directory* of the National Wildlife Federation (NWF), which for 30 years has identified organizations concerned with resource use and management.[45] The number of national, international, and interstate organizations listed more than doubled, from 185 to 387 groups, between 1968 and 1986. The rate of growth dramatically slowed, however, from 40 percent in 1972–78 to 10 percent in 1980–86. Cross-sectional data provide another view of organizational growth. The 108 national wildlife and humane organizations identified for this study are arrayed by founding date in Table 2.2.[46] The recent origin of these groups is evident; while 14 percent had been founded before 1940, 68 percent had been founded since 1966. The decade surrounding Earth Day accounted for 40 percent of all groups. It is notable that groups with a humane or single-species focus are much newer than other broader-purpose wildlife and environmental organizations. In particular, whereas 52 percent of humane groups and 38 percent of single species groups were founded in the decade 1976–85, only 14 percent of other groups were founded during this period. This is not surprising in view of the life histories of these older organizations, which show an evolution from special purpose to general purpose. It is much easier for an

Table 2.2
Founding Dates of 108 Wildlife Organizations

Year Founded	All NGOs		NGOs with humane orientation		NGOs with species orientation	
	(number)	(percent)	(number)	(percent)	(number)	(percent)
—1940	15	14	2	10	0	0
1941–1950	0	0	0	0	0	0
1951–1960	13	12	3	14	4	14
1961–1965	7	6	0	0	3	10
1966–1970	20	19	3	14	3	10
1971–1975	23	21	2	10	8	28
1976–1980	15	14	6	29	3	10
1981–1985	15	14	5	24	8	28
Totals	108	100	21	101	29	100

Sources: National Wildlife Federation, *Conservation Directory* (Washington, D.C.: National Wildlife Federation, various years); Denise Akey, ed., *The Encyclopedia of Associations—1986*, 20th ed., 1986 (Detroit: Gale Research, 1985); publications of various organizations.

established organization to devote resources to an expansion in scope than for a new organization to mount a broad-scale campaign on a wide range of issues.

Organizations arise out of a wide variety of circumstances; voluntary and, more particularly, public interest organizations from a somewhat narrower set. Two broad theories, associated with the names of David B. Truman and Robert H. Salisbury, suggest environmental disturbance and entrepreneurial exchange as primary explanations. The former holds that groups provide pluralistic balance in a democratic society. When disturbances move the balance of interests from equilibrium, new configurations emerge to claim the potential gains from change. The latter theory, addressing the observation that groups do not always arise spontaneously to take advantage of opportunities for gain, suggests that organizational entrepreneurs package deals in which members join groups in exchange for personal benefits of a material, solidary, or purposive nature.[47] These mechanisms are closely linked. Indeed, Jeffrey M. Berry suggests that by considering entrepreneurial activity as a form of disturbance, Salisbury's theory might be seen as a special case of Truman's more general explanation. Insofar as each approach presumes the primacy of one variable, the theories are distinct and provide a basis for empirical test. Berry's data on 83 national public interest groups indicate that entrepreneurial motives are more often the primary driving force, and this finding is particularly strong for environmental and consumer groups.[48] The entrepreneurial approach is appealing to other analysts as well. Donald Fleming, asking why the environmental movement suddenly flared up in the 1960s, initially asserts that it "must be that an extraordinarily diverse concatenation of impulses suddenly flashed together." But he then goes on to support the entrepreneurial view by "traversing the routes by which the principle leaders of the New Conservation movement arrived at an unexpected rendezvous."[49]

Entrepreneurship alone is not usually sufficient. Although the expectation of future membership benefits can generate a growing membership base, the essential entrepreneurial ingredient may be outside financial backing to meet start-up costs. Jack L. Walker found, in his 1983 study, that 60 percent of all nonprofit and 89 percent of citizens groups received financial aid from an outside source that facilitated the birth of the organization.[50] These outside sources include foundations, which provided funding for the Natural Resources Defense Council (NRDC), the Environmental Defense Fund

(EDF), and the Wildlife Conservation Fund of America (the tax-exempt affiliate of the Wildlife Legislative Fund of America), and they include other NGOs, which provided funding for Trade Records Analysis of Flora and Fauna in Commerce (TRAFFIC). The World Wildlife Fund, sponsor of the TRAFFIC network, was itself founded by the International Union for the Conservation of Nature and Natural Resources (IUCN) as a fund-raising arm for the international conservation community.

Organizational Scope

The circumstances surrounding the creation of an organization describe, in great measure, its initial scope, but once established, this scope can and does change in response to the goals and skills of directors, staff, and members; financial resources; organizational environment; and external disturbances. The change most generally observed, arising out the increased clarity with which the complexity of environmental problems is understood and out of the competitive search for supporting constituencies, is an expansion in the range of issues addressed. Defenders of Wildlife began in 1925 as the Anti-Steel Trap League, grew into Defenders of Furbearers, and finally into its current descriptive title. "As the world has grown more complex, Defenders' niche has expanded accordingly. . . . We realize that our proper concerns now include the kinds of environmental insults that may not kill animals directly and dramatically, but despoil or diminish their dwelling places."[51] Another example may be found in the Peregrine Fund, "created in 1970 to prevent the extinction of the Peregrine Falcon," which recently opened the World Center for Birds of Prey, symbolizing the fund's expansion "to include national and international conservation of birds of prey and other wildlife."[52]

The National Audubon Society (NAS) has gradually expanded its sphere of interest from the preservation of nongame birds to a broad spectrum of environmental concerns, a trend that accelerated under the leadership of Russell Peterson. An early task in his new administration was the development of the "Audubon Cause," the organization's mission statement. "Over its seventy-five years, the society, through the study of bird life, has become increasingly aware of the interconnectedness of all life, and of the major cumulative impact of humankind's activities on the health of life-support systems—the air, water, and land." The seven goals that encompass the Cause concern the conservation of wildlife and life-support systems, the promotion of rational strategies for energy development, the protection of life from pollution, radiation and toxics, the wise use of land and water, the protection of public lands, the global environment, and stabilization of world population.[53] Did Peterson see any danger that NAS was casting its net too widely? "Absolutely not. . . . Audubon's mission is to train people to think holistically. So we really have only one thing on our plate: the environmental health of the planet."[54] The expansion of organizational breadth promoted by Peterson remains in place under his successor, Peter A. A. Berle. *The Audubon Activist* (the bimonthly publication available to members by subscription since 1986) contains in its first 16-page issue articles on Superfund, the spotted owl, nuclear dump sites, phaseout of lead shot, the national debt, soil conservation, global warming, the Columbia River Gorge, billboards, state conservation budgets, off-road vehicles, and world population. Berle wrote in the welcoming editorial, with curious metaphor, "In Audubon, you don't have to wear a label or fit into a mold. Because the organization is diverse and far-flung, there are unlimited opportunities to plug your energies into the Audubon machine."[55]

For some groups, expansion of scope had become counterproductive. The National Parks and Conservation Association was founded in 1919 as the National Parks Association by Stephen Mather, first director of the National Park Service. The journal of the new organization was the *National Parks Magazine.* In April 1970 the organization assumed its present, broader name, and its journal became *National Parks and Conservation Magazine: The Environmental Journal.* In 1979 prospective contributors could be told that the organization had "broadened its horizons and is working for ecological forestry, protection of endangered species, air and water quality, protection of our rural land, alternate sources of energy, environmental management of river basins, in short . . . conservation of the total environment." The following year, having reorganized around the limited special interest that underlay its creation, the association issued a policy statement noting that the association is "unique among conservation organizations, because it is the only national organization that focuses on protecting, promoting, and expanding our national parks." With the June 1980 issue the journal's subtitle was dropped, and since January 1981 the magazine has been known simply as *National Parks.*

Organizations seek to distinguish themselves, certainly in their achievements, but also in their structures and scope:

- The Wilderness Society is "the only national environmental organization to focus exclusively on public lands."
- The National Wildlife Refuge Association is "dedicated to a single mission: to preserve and sustain the National Wildlife Refuge System for all Americans and their descendants."
- The Wildlife Legislative Fund of America "is the only organization solely devoted to protecting sportsmen's rights."
- World Wildlife Fund–US is "the one United States organization uniquely concerned with international wildlife."
- Wildlife Conservation International (a division of the New York Zoological Society) "is the only American conservation group that is truly international in scope."
- The Natural Resources Defense Council (NRDC) "has the largest legal and technical staff of any environmental organization in the country."
- The Animal Legal Defense Fund "was *created specifically* to provide full-time legal effort to . . . insure that animal cruelty and abuse will come to an end soon. The approach which our staff . . . takes is unique."

These distinctions reflect in part the efficiency that division of labor can bring, but they also reflect strategic organizational posturing designed to create a favorable distribution of the total available support.

A second dimension for change has been in the range of tactics employed to achieve organizational goals. The World Wildlife Fund–US (WWF–US), primarily a grant-making organization that has presented itself as a "united fund" for international conservation, "has traditionally not sought a role among the environmental community as a militant, activist organization." Although it expects to continue in this tradition, "we have been increasing our involvement in the resolution of public issues . . . [that] are central to our concerns."[56] It established an office of governmental affairs in 1981, and since that time, although "we are not a lobby in any active or official sense," it has slowly but surely increased its presence on Capitol Hill. Similarly, NRDC, finding that it was "winning the cases, but losing the war," has been gradually transformed from an environmental law firm into a broader-purpose environmental organization with education and lobbying functions.

A third change reflects the expansion of national NGOs into the international and local policy arenas, a change fostered both by the promise of substantive and organizational gains and by diminishing returns in some realms of national policy. States are increasingly responsible for administering national environmental legislation, and in the absence of aggressive federal leadership, states have taken the initiative in a number of policy areas. Audubon, relying on its extensive network of 504 chapters and 10 regional offices, expects to provide "the diversity necessary to develop solutions tailormade to the local situation." EDF has inaugurated the Environmental Information Exchange (EIE), "which gives state-level groups access to EDF's professional expertise through a computer-assisted network." The Environmental Task Force (ETF), performing similar functions, predates these efforts. Founded in 1980, "ETF is the *one* national group established solely to strengthen and unify America's grass-roots environmental organizations and to build networks among citizens' groups at the local, state and national levels."[57]

Certain changes follow, not from the life histories of individual organizations, but from the collective life histories of the community of organizations that have coevolved with the environmental movement. By the late 1970s, legislative initiatives were in place in many areas of environmental policy. As the cost of making substantive progress in implementation became better understood, the federal government sought increasingly to justify new regulations here as in other arenas, through the logic of cost-benefit analysis and other regulatory review procedures. This development called forth from the environmental community a more studied, more analytical, and less confrontational style, focusing more on efficiency and less on fairness. Consequently, organizations have become increasingly skilled in research and policy analysis. The Wilderness Society, with a $620,000, three-year grant from the Richard King Mellon Foundation, created the Natural Resource Policy Analysis Unit in 1980, "the first of what must become a standard element of every significant conservation and environmental group. In 10 years, we'll wonder how we ever got along without units such as these."[58] This unit has evolved into the Resources Planning and Economics Department, currently in the midst of a four-year, $4 million program ("probably the largest—and most expensive—conservation program ever undertaken by an environmental organization") to review all 124 national forest plans now being prepared by the forest service.[59] EDF has developed expertise in energy modeling and has promoted market-oriented approaches to controlling the production of ozone-damaging chlorofluorocarbons and to conserving scarce Western water resources.[60]

The evolution of the environmental issue area has been explicitly identified as the theoretical underpinning for this change. Frederic D. Krupp, executive director of EDF, argues that the third stage of environmentalism is upon us. Whereas the first phase was to halt "truly rapacious exploitation of natural resources" and the second was to work to halt abusive pollution through lobbying, lawsuits, and other direct actions, the third phase is to find alternatives "to answer the legitimate needs that underlie ill-advised projects like destructive dams" and present them convincingly. The movement needs thinkers who can "envision and persuasively lead this nation toward environmentally-sound economic growth." EDF is "the first environmental group to begin to fill this exciting new environmental niche."[61] But if the larger and older groups have adopted a less confrontational, more analytical, and more homogeneous stance in response to the practical politics of the environment, other groups, younger and perhaps more brash, have arisen to fill the organizational space created by this move to the center. The dynamics of the industry are further addressed in Chapter 6.

Setting Agendas

A given organizational scope and set of tactics are consistent with a wide range of specific actions that might constitute the organizational agenda. Indeed, scope and tactics are themselves agenda items. Boards of directors, advisory councils, staffs, and members, acting formally and informally and in various combinations, determine the specific actions to which organizational resources are devoted. Boards provide broad policy guidelines, and occasionally individual members focus the organization on specific problems or tasks. Boards also appoint the president, executive director, or chief executive officer, who in turn can be expected to exercise major influence over the organizational agenda. The working agenda is set by staff, both paid and volunteer, and with more or less input from members (or from contributors who make restricted gifts).[62] One respondent in the present study reported that his organization selected issues according to its ability to affect the outcome, the availability of the resources required to achieve the desired impact, and to a limited extent, whether other groups were already working in the area. Another respondent suggested, similarly, that his organization selected wild- life policy issues according to the importance of the issue, the cost- effectiveness of involvement (recognizing that existing expertise developed through past selection would affect the choice), and on expected impact.

The development of day-to-day agendas, especially for lobbying activities, is more reactive than strategic. "We move wherever we can." "The issues pick themselves." "The name of the game is what is possible." One former Friends of the Earth staffer, in search of the origins of the organization's whale campaign, concluded that

it would be reassuring, but deceitful, to say that options are carefully consid- ered, pros and cons finely weighed on deeply scientific and political grounds, arguments analyzed and measured decisions finally arrived at. In fact enthusiasm, personal commitment, popular opinion, strong hunches and the availability of desk space and funding are just as important as purely intellectual factors.[63]

Among the important tasks often shunted aside is a systematic assess- ment of organizational resources, goals, and strategies. This outcome may well represent reasoned choice under conditions of impoverish- ment, where investing in tomorrow risks starvation today; it may foster a kind of fervor and accompanying good work that is lost under cooler circumstances; but it may also result from inexperience and poor management. Indeed, especially among the larger groups, there is a general move toward professionalization in all areas of organiza- tional life: the development and presentation of information, fund raising, accounting, strategic planning, and general administration.

The role of members in agenda setting varies widely. Some organi- zations emphasize their participatory nature, involving members in the election of board members and the setting of organizational priorities. Organizations must balance efficiency of operation against member participation and control. On the one hand there is Com- mon Cause, in which the internal control structure mirrors the larger open, participatory policy structure that the organization seeks to create.[64] At the other extreme are staff organizations that may have public support but no memberships or members with no privileges. The Wilderness Society makes a certain point of the remove at which it keeps members. There are no local chapters, no membership com- mittees, and no volunteer opportunities. Members join because they want to support the work of the organization and its professional staff. "The organization isn't being tugged in eighteen different directions by volunteer activists."[65]

Until its reorganization in 1986, Friends of the Earth (FOE), headquartered in San Francisco and with a Washington office, regional offices, local chapters, and international affiliates, was among the more decentralized of the organizations examined. Indeed, when the organization was created in 1969, its president was based in San Francisco, its executive director in New York, its governmental relations staff in Washington, and its membership and finance in Albuquerque.[66] One of the organization's first campaigns involved forming the coalition against the SST. According to George Alderson, FOE's first legislative director, the executive committee decided that "what we wanted to do immediately was something that other conservation groups haven't done: focus on runaway technology, that is, technology for no rational reasons. We looked around and the SST seemed like a good thing to go after."[67] Other groups, although opposed, were committed to other issues and were reluctant to oppose Senator Henry Jackson (D. Wash.), chairman of the Senate Interior Committee and usual ally of the conservation community but strong supporter of the Boeing-contracted plane.

The broadest agenda and management decisions were guided by the board and national staff, but within those decisions, policy and initiative depended on the interests and perceptions of staff members and even volunteers. The Washington lobbyist who followed the Endangered Species Act through two years of amendments "because that was clearly the most important wildlife issue at the time" shifted largely to coastal issues in 1980 because of a national staff decision to play a major role in the formation and support of the Coast Alliance. With the exception of marine mammals, wildlife was "put on the shelf for a year," at least in the Washington office. FOE's interest in the California condor recovery program stemmed largely from the personal interest of former president David Brower and of David Phillips, a California staff member who was initially able to raise his own support for this work. According to one staffer, "people come and start to work for us who have a passionate interest in something." Specialties tend to remain vested in individuals rather than in the organization. Following the recent restructuring of FOE, Phillips joined Brower at the Earth Island Institute, establishing an interest in the condor there and removing it from FOE's organizational agenda.[68] While FOE's position on the condor issue has not changed, it is not an issue on which the organization believes it can make much of a difference, given its limited resources and other staff interests. The decentralized development of policy within the organization causes FOE to find itself allied variously with moderate or extreme environmental groups, with nonenvironmental public interest groups, with labor, or in the case of the organization's support for Native American quotas on bowhead whale, with none of these groups.[69]

The FOE structure on the international level replicates the decentralized structure in the U.S. What began as a set of David Brower's personal representatives stationed in various nations had grown by late 1987 into a network of affiliated organizations in 32 countries, loosely coordinated by Friends of the Earth International. The organizations differ widely in their structure, staffing, and role. The Mexican affiliate, for example, is a network of 300 village-based groups emphasizing environmentally sound food production.[70] Some national groups are themselves umbrella organizations for local, largely independent affiliates that raise their own revenues, set their own agendas, and carry out their own projects. In the United Kingdom, for example, local groups raised and spent in 1980 an amount equal to that of the national group.

Some organizations have institutionalized very systematic procedures for setting agendas and allocating organizational resources. The International Association of Fish and Wildlife Agencies (IAFWA) supports several standing committees (including endangered wildlife, fur resources, hunter education, Indian relations, and predator policy) that meet as needed to complete assigned tasks and develop resolutions concerning future work.

For example, the legislative committee met in December 1978 to review the major issues of the past year and establish new priorities. Issues were assigned Priority 1 (begin immediate and active participation, aggressive involvement and advocacy), Priority 2 (establish posture but pursue active role only as required), or Priority 3 (monitor only). For Priority 1 issues, specific courses of action were outlined (such as, "prepare to testify at an early date"). The executive committee charged the legislative committee to examine the matter of "progressive and persistent erosion of state jurisdiction over fish and resident wildlife" and to report at the annual meeting in March. Specific tasks were assigned to individuals and other committees (such as, "ask each regional Association to provide specific examples of erosion of jurisdictional authority over fish and wildlife" and "prepare a résumé of court decisions applying to State jurisdictional issues"). Among alternative strategies identified for resolving the problem were development of a memo of understanding between the association and the director of the U.S. Fish and Wildlife Service (FWS), development of a legislative proposal to clarify jurisdictions, and development of a program to inform Congress of the problem.[71] This issue was later to unfold as the controversial fish and wildlife policy of the service, discussed in Chapter 5. The association subsequently established an ad hoc states' rights committee, which proposed legislative solutions to the problem of the migratory boundary separating federal and state jurisdictions.[72] The public policy interests of the association are pursued by a Washington staff of two lobbyists. They are generally guided by the resolutions of the executive and legislative committees, but they respond as events require in the interest of the organization.

Members

Members and supporters provide NGOs with financial resources, volunteer labor, and organizational legitimacy in exchange for private and public goods. Mitchell, extrapolating from membership figures for major national environmental organizations and analyzing data collected in a 1974–75 national telephone survey, estimated a total membership of 3.7 percent of the adult U.S. population, or 5 million members.[73] Kellert derived an estimate of 11.3 percent, but this number includes, for example, sportsmen's and natural history organizations as well as the public interest conservation organizations studied by Mitchell. This broader description seems appropriate for the present study, in that it more closely corresponds to the boundaries of the wildlife industry.[74]

The logic of membership in groups such as the National Geographic Society is not complex. Its 10 million members, in addition to supporting the production of public goods through research and education, receive private goods that feature the organization's well-known monthly magazine, at a total annual membership fee that is certainly less than a proprietary competitor would charge for the magazine alone. But the logic of membership grows more problematic as the proportion of public to private goods grows. Indeed, the founding and persistence of such groups has sparked a lively academic debate.[75]

Strategic decision making would suggest that individual membership can be justified only if the benefits of membership exceed the costs of joining. For public interest groups producing nonexclusive public goods, membership can be justified only if the quantity of public goods consumed by the member is highly valued and otherwise unlikely to be forthcoming, or if private goods are included to tip the balance. These private goods need not be limited to material benefits such as colorful magazines, informative newsletters, or opportunities for group travel, but may include moral fulfillment and guilt avoidance. And, of course, the tax-exempt status of many organizations reduces the cost of giving for some donors, thereby increasing the number of individuals who are willing to accept a given package of public/private benefits. Furthermore, as Terry M. Moe argues, it is the perceived costs and benefits, rather than their objective values, that preconditions membership decisions. Group leaders may therefore manipulate perceptions to attract support among certain audiences. The decision to join may be further enhanced, he suggests, by the inclination of individuals to overestimate their political efficacy.[76] This kind of rational calculus need not be called upon to provide the entire basis for membership. Habits of culture, social class, and personality surely combine to explain a certain "irrational" component to giving behavior.

Mitchell offers another perspective, noting the asymmetry of the benefits for environmental quality experienced by the prospective group member. If marginal benefits can be assumed to diminish as environmental quality increases, a given increase in environmental quality adds less benefit than would be sacrificed by a reduction in environmental quality of equal magnitude. The avoidance of environmental bads, rather than the provision of environmental goods, therefore provides a significant membership incentive. As Mitchell observes, this logic is not lost on the groups, which in their solicitations are more likely to ask for support to prevent deterioration in environmental quality than to achieve an improvement.[77] The consequences of reductions in quality are all the more serious when they involve the risk of an irreversible loss such as extinction. In a 1987 solicitation for funds to protect the mountain gorilla, WWF–US concluded: "Imagine how *you* will feel if this magnificent species vanishes from our planet—forever. Please rush your gift to the World Wildlife Fund today!"

Although this modification cannot easily explain the vast numbers who fail to take advantage of the same opportunities to avoid the risk of diminutions in environmental quality, it is consistent at the margin with the growth in membership in some organizations following the 1980 election and the appointment of James Watt as primary guardian of the nation's natural resources. The likelihood of deteriorating quality was widely perceived to have increased, and some former free riders were induced to exchange the certain loss of membership fees for a reduction in the probability of suffering the costs of those quality reductions. A spokeswoman for the League of Conservation Voters reported, for example, that "everyone who sends us a check says 'I'm really scared about the way the government is going.'"[78] Organizations, on their part, have lost no time in playing on these motivations by detailing the possible consequences of the projected resource management.

Membership size and growth is shown in Table 2.3 for eight organizations representing a variety of wildlife constituencies. While the figures are consistent representations for organizations individually, they cannot be compared across organizations. Nor do all organizations make clear just what the numbers represent. (This is further complicated by the fact that the figures variously represent year-end, mean annual, or some other unique measure of support). The basic distinctions are among memberships, members, and contributors or supporters. Most membership organizations report the number of active memberships (current year plus renewal grace period of three-to-four months). NAS estimates in addition the number of members, assuming any membership held at the "family" level of support or above to include two members. WWF–US, which initiated a formal membership program only in 1981, maintains a historically consistent, but not public, definition of membership, reported to be less than the number of all supporters but more than the number who have given the basic membership amount within 18 months. The National Wildlife Federation identifies several categories of supporters. Associate memberships, including those who join directly through the national office, are counted as by other membership organizations; junior members receive *Ranger Rick* magazine; state affiliate members, numbering approximately 1 million, belong to the federation through membership in state organizations; and contributors who respond to mailings offering conservation stamps or who purchase cards and gifts are counted among the total number of supporters reported by the organization, now approximately 4,600,000. This comprehensive number is likely to represent some amount of double

Table 2.3
Members and Supporters of Eight Wildlife Organizations, 1970–1986 (in thousands)

	1970	1971	1972	1973	1974	1975	1976	1977	1978	1979	1980	1981	1982	1983	1984	1985	1986
Defenders	13	14	15	21	26	32	32	37	47	48	44	50	57	63	66	73	75
EDF	11	27	30	33	36	37	43	45	43	45	45	47	50	50	50	50	50
Greenpeace						5			21			250			400	550	600
HSUS											48		66		116		310
NAS																	
memberships	105	139	164	218	237	251	269	287	298	300	311	328	357	399	446	443	456
members									388	392	412	436	468	498	506	502	516
NWF																	
associates	540	505	525	556	594	612	598	571	798	877	859	786	735	725	815	854	877
junior															682	677	704
all supporters (in millions)	2.7	2.9	2.9	3.1	3.2	3.4	3.4	3.9	4.1	4.2	4.7	4.2	4.1	4.1	NA	4.5	4.6
TNC								48	56	72	100	130	153	194	237	275	311
WWF–US									44	44	45	58	85	94	133	172	222

Sources: Data provided by organizations in response to inquiry and drawn from NGO publications. Data for Defenders of Wildlife, 1970–1979, and the NWF associate memberships, 1970–1975, were provided by Robert Cameron Mitchell.

counting, since state affiliate members may independently join the organization as associate members. They may also respond to merchandise offers, and their children may receive *Ranger Rick* magazine. For Greenpeace the numbers represent all supporters. For the Humane Society of the U.S. (HSUS), the precise derivation of the numbers was not made available. The numbers do not include all supporters but "similar and representative membership categories." As suggested by this discussion, organizations were willing and able to respond to requests for information to differing extents. Some organizations could respond only with great difficulty or not at all, since the data was in storage, misplaced, or handled by outside consultants. There is great variation in the quality of organizational memory.

The membership growth patterns differ significantly across organizations. The NWF, founded in 1936 and by far the largest organization in 1970, has shown steady but slow growth over 16 years, its associate memberships increasing 62 percent. The EDF, on the other hand, founded in 1967, saw memberships quadruple in the early 1970s, followed by modest growth, followed by no growth. The Nature Conservancy and WWF–US have enjoyed substantial growth since 1980, tripling and quintupling, respectively. Two periods in which rapid membership growth might have been expected are the post-Earth Day years of the early 1970s, during which time Congress passed the landmark conservation legislation concerning air and water quality and endangered species, and the early 1980s, following the election of Ronald Reagan and his appointment of Watt as Secretary of the Interior. The pattern is not clearly supported by the experiences of these groups. EDF, which saw dramatic growth in the early period, saw very little in the second. NAS grew substantially during both periods, adding approximately 150,000 members during the first half of each decade. NWF grew slowly in the first period but declined in the second. The two national environmental organizations that made the largest and most permanent gains during the early Reagan years are not represented here. The Wilderness Society and the Sierra Club, both of which follow public lands issues, drew substantial attention to Watt's Interior Department and mobilized popular opinion against the outspoken secretary. The Sierra Club nearly doubled its membership, to 335,000, between 1980 and 1983, and the Wilderness Society more than doubled its membership, to 100,000, during the same period.[79] NAS, EDF, and Defenders showed relative or absolute stagnation during the late 1970s, a time when

environmental values were strongly represented in the Carter administration and potential new members were perhaps not threatened by
environmental deterioration.

Budgets

Revenue and expenditure data for a sample of 18 wildlife NGOs
for 1985 reveal a range of budgetary patterns as broad as the range
of the scopes, purposes, and activities of the organizations in the
industry.[80] These organizations reported combined revenues of $291
million, with a mean of $16.6 million and a median of $3.6 million.
The five largest organizations—the Nature Conservancy, New York
Zoological Society (NYZS), Ducks Unlimited (DU), National Wildlife
Federation (NWF), and National Audubon Society (NAS)—accounted
for 85 percent of the total. The Nature Conservancy alone, with revenues of $83.7 million, received 29 percent of the total of all NGOs.
The five smallest—the Animal Welfare Institute (AWI), American
Horse Protection Association (AHPA), Wildlife Legislative Fund of
America (WLFA), Monitor, and Boone and Crockett Club—accounted
for less than 1 percent of the total, but even these organizations,
with the exception of the very small Monitor, generate annual revenues in the range of $300,000–500,000.[81]

Total expenditures amounted to $216 million, or 74 percent of
revenues. This sizable operating surplus is largely accounted for by
the Nature Conservancy ($51.8 million) and the NYZS ($19.2 million). Of the remaining sixteen organizations, eight recorded operating
losses that ranged from 4 to 41 percent of revenues. The eighteen
organizations had a combined end-of-year net worth of $449 million,
just over two times annual expenditures. But this result is largely
driven by the Conservancy, the expenditures for which were but 11
percent of net worth. At the other extreme were NGOs with expenditures exceeding net worth by multiples of 6 (EDF), 34 (Greenpeace),
47 (Monitor), and 87 (AHPA).

All NGOs routinely allocate expenditures among program, management, and fund-raising activities. For all organizations taken together,
80 percent of expenditures are allocated to programs and, with the
exception of a low value of 37 percent for Boone and Crockett, the
distribution is quite narrow, with 13 NGOs reporting 70–90 percent
of expenditures for programs. Management expenses account for 8
percent overall and, with the exception of Boone and Crockett at 64

percent and NAS at 26 percent, all NGOs report management expenses at 4–15 percent. Fund raising accounts for 12 percent of total expenses, with reported figures ranging from 0 percent (Boone and Crockett and Monitor) to 27 percent (AHPA).

The division of program expenditures into specific programs reveals a wide range of NGO activity. For example, the $7.8 million program budget of Greenpeace is divided into 14 programs ranging from "Operation of merchandise operations which promotes Greenpeace USA's charitable purpose" ($1.6 million) and "Protection of harp seals in Canada and population assessments" ($1.3 million) to "stop the exploitation of the outer continental shelf" ($35,643) and "stop the slaughter of sea turtles" ($15,203). The $39.9 million program budget of DU is devoted largely to acquisition and maintenance of waterfowl habitat: $26 million was distributed to DU (Canada) and $1.2 million to DU (Mexico). Another $6.9 million is allocated to U.S. habitat protection. Other expenses include conservation education ($3.1 million), membership services ($1.8 million), national and international operations ($.2 million), and other programs ($.7 million). The Wildlife Legislative Fund of America divides its $308,000 of program services into research and information ($101,000), legislative research and monitoring ($80,000), legislative services ($74,000), and membership services ($54,000). The AHPA devotes its program budget of $211,000 to a single program, "protection of horses and burros from abuse through public education and field activities."

NGOs would prefer to report high program expenditures relative to maintenance functions. Donors could then be confident that their contributions were devoted to achieving the basic goals of the organization.[82] The division of expenses among programs leaves a certain amount of discretion to the organization, since many activities that raise funds also educate members or solicit their participation in achieving organizational goals. The New York State annual financial report for charitable organizations asks filers whether or not they "allocate costs of multipurpose activities between program services and fundraising," and, if so, directs them to append an explanatory statement. Organizations that do not allocate costs may include all costs of direct mail that includes any program content whatsoever as program expenses. Greenpeace allocates $.96 million in canvassing expenses in equal parts to fund raising and education. Of the $4.12 million direct mail budget, payments to fund raisers, "continuing costs," and mailings without program content are charged to fund raising, whereas direct costs of mailings with program content are charged to programs. By this method, less than one-third of direct mail expenses are charged to fund raising. Similarly, WWF–US allocated 30 percent of its $2.75 million direct mail campaign to fund raising, the remainder covering membership development (32 percent) and public information combined with fund-raising (38 percent). HSUS, which does not allocate costs, reported $233,765 (3 percent of total expenses) as fund-raising expenses but also identified "membership development mailing," as a program service receiving over $2 million (29 percent of total expenses). In addition, the largest program category, "humane education, membership and program services," might also include activities related to fund raising. Similarly, the NWF allocates approximately 8 percent of its $40-million budget to fund raising but spends $1.4 million to rent mailing lists, of which only $118,604 is included as fund-raising expense.

Organizations provide functional as well as programmatic expense data. Employee compensation among the 18 NGOs accounts for 28 percent of total expenses, ranging from 14 percent (Greenpeace) to 62 percent (Monitor). Salaries of executive directors (not available for all organizations) can be divided into three groups. In the larger organizations (WWF–US, NAS, Nature Conservancy, NYZS, and NWF), salaries lie in the $100,000–120,000 range; for the next tier of organizations (such as EDF and Defenders), top salaries are about $75,000; for the smaller organizations, salaries lie in the $40,000 range. The larger organizations support large bureaucratic structures and salaries to match. NAS, for example, identifies 26 full-time vice-presidents who received an average of $51,000 during the year.[83] In addition, the organization supports 35 employees at salaries above $30,000, of whom at least 5 earn in excess of $50,000. The Nature Conservancy compensates 18 officers (excluding the president) an average of $61,000. Among midsized organizations, EDF, for example, employs 9 persons at salaries in excess of $30,000, none of whom (except the executive director) earns in excess of $50,000. Greenpeace, on the other hand, has no officers or employees who earn more than $30,000; indeed, no listed salary exceeds $20,000.

Revenues may be divided by source into direct public support (from individuals, corporations, and foundations), indirect public support (for example, from federated fund-raising campaigns), government grants, program revenues (sales and admissions), and property income (interest, dividends, capital gains, and royalties). Public (non-government) sources provide a mean of 77 percent of NGO revenues but range from 38 to 99 percent. The variety of experience is suggested by three examples. The NYZS reports $21.1 million in non-governmental public support (42 percent of total revenues), deriving 47 percent from foundations and trusts, 28 percent from bequests, 12 percent from individuals, 5 percent each from members and businesses, and 3 percent from fund-raising events. WWF–US received $9.9 million of direct and indirect public support (83 percent of total revenues), of which 10 percent derives from foundations, 13 percent from bequests, 43 percent from individuals (of which about one-half is direct mail, one-third is personal contact, and the remainder is telephone generated), 17 percent from members, 5 percent from corporations, and 12 percent from federated fund raising. Finally, Greenpeace received $8.4 million in direct and indirect public support (83 percent of total revenues), 79 percent of which is derived from direct mail campaigns, 14 percent from door-to-door canvassing, and 4 percent from unsolicited gifts. An additional 3 percent is derived from affiliate organizations. Government support is of substantial importance only for the NYZS, which derived 17 percent of its $50.8 million in revenues from New York City (14 percent), New York State (3 percent) and the federal government (0.4 percent). These data understate the importance of government support, in that they do not include the city's capital expenditures. Government grants and contracts are a minor source of revenue for seven other NGOs, accounting for less than 4 percent in each case; nine NGOs receive no government support.

Interest and dividend income of $13.4 million represents 5 percent of total revenues for the 18 NGOs and exceeds 10 percent only for one organization (HSUS). Income from merchandise sales was reported by nine organizations and is a significant revenue factor for AWI (30 percent), Boone and Crockett (34 percent), NWF (37 percent), NAS (11 percent), and Greenpeace (16 percent). (Note, however, that the NYZS reports zoo admissions and visitor services as program revenue rather than as gross sales.) Program revenues are of particular significance, for the Wildlife Management Institute (WMI, 16 percent), NYZS (25 percent), and the Nature Conservancy (19 percent). Ducks Unlimited (DU) generated just over half of its $48.3 million by fund-raising banquets held across the nation. A final revenue source of note is the mineral royalty—nearly $1 million in 1985—

generated for NAS through gas wells on its Rainey Sanctuary in Louisiana. The demonstrated willingness of NAS to subsidize environmental protection with revenues from carefully managed resource extraction is frequently cited by commentators who recommend a greater reliance on prices and markets in managing the land and its resources.[84]

Proprietary Sector

Business organizations in general, and large corporations in particular, are often pitted against the environmental community as if their goals, methods, and, indeed, entire world views excluded one another. Indeed, numerous specific conflicts arise in allocating access to public lands, setting pollution control standards, and protecting endangered species. It may seem no surprise that, as previously indicated, the business sector does not feature prominently in the support upon which wildlife NGOs can depend in pursuing their goals. In his 1979 address, "Preserving Our Natural Heritage," Joseph Cullman III, retired CEO and chairman of Philip Morris, Inc. and then-chairman of the World Wildlife Fund–U.S. (WWF–US) Executive Committee, argued not only for substantial growth in total corporate philanthropy but also for a major new commitment to conservation and the environment. "Considering the deep public interest in such matters," the 2 percent of corporate gifts now directed to these areas represents "a gross lack of performance by corporations." He singled out 11 national organizations among many worthy of support and observed that corporate expertise as well as money would be welcomed.[85]

Corporate giving for wildlife and the environment is constrained by the overall level of corporate giving, currently representing about 5 percent of total giving and 2 percent of the income of nonprofit organizations. Corporate charity in 1984 is recorded at $3.8 billion, which at about 1.5 percent of pretax net income represents approximately half the rate of individual giving.[86] Almost all giving is by the largest firms. In particular, in 1977 the largest .1 percent of firms made 50 percent of corporate gifts. Of these amounts, however, little has been directed to conservation and environmental protection. A 1982 survey of 534 corporations giving $1.2 billion shows that "environment and ecology" received 1.1 percent of the total (even less than Cullman's 2 percent), as compared, for example, to higher education (25.7 percent) and culture and the arts (11.4 percent).[87]

There are two groups of NGOs that have historically tapped corporate philanthropy with some success. The first includes sportsmen's organizations that derive funding from sporting arms and ammunition manufacturers and dealers. The Wildlife Management Institute, founded in 1911 as the American Game Protective and Propagation Association with a five-year industry gift, continues to receive industry support; the NWF, founded in 1936, received industry support for a decade; the National Shooting Sports Foundation is supported by contributions from 90 firms and 279 arms dealers and distributors.[88]

A second group that receives corporate gifts includes NGOs perceived to be nonconfrontational. Examples are Cullman's own WWF–US and the Nature Conservancy. WWF–US launched a corporate contributions campaign in 1977. Its slick fund-raising brochure explains that "we understand the need to balance environmental and economic values. We seek cooperation, not confrontation. . . . The Fund has been called one of the most balanced, objective, and responsible of the American-based conservation organizations."[89] The brochure offers testimonials from the chairmen of the Atlantic-Richfield, IBM, and Ford Motor Corporations and names corporations that have become "associate," "sponsor," or "patron" members by contributing $1,000 or more annually. In fiscal 1980, 150 corporations had contributed $522,000.[90] In subsequent years annual corporate contributions have remained at about this level, representing a substantial decline in proportional importance.

The Nature Conservancy exudes moderation and balance. The organization, variously called the "real estate arm of the conservation movement" and a cross between Century 21 and the Sierra Club,[91] acquires ecologically significant properties through gift or purchase, transferring some to governments or local conservation organizations and managing others as part of what has become a half-million-acre network of reserves. In 1980 over 300 corporations contributed nearly $1.7 million in cash, but this total does not include corporate gifts of land, which over the period 1975–80 totaled $40 million at estimated fair market value.[92] Cash grants from corporations have grown only modestly, to an annual rate of about $2.4 million in 1985, and have generally retained their proportional importance among revenue sources. Corporate associates have increased in number to 442.

Corporate support for the conservancy in particular is suggested by the extent to which the organization, through its style of preservation, validates the existing distribution of property rights in land and thereby confirms corporate values. Interior Secretary William Clark, in praising a 120,000-acre gift through the conservancy to the National Wildlife Refuge System, remarked on the organization's "unique ability to bring the public and private sectors together and build a bridge between ecology and economics."[93] From the conservancy's point of view, corporate support recognizes the "compatibility between a selective, business-like approach to land conservation and essential economic growth."[94] An executive of Consolidation Coal Company, donor of one of the largest corporate gifts to the conservancy, reported that the group acquires land "for, I believe a very good purpose, but do[es] so within the framework of the free-market system. They do not seek to change the law or public opinion so as to deprive individuals or businesses of their just property rights."[95]

Donations of land or sales below market price have favorable tax consequences for donors and may otherwise reflect sound business practices. Robert A. Beck, chairman and chief executive officer of Prudential, said of the aforementioned transfer, "It has never been our intention to develop all of our North Carolina holdings for commercial purposes. We believe that we have now maximized the private value of this resource and that the timing is right to seek a highest and best alternative use."[96] Furthermore, the value to corporations of donated lands may already have been diminished or threatened by redistributive environmental legislation promoted by other NGOs. Indeed, the conservancy looks favorably on groups that are more issue directed. "They have created a climate of public opinion generally favorable to environmental protection, made it an important issue."[97]

Beyond support for these categories of NGOs, there is sporadic corporate support for other NGO projects. The Celanese Corporation, for example, awarded the NAS $400,000 to support research on four species of endangered birds. John McComber, the Celanese president, remarked that the grant was made to "establish a precedent of cooperation between business and conservation groups and encourage a sharing of resources to save nature's diversity for future generations. . . . The chemical industry as a whole is acutely aware of its responsibilities" to the environment.[98]

These instances of cooperation between the business and environmental communities reflect genuine corporate concern for environmental quality, but they also reflect corporate concern for the profitability of the individual enterprise in particular and for the viability of free enterprise in general. Corporate philanthropy is but one element in a larger pattern of activities responding to the perceived threats that environmentalism and the public interest movement offer to corporate influence over political and economic life. Political confrontation is costly regardless of the outcome, and organizational resources devoted to reducing its frequency of occurrence or increasing the likelihood of successful outcomes may be wise investments. Other important elements in such an investment strategy include public service advertising, such as that offered by Mobil Oil Corporation's "op-ed" defense of deregulation and free enterprise, and a substantially enlarged Washington presence in lobbying and electoral politics.

Corporations have often found themselves the losers in litigation brought by public interest representatives, either against business directly or against agencies for failure to enforce or develop regulatory standards that impinge on business activity. The corporate response has been the creation of countervailing public interest law foundations, such as the Pacific, Southeastern, and Mountain States legal foundations, the latter of which served as Watt's springboard into the Reagan Interior Department. Costly litigation has also led to support for less confrontational dispute resolution mechanisms such as environmental mediation and negotiated rule making. Corporations have provided instrumental support for new organizations seeking to identify solutions to specific environmental concerns. Clean Sites, Inc., for example, a nonprofit, industry-funded corporation to promote voluntary cleanup by industry of hazardous waste sites, was created in 1984 by a coalition of industrial and environmental leaders coordinated by the Conservation Foundation. During its first year, more than 100 corporations provided 88 percent of its $2.5 million budget.[99] Finally, business has fostered grass-roots political activity in its sponsorship of Big Business Day and Growth Day, modeled after the successful series of Earth Days staged by the environmental community beginning in 1970. The corporate community has fostered the development of voluntary organizations that mimic citizens groups but work toward different goals. Keep America Beautiful, recommending a voluntary approach to litter control, was an early example sponsored by the beverage container industry. More recent examples include Citizens for Sensible Control of Acid Rain, funded by utilities and lobbying against restrictive acid rain legislation, and the St. Vrain Environmentalists and the Auburn Naturalists, promoting construction of water projects.[100]

In utilizing these strategies, the proprietary, and particularly the corporate, sector is meeting the environmental community on its own ground. The perceived need for this activity ranks as an important indicator of the success of the environmental movement. But it must be recalled that the proprietary sector exercises control over the policy process at a more fundamental level than that represented by these skirmishes. Charles E. Lindblom, in one assessment of the "privileged position of business in policy making," concludes that

the precise extent of business control appears to wax and wane. Over the long run, government regulation of business appears to grow. But so also do new supports or indulgences for business. . . . In market systems, since business performs only when induced to do so, government must follow policies that provide the necessary inducements. If from year to year or decade to decade, the pattern of inducement alters, the basic necessity remains.[101]

Whatever indirect control the corporate sector maintains over policy making, organizations have direct impacts on wildlife through the conduct of normal business activities of resource extraction, manufacturing, building, transporting, and disposing. Most of these impacts are regarded as costs external to the otherwise desired activities of the proprietary sector, but these activities may also have associated with them certain external benefits of a parallel nature. The endangered manatee, for example, finds expanded habitat at the warm water discharges (called "thermally enriched effluent" by utilities and "heat pollution" by the public interest community) of Florida's power plants. Many species benefit from the edge environments maintained along utility rights-of-way.[102] These and other benefits are fortuitous consequences of normal business activities, enhanced in some cases by corporate philanthropy.

For obvious reasons, corporations are beginning to identify and promote the beneficial environmental impacts of their activities. This increased corporate awareness may signal a shift in corporate strategy from the support of nonprofit organizations to the direct support of wildlife management programs. As one publicist suggested, "people simply love animals. If your company is associated with kindness to animals, some of that love will rub off on you."[103] The DuPont Chemical Company and General Wine and Spirits, Inc., a division of Joseph E. Seagrams, have each contributed to the restoration of the bald eagle, the former through a series of annual $50,000 grants for research and captive breeding facilities and the latter through wide distribution of printed materials in conjunction with the marketing of the firm's Rare Eagle Bourbon. A spokesman for the Fish and Wildlife Service reported that "Seagrams has done more to publicize the plight of the eagle than the federal government has ever done, or ever will do. The government simply doesn't have the money to match Seagrams' work."[104] DuPont's director of environmental affairs reported, "We've made contributions (to private groups) for years, but often we didn't know whether our money went to buy paper clips or what. We decided we wanted a 'hands-on' identity for future projects, and the eagle program just fit perfectly."[105]

Other corporate support since the late 1970s has helped to underwrite the reintroduction of the peregrine falcon in Manhattan (Manhattan Life Insurance Co.), document and publicize the California condor recovery program (Sony Corporation, Televideo-San Diego, and three national networks), improve the habitat of the bighorn sheep (Martin-Marietta), increase public awareness of the manatee (Florida Light and Power), and publicize the plight of endangered species (Health-tex).

Some corporations, in response to consumer boycotts and other publicity, have modified business practices to reduce certain threats to wildlife. In 1983, Burger King and the Long John Silver Seafood Shoppes halted their purchases of Norwegian fish to protest that nation's refusal to abide by the International Whaling Commission ban on the cold harpoon. In 1986, Burger King, because of alleged complicity in tropical deforestation through the purchase of Central American beef, became the target of a boycott organized by the Rainforest Action Network, and, in September 1987, the corporation cancelled a major contract with Costa Rican ranchers. In 1988, Burger King once again became the object of a protest, this time to encourage the corporation to join an international boycott against Icelandic fish in response to that nation's continued whaling.[106]

Corporate programs that benefit wildlife may grow at the expense of the nonprofit sector or they may represent additional resources drawn into the wildlife industry that will generate further support for the nonprofit sector. As this inquiry expands in scope in the subsequent chapters of this book, it builds to this industrywide perspective. The initial step in this direction is taken in the case studies of Chapters 3 and 4. Each focuses on the management problems associated with a single species—the California condor in Chapter 3 and the bobcat in Chapter 4—but each is principally organized around the roles of NGOs, not only in keeping with the themes of this book but in recognition of the instrumental roles that NGOs have played as these cases unfolded. The intent in presenting these cases is to explore the intricacies of the policy process and to identify several critical issues in the wildlife policy arena. These issues include a divided jurisdiction over wildlife between the state and federal governments; conflict between scientific and popular decision making; disagreements among advocacy groups and among experts; the division of labor among the congressional, administrative, and judicial realms; and action in the face of uncertainty. These themes will be returned to throughout the remainder of the book.

NOTES

1. Already there are problems. First, some groups, individuals, and agencies concerned with wildlife as defined here are also concerned with domesticated and laboratory animals, including newly created life-forms. Second, the definition obscures the boundary between domestic and wild animals and the policy issues surrounding passage from one status to the other. Free-roaming feral populations of horses and burros on the public domain, for example, have generally been protected as "an integral part of the natural system of the public lands." Wild Free-Roaming Horses and Burros Act, 85 Stat. 649 (1971). The patterns of control over captive-bred wildlife and the creation of private rights in wildlife to promote efficiency in resource use raise additional concerns.

2. For example, see Frederic Scherer, *Industrial Market Structure and Economic Performance*, 2nd. ed. (Chicago: Rand McNally, 1980). For a related industry study, see Joel F. Handler, Betsy Ginsberg, and Arthur Snow, "The Public Interest Law Industry," in *Public Interest Law: An Economic and Institutional Analysis*, Burton A. Weisbrod, study director, in collaboration with Joel F. Handler and Neil K. Komesar (Berkeley: University of California Press, 1978), pp. 42-79.

3. Erik Eckholm, "Species are Lost Before They're Found," New York *Times*, September 16, 1986, p. C1; Roger Lewin, "Damage to Tropical Forests, or Why Were There So Many Kinds of Animals?" *Science* 234 (October 10, 1986): 149-50. These estimates, based on small samples taken in tropical environments, are larger by a factor of three than estimates made five to ten years ago. For example, the 1980 *Global 2000* report estimates 3-10 million species. Council on Environmental Quality and U.S. Department of State, *The Global 2000 Report to the President: Entering the Twenty-first Century*, vol. 2 (Washington, D.C.: Government Printing Office, 1980), p. 327.

4. Eckholm, "Species are Lost," p. C1.

5. Paul Erlich and Anne Erlich, *Extinction: The Causes and Consequences of the Disappearance of Species* (New York: Random House, 1981), p. 17.

6. These counts are sensitive at the margin to the ongoing debates within systematics between the splitters, who tend to recognize fine distinctions among populations or related species, and lumpers, who do not. They are sensitive as well to cross-breeding and isolation, which may eliminate or create species. The policy implications of species delineations can be significant. For a critical view, see William Tucker, *Progress and Privilege: America in the Age of Environmentalism* (Garden City: Anchor Press, Doubleday, 1982), Chapter 7.

7. David M. Raup, "Biological Extinction in Earth History," *Science* 231 (March 28, 1986): 1528-33.

8. Greta Nilsson, *The Endangered Species Handbook* (Washington, D.C.: Animal Welfare Institute, 1983), pp. 6-7.

9. Among them are the Texas Henslow's sparrow, the Tarahamaro frog, and the Wyoming toad. See testimony of Michael J. Bean in U.S. Congress, Senate, Subcommittee on Environmental Pollution of the Committee on Environment and Public Works, *Endangered Species Act Authorizations, Hearings on S.725*, April 16 and 18, 1985, 99th Cong., 1st sess., S. Hrg. 99-70, pp. 186-212.

10. See, for example, Nilsson, *Endangered Species Handbook*, pp. 2-24.

11. F. Wayne King, "Preservation of Genetic Diversity," in *Sustaining Tomorrow: A Strategy for World Conservation and Development*, edited by Francis R. Thibodeau and Hermann H. Field (Hanover, N.H.: published for Tufts University by University Press of New England, 1984), p. 42.

12. Council on Environmental Quality, *Global 2000 Report*, pp. 328–31, and testimony of Thomas B. Stoel, Jr., in U.S. Congress, House, Subcommittee on Human Rights and International Organizations of the Committee on Foreign Affairs, *U.S. Policy on Biological Diversity, Hearing*, 99th Cong., 1st sess., June 6, 1985, pp. 45-46.

13. See Norman Myers, *A Wealth of Wild Species: Storehouse for Human Welfare* (Boulder, Colo.: Westview, 1983); Margery L. Oldfield, *The Value of Conserving Genetic Resources*, U.S. Department of the Interior, National Park Service (Washington, D.C.: Government Printing Office, 1984); and Christine Prescott-Allen and Robert Prescott-Allen, *The First Resource: Wild Species in the North American Economy* (New Haven: Yale University Press, 1986).

14. Erik Eckholm, "Quest for Cancer Drugs: U.S. Devises Major New Strategy," New York *Times*, December 23, 1986, p. C1.

15. On the history of wildlife on the land, see Durward L. Allen, *Our Wildlife Legacy* Rev. ed. (New York: Funk & Wagnalls, 1962); Peter Mattheissen, *Wildlife in America* (New York: Viking, 1959); James Trefethen, *Crusade for Wildlife: Highlights in Conservation Progress* (Harrisburg, Pa.: Stackpole Company and Boone and Crockett Club, 1961); and James A. Tober, *Who Owns the Wildlife? The Political Economy of Conservation in Nineteenth-Century America* (Westport, Conn.: Greenwood, 1981).

16. On the condor, see Chapter 3 of this book. Also see, generally, the case studies in National Audubon Society, *Audubon Wildlife Report* (New York: National Audubon Society, annual), and in U.S. Department of the Interior, Fish and Wildlife Service, *Restoring America's Wildlife, 1937-1987* (Washington, D.C.: Government Printing Office, 1987). See also Council on Environmental Quality, *Environmental Quality—1984* (Washington, D.C.: Government Printing Office, 1984), Table A-39.

17. Peter Steinhart, "Abundance," *Audubon*, January 1987, pp. 8-11.

18. Stephen R. Kellert, *Phase II: Activities of the American Public Relating to Animals*, U.S. Fish and Wildlife Service, April 1980. These data are generally confirmed by the more narrowly focused U.S. Department of the Interior, Fish and Wildlife Service, and U.S. Department of Commerce, Bureau of the Census, *1980 National Survey of Fishing, Hunting, and Wildlife-associated Recreation* (Washington, D.C.: Government Printing Office, 1982).

19. Amanda Jorgenson, "Biologists Express Concern for Huge Trade in Bullfrogs," *Traffic (USA)*, April 1985, p. 25; Prescott-Allen and Prescott-Allen, *The First Resource*, p. 92; and Doug Fuller, "American Ginseng: Harvest and Export, 1982-1984," *Traffic (USA)*, June 1986, p. 7.

20. Kellert, *Phase II*, Tables 18, 19, 20, 22, 41, 43, and 44; see also U.S. Departments of the Interior and Commerce, *1980 National Survey*.

21. Stephen R. Kellert and Joyce K. Berry, *Phase III: Knowledge, Affection and Basic Attitudes toward Animals in American Society*, U.S. Fish and Wildlife Service, 1980, pp. 11-27.

22. Ibid., Table 2, p. 9.

23. Ibid., Figures 3, 4, pp. 24, 28.

24. Council on Environmental Quality, *Public Opinion on Environmental Issues: Results of a National Public Opinion Survey* (Washington, D.C.: Government Printing Office, 1980).

25. Roger W. Cobb and Charles D. Elder, *Participation in American Politics: The Dynamics of Agenda-Building*, 2nd ed. (Baltimore: Johns Hopkins University Press, 1983), Chapter 1.

26. Kellert and Berry, *Phase III*, pp. 10, 27, 31-42. Elsewhere, Kellert identifies eight factors "significantly affecting public support for protecting endangered species:" aesthetics, phylogenetic relatedness, reason for endangerment, tangible economic value of species, number and types of people affected by efforts to protect species, knowledge and familiarity, cultural and historical relationship, and perceived humaneness of activity threatening the species. Stephen R. Kellert, *Phase I: Public Attitudes toward Critical Wildlife and Natural Habitat Issues*, U.S. Fish and Wildlife Service, October 15, 1979, p. 34. See also the member surveys of Defenders of Wildlife showing relative species preferences. *Defenders*, September-October 1984, p. 42; November-December 1985, p. 43.

27. Kellert, *Phase I*, Table 10A/B, pp. 19-20.

28. Ibid., Table 13, p. 27.

29. Ibid., Table 45, p. 106.

30. E. J. Kahn, "The Indigenists," *New Yorker*, August 31, 1981, p. 60.

31. On the Endangered Species Act amendments of 1978, see the section on congressional action in Chapter 5; on the press treatment of the controversy, see Carroll J. Glynn and Albert R. Tims, "Environmental and Natural Resource Issues: Press Sensationalism," in *Transactions of the Forty-fifth North American Wildlife and Natural Resources Conference* (Washington, D.C.: Wildlife Management Institute, 1980), pp. 99-109.

32. Recent surveys include Graham K. Wilson, *Interest Groups in the United States* (New York: Oxford University Press, 1981); Jeffrey M. Berry, *The Interest Group Society* (Boston: Little, Brown, 1984); and Allan J. Cigler and Burdett A. Loomis, eds., *Interest Group Politics*, 2nd. ed. (Washington, D.C.: Congressional Quarterly Press, 1986).

33. See Robert Cameron Mitchell, "From Conservation to Environmental Movement: The Development of the Modern Environmental Lobbies," Resources for the Future, Discussion Paper QE85-12, June 1985, and Burdett A. Loomis and Allan J. Cigler, "Introduction: The Changing Nature of Interest Group Politics," in *Interest Group Politics*, 2nd. ed., edited by Cigler and Loomis (Washington, D.C.: Congressional Quarterly Press, 1986), pp. 1-26.

34. Robert H. Salisbury, "Washington Lobbyists: A Collective Portrait," in *Interest Group Politics*, p. 149.

35. Arthur C. Close, John P. Gregg, and Regina Germain, eds., *Washington Representatives-1986* (Washington, D.C.: Columbus Books, 1986).

36. Mitchell, "From Conservation to Environmental Movement," p. 38.

37. E. Donald Elliott, Bruce A. Ackerman, and John C. Millian, "Toward a Theory of Statutory Evolution: The Federalization of Environmental Law," *Journal of Law, Economics, and Organization* 1 (1985): 313-40.

38. Hugh Heclo, "Issue Networks and the Executive Establishment," in *The New American Political System*, edited by Anthony King (Washington, D.C.: American Enterprise Institute, 1978), pp. 97, 99, 100.

39. Robert Cameron Mitchell and J. Clarence Davies, III, "The United States Environmental Movement and Its Political Context: An Overview," Resources for the Future Discussion Paper D-32, May 1978; Mitchell, "From Conservation to Environmental Movement"; Stephen Fox, *John Muir and His Legacy: The American Conservation Movement* (Boston: Little, Brown, 1981); and David L. Sills, "The Environmental Movement and Its Critics," *Human Ecology* 3 (1975): 1-41.

40. Robert Cameron Mitchell, "Public Opinion and Environmental Politics in the 1970s and 1980s," in *Environmental Policy in the 1980s: Reagan's New Agenda*, edited by Norman J. Vig and Michael E. Kraft (Washington, D.C.: Congressional Quarterly Press, 1984), pp. 51-74.

41. See, for example, Philip Shabecoff, "Thousands Hail Earth Day '80 Tomorrow and Map Battles for a New Decade," New York *Times*, April 21, 1980,

p. A16; Luther J. Carter, "Environmentalists Seek New Strategies," *Science* 208 (May 2, 1980): 477–78.

42. Other typologies may be found in Elvis J. Stahr and Charles H. Callison, "The Role of Private Organizations," in Council on Environmental Quality, *Wildlife and America, Contributions to an Understanding of American Wildlife and Its Conservation,* edited by Howard P. Brokaw (Washington, D.C.: Government Printing Office, 1978), pp. 498–511; Mitchell and Davies, "United States Environmental Movement," Table 1; David P. Forsythe, "Humanizing American Foreign Policy," Program on Non-Profit Organizations, Yale University, Working Paper No. 12, 1980; Charles H. W. Foster, "Counsel for the Concerned," in *Law and the Environment,* edited by Malcolm F. Baldwin and James K. Page (New York: Walker, 1970), pp. 277–88; and Kellert, *Phase II.*

43. On the nineteenth-century history of national sportsmen's associations, see James A. Tober, *Who Owns the Wildlife? The Political Economy of Conservation in Nineteenth-Century America* (Westport, Conn.: Greenwood, 1981), pp. 185–89.

44. Virginia Ann Hodgkinson and Murray S. Weitzman, *Dimensions of the Independent Sector: A Statistical Profile,* 2nd. ed. (Washington, D.C.: Independent Sector, 1986), Tables 1.4 and 1.6.

45. Author's counts. NWF compilation procedures suggest that directories are likely to omit new organizations and retain some no longer in existence.

46. Included are wildlife groups and national conservation groups otherwise considered in this book (such as Friends of the Earth), but omitted are humane groups that focus only on antivivisection or domestic animals. For comparative data, see Jeffrey M. Berry, *Lobbying for the People: The Political Behavior of Public Interest Groups* (Princeton, N.J.: Princeton University Press, 1977), Table II.3, p. 34, and Philip Lowe and Jane Goyder, *Environmental Groups in Politics* (London: Allen & Unwin, 1983), Figure 2.1, p. 16. For data suggestive of the permanence of groups, see Kay Lehman Schlozman, "What Accent the Heavenly Chorus? Political Equality and the American Pressure System," *Journal of Politics* 46 (1984):1021–25.

47. David B. Truman, *The Governmental Process,* 2nd. ed. (New York: Knopf, 1971), and Robert H. Salisbury, "An Exchange Theory of Interest Groups," *Midwest Journal of Political Science* 13 (February 1969): 1–32; see also Berry, *Lobbying for the People,* pp. 18–24, and J. Craig Jenkins, "Nonprofit Organizations and Policy Advocacy," in *The Nonprofit Sector: A Research Handbook,* edited by Walter W. Powell (New Haven: Yale University Press, 1987), pp. 298–303.

48. In particular, he found 17 of 21 environmental groups and all 13 consumer groups in his sample to have entrepreneurial origins. Jeffrey M. Berry, "On the Origins of Public Interest Groups: A Test of Two Theories," *Polity* 10 (Spring 1978): 379–97.

49. Donald Fleming, "Roots of the New Conservation Movement," in *Perspectives in American History,* vol. 6, edited by Donald Fleming and Bernard Bailyn.

(Cambridge, Mass.: Charles Warren Center for Studies in American History, Harvard University, 1972), p. 7.

50. Jack L. Walker, "The Origins and Maintenance of Interest Groups in America," *American Political Science Review* 77 (1983): 390–406.

51. Malcolm Forbes Baldwin, "Defenders' Distinctive Niche," *Defenders*, January–February 1986, p. 46.

52. Peregrine Fund, "World Center for Birds of Prey," undated brochure.

53. "The Audubon Cause," *Audubon*, January 1980, pp. 78–79.

54. *Audubon Action*, June 1985, p. 8.

55. *Audubon Activist*, September 1986, p. 2.

56. World Wildlife Fund–US (WWF–US), *Annual Report 1978*, p. 2.

57. *Audubon Activist*, September 1986, p. 6; Environmental Defense Fund, *Annual Report 1986*, pp. 2, 9; Environmental Task Force, "Case Statement," Washington, D.C., December 12, 1985.

58. *Living Wilderness*, September 1980, p. 39; New York *Times*, April 19, 1981, p. 1.

59. *Wilderness*, Spring 1986, p. 10.

60. Environmental Defense Fund, *Annual Report 1986*.

61. *EDF Letter*, August 1986, p. 4.

62. Berry found, for example, that decision making in 69 percent of groups was staff dominated and in only 10 percent of groups board dominated. The board played no role at all in 68 percent of the groups in his sample. Berry, *Lobbying for the People*, pp. 196–97.

63. Cited in Tom Burke, "Friends of the Earth and the Conservation of Resources," in *Pressure Groups in the Global System: The Transnational Relations of Issue-Oriented Non-Government Organizations*, edited by Peter Willetts (New York: St. Martin's, 1982), p. 129.

64. Andrew S. McFarland, *Common Cause: Lobbying in the Public Interest* (Chatham, N.J.: Chatham House, 1984).

65. Interview with outgoing president, William Turnage, *Wilderness*, Summer 1985, p. 46.

66. Jamie Heard, "Washington Pressures/Friends of the Earth Give Environmental Interests an Activist Voice," *National Journal*, August 8, 1970, p. 1711.

67. Ibid., p. 1713.

68. In 1986 Friends of the Earth emerged from a bitter two-year internal fight over leadership, goals, and location. One of the few public personalities in the environmental movement, Brower had founded FOE in 1969 after being forced to resign as director of the Sierra Club (which he had substantially revitalized). He was dismissed as FOE chairman in 1984 for failure to support the decision of the board to address the organization's substantial debts through staff reductions. He was reinstated through a procedural challenge. To reduce these debts, the directors then voted 8 to 7 to consolidate the organization by moving the headquarters from San Francisco to Washington, location of the

legislative office, a move opposed by Brower and his allies, who believed it would cost FOE its identity. The minority members placed a measure on the 1986 membership ballot to recall the majority directors. The majority position prevailed, the move was made, and Brower and other staff members resigned. With the hiring of movement veteran Cynthia Wilson as executive director in October 1986, FOE was prepared to move forward (smaller in membership and leaner in budget) in a somewhat uncertain search for a place in the environmental community. New York *Times*, July 7, 1984, p. 1, August 2, 1984, p. A10, and January 3, 1986, p. A9, and numerous FOE mailings to the membership.

69. Toby Cooper, "Blow by Blow: Calling the Punches in Washington's Battle of the Bowhead," *Defenders*, February 1978, pp. 58-61.

70. Burke, "Friends of the Earth and the Conservation of Resources," pp. 106-8.

71. International Association of Fish and Wildlife Agencies, *Proceedings of the Sixty-eighth Convention*, September 10-13, 1978, pp. 154-56.

72. International Association of Fish and Wildlife Agencies, *Proceedings of the Seventy-first Convention*, September 13-16, 1981, pp. 129-30, 239-48.

73. Robert Cameron Mitchell, "National Environmental Lobbies and the Apparent Illogic of Collective Action." In *Collective Decision Making: Applications from Public Choice Theory*, edited by Clifford S. Russell (Baltimore: John Hopkins University Press, 1979), pp. 96-98. Mitchell's more recent estimate of two million members is limited to major national groups and includes an estimated correction for multiple memberships. (Robert Cameron Mitchell, "Public Opinion and Environmental Politics in the 1970s and 1980s," in *Environmental Policy in the 1980s*, p. 60.

74. Kellert, *Phase II*, pp. 73-82.

75. The debate was initiated by Mancur Olson, *The Logic of Collective Action* (Cambridge, Mass.: Harvard University Press, 1965); subsequent contributions have included Mitchell, "National Environmental Lobbies"; Terry M. Moe, *The Organization of Interests: Incentives and the Internal Dynamics of Political Interest Groups* (Chicago: University of Chicago Press, 1980); David P. Forsythe and Susan Welch, "Citizen Support for Non-Profit Public Interest Groups," Program on Non-Profit Organizations, Yale University, Working Paper No. 35, n.d.; and V. Kerry Smith, "The Green Lobby," *American Political Science Review*, 79 (1985): 133-47.

76. Moe, *Organization of Interests*, pp. 30-34.

77. Mitchell, "National Environmental Lobbies," pp. 112-17. A more cynical view is offered by Jeremiah Allen. "The product of most firms in the conservation sector consists of information which is distributed to consumers. The purpose of the information is to cause the consumers to experience a reduction in satisfaction, which, in turn, will leave them in a state of disequilibrium." Consumers can restore equilibrium by allocating real income to the pursuit of the

firm's goals. "Anti-Sealing as an Industry," *Journal of Political Economy*, 87 (1979): 423-28.

78. Brattleboro *Reformer*, April 17, 1981, p. 13.

79. On the Sierra Club, see Mitchell, "Public Opinion and Environmental Politics," p. 61; on the Wilderness Society, see *The Living Wilderness*, Spring 1981, p. 44; and *Wilderness*, Spring 1984, p. 48.

80. These data are derived from IRS Form 990 tax returns, from annual financial reports filed with the New York State Department of State, Office of Charities Registration, and from financial data supplied by the organizations in annual reports and other publications.

81. The remaining eight NGOs are the African Wildlife Foundation, Defenders of Wildlife, Environmental Defense Fund (EDF), Fund for Animals, Greenpeace, Humane Society of the U.S. (HSUS), Wildlife Management Institute (WMI), and World Wildlife Fund-U.S. (WWF-US).

82. On fund-raising costs, see Susan Rose-Ackerman, "Charitable Giving and 'Excessive' Fundraising Costs," *Quarterly Journal of Economics* 97 (1982): 193-212.

83. Due to terminations and additions, the salaries for seven of these represent compensation for partial years. The mean annual salary is thereby understated.

84. See, for example, Richard L. Stroup and John A. Baden, *Natural Resources: Bureaucratic Myths and Environmental Management*. Pacific Studies in Public Policy. (Cambridge, Mass.: Ballinger, 1983), pp. 50, 107-109, and Tucker, *Progress and Privilege*, pp. 145-46.

85. Joseph F. Cullman, 3rd., "Preserving Our Natural Heritage," New Directions in Corporate Giving, Waldorf-Astoria Hotel, April 10, 1979, reprint distributed by Philip Morris, Inc. The organizations named range from the Smithsonian Institution to Friends of the Earth to the Atlantic Salmon Foundation.

86. Hodgkinson and Weitzman, *Dimensions of the Independent Sector*, p. 49. This may be an understatement, due to the corporate practice of deducting contributions as a business expense rather than reporting them as charitable contributions. Ibid.

87. Kathryn Troy, *Annual Survey of Corporate Contributions, 1984 Edition* (New York: Conference Board, 1984), cited in Michael Useem, "Corporate Philanthropy," in *The Nonprofit Sector*, pp. 342-44. See also Hodgkinson and Weitzman, *Dimensions of the Independent Sector*, Tables 3.51-3.53.

88. National Shooting Sports Foundation, *Annual Report 1978/79*.

89. WWF-US, "Invest in the Future." See also *Annual Report 1986*, p. 12. "WWF's effectiveness is bolstered by its nonconfrontational approach to public policy." Ibid.

90. WWF-US, "Invest in the Future," and WWF-US, *Annual Report 1979-80*, pp. 7, 41-43.

91. Peter Wood, "Business-Suited Saviors of Nation's Vanishing Wilds," *Smithsonian*, December 1978, pp. 77–84; Bil Gilbert, "The Nature Conservancy Game," *Sports Illustrated*, October 20, 1986, pp. 86–100.

92. Nature Conservancy, *Annual Report 1980*, p. 28.

93. U.S. Department of the Interior, news release, March 26, 1984.

94. Nature Conservancy, *Annual Report 1980*, p. 27.

95. Remarks of Jarvis B. Cecil, executive vice-president for finance and corporate affairs. Quoted in Gilbert, "Nature Conservancy Game," p. 94.

96. U.S. Department of the Interior, news release, March 26, 1984.

97. Conservancy president Bill Blair, quoted in Gilbert, "Nature Conservancy Game," p. 90.

98. New York *Times*, March 26, 1980, p. A18.

99. See, for example, Steering Committee on Hazardous Waste Cleanup, *Clean Sites and Private Action: A Plan to Accelerate Private Hazardous Waste Cleanup* (Washington, D.C.: Conservation Foundation, May 1984).

100. *Not Man Apart*, September–October 1986, p. 4; Jon R. Luoma, "Forests Are Dying but Is Acid Rain to Blame?" *Audubon*, March 1987, p. 48.

101. Charles E. Lindblom, *The Policy-making Process*, 2nd. ed. (Englewood Cliffs, N.J.: Prentice-Hall, 1980), p. 82.

102. Frank Graham, Jr., "A New Hand in the Wildlife Business," *Audubon*, May 1979, pp. 94–113; Council on Environmental Quality, *Environmental Quality 1983*, pp. 164–75.

103. Quoted in Robert A. Jones, "Businesses Move to Save Wildlife," Los Angeles *Times*, January 24, 1983, p. 1.

104. Quoted in ibid. See also "Using the Bald Eagle to Promote Bourbon," *Business Week*, September 4, 1978, unpaged reprint.

105. Quoted in Jones, "Businesses Move," p. 1.

106. *International Wildlife*, September–October 1983, p. 28A; letter from Monya Prince, Burger King Corporation, August 31, 1983; *Earth Island Journal*, Spring 1988, pp. 8–9; Brattleboro *Reformer*, August 13, 1988, p. 13.

3

The California Condor

On April 19, 1987, the last known wild California condor was captured on the Bitter Creek National Wildlife Reserve, northwest of the Los Angeles metropolitan area, and transported to the San Diego Wild Animal Park. The bird, a 7-year-old male known as AC-9 (adult condor 9), had been trapped before and carried a small radio transmitter on its wing. Although followed closely by the staff of the California Condor Research Center in Ventura, AC-9 had eluded final capture for many months. Netted at last, the bird joined the 26 others of its species known to exist on this earth, which presently reside in the "condorminiums" at the Los Angeles and San Diego zoos. The descendents of these two captive populations may one day occupy some portion of the historical range of the species. With the exception of Topa Topa, a male condor held in the Los Angeles zoo since 1967, the birds have been taken into captivity in the past six years— as eggs, as chicks, and as free-flying birds—to implement a controversial recovery program. On April 29, 1988, Molloko, the world's first captive-bred California condor, hatched at the San Diego Zoo's Wild Animal Park.

The decision to remove all of the birds from the wild was neither easily reached nor smoothly implemented. Indeed, the declaration of this policy in December 1985 by the U.S. Fish and Wildlife Service (FWS), the agency with legal responsibility for managing the birds under the federal endangered species act, prompted the National Audubon Society (NAS) the initiator, financial supporter, and partner in the recovery effort, to seek an injunction prohibiting the capture of six birds then in the wild. Audubon's case was built on the assertion that the FWS action, reversing the recently achieved policy consensus, was arbitrary, based on no new scientific evidence, and taken without proper consultation with interested parties. The legal proceedings, which one observer characterized as featuring more lawyers in the courtroom than condors in the wild,[1] produced the desired injunction in February 1986. Four months later the appeals court overturned the injunction, and the final round of captures began.

The California condor (*Gymnogyps californianus*), a huge vulture with a nine-to-ten-foot wingspan, once ranged throughout the Pacific coastal region from British Columbia to Baja California and also as far east as Florida. Its numbers have been drastically reduced during historic times, and for nearly 100 years its range has been confined to a wishbone-shaped region of some 50,000 square miles stretching from the northern edge of the Los Angeles metropolitan area along the mountain ridges that surround the San Joaquin Valley, about one-third of which lies within the national forests.[2] The factors accounting for the decline of the species are not fully understood. Documented takings of birds and eggs by hunters and collectors in the late nineteenth century represent a significant impact. More recently, land use changes associated with ranching, farming, mining, recreation, and housing and the accompanying uses of pesticides and poisons, together with accidental and malicious shootings, lead poisoning from ingesting bullet fragments, and power line collisions, combined to threaten the remaining birds.

Long an object of naturalists' curiosity and a source of Native American ceremonial goods, the condor did not benefit from organized concern until the 1930s. A small but critical condor sanctuary was created in 1937 in the wake of an unsuccessful effort by the U.S. Forest Service (USFS) to build a road through Sisquoc Canyon in Los Padres National Forest. In 1939 the NAS sponsored a multiyear study on the status and prospects of the species, undertaken by naturalist Carl Koford. Although Audubon did not publish Koford's work until 1953, his findings were clear much earlier: there were perhaps 60 birds, and there was little cause for optimism.

In 1947, based in part on the knowledge gained through Koford's investigation, the 35,000-acre Sespe condor sanctuary was created within the national forest.[3] At NAS urging, the Forest Service named a California Condor Advisory Committee to guide its management of the reserve.[4] The committee enjoyed moderate success in its early years. No new mineral claims were permitted within the sanctuary, and surface activity within existing claims was prohibited near nest sites. In 1950 the San Diego zoo secured the necessary state permits to initiate a captive breeding program, but the advisory committee refused to allow entry into the sanctuary where known nests were located. Zoo personnel were unable to discover nests elsewhere, nor could they capture adult birds before Audubon prevailed upon the state legislature, in 1953, to prohibit the taking of the condor at all times, existing permits notwithstanding. Some advocates of the current captive breeding program have observed that, had these earlier efforts gone forward, the outlook for the species today would be considerably less bleak.

In 1961, concerned that there was little basis on which to assess the progress of the species under its limited management regime, the NAS commissioned a new study by ornithologist Alden Miller and rancher/naturalists Ian and Eban McMillan, the latter of whom had assisted Koford in his earlier investigation. The Miller-McMillan report, published by Audubon in 1965, suggested that the decline of the species had not been arrested and that the threats to the condor were not being addressed by the present management. Few forest rangers and wardens knew or cared about the condor; the warden of the Sespe sanctuary, it was reported, "couldn't tell a condor from a turkey vulture."[5] The habitat was regularly traversed by hunters, and poisons were widely used to protect livestock and crops.

The advisory committee, inactive for a decade, was called to life in 1964 by a proposal, never funded, to dam the creek running through Sespe sanctuary. The following year, FWS assigned a full-time biologist to research the condor and evaluate the impact of the proposed dam. In the same year the NAS dispatched John Borneman as full-time naturalist and public relations agent to "represent" the condor and the society before the public.

Heightened concern over the fate of the condor renewed the debate over the merits of captive breeding. In 1965 the FWS opened the Patuxent Wildlife Research Center in Maryland, thereby initiating a federal commitment to research in captive breeding as a strategy for responding to the needs of endangered species. In 1966 Andean condors, the relatively abundant South American relatives of the California species, were brought to the center, signaling the first step in an implicit contingency plan to save the endangered bird.

With the passage of the Endangered Species Act in 1966 and the designation of the condor as endangered in 1967, the FWS joined the State of California (which had offered nominal protection under a 1901 nongame bird law) as guardian of the rare birds. The federal act was replaced by a more comprehensive law in 1969, and this was followed by the passage of a California endangered species statute in 1970. The condor did not receive its first specific federal protection until 1972, when the migratory bird treaty with Mexico was amended to include vultures. The passage of the third federal Endangered Species Act, in 1973, invited a more aggressive approach to species preservation. The act mandates the designation of recovery teams to develop strategies for removing species from the endangered species list and the designation of critical habitats to facilitate their recovery. In December 1975 the first critical habitats under the act were proposed for the condor and five other species, and in September 1976 the critical habitat for the condor, covering several hundred square miles of nesting and feeding grounds in nine dispersed parcels, was identified.[6]

The condor recovery team, staffed by FWS, USFS, and state personnel and by the NAS condor advocate, put forth a recovery plan in 1975 that contained only the most general suggestions leading to the growth of the condor population to about 50 birds and its subsequent maintenance. In addition the team developed a contingency plan to be implemented should the recovery plan fail to halt the decline of the species. That plan, as it emerged through several drafts, provided for a captive breeding program, but it did not detail such a program enough to inspire much confidence in its efficacy.[7]

Audubon's third round of concern over the fate of the condor began as the recovery plan was unveiled. With the support of its board of directors and with a grant from the Andrew W. Mellon Foundation, Audubon invited the cooperation of the American Ornithologists' Union (AOU) in appointing an advisory panel to review "every aspect of the condor problem, . . . the adequacy of the Recovery Plan, and the wisdom of executing the Contingency Plan in its present format and at this time." The May 1978 report, strongly endorsed by the Audubon board, concluded that "the future of the California Condor's habitat is dim," and it argued that the survival of the birds "demands drastic action requiring a firm commitment over two to four decades" and "depends on conscientious human intervention." It recommended that the recovery plan goals be substantially enlarged to provide for a population of several hundred individuals, distributed widely throughout the species' present and former range, that this be achieved through a program of captive breeding requiring the capture of a large proportion of the population and leading to the production of at least 100 second- and third-generation birds for release into the wild, that large expanses of habitat be immediately identified and preserved, and that research on free-living condors be intensified.[8]

The report was adopted by the Interior Department and became the basis for the revised recovery plan, approved in February 1980.[9] FWS, however, made no secret of the fiscal limitations, which would make implementation difficult if not impossible. Audubon undertook the task, with FWS backing, of seeking supplemental and add-on appropriations for fiscal 1979 and 1980 in amounts totaling $706,000. Audubon's effort, carefully engineered and ultimately successful, was aided by its own commitment to raise and spend $500,000 over five years in support of its own participation in the recovery effort.

Retiring NAS president Elvis J. Stahr and FWS Director Lynn Greenwalt testified before the House Interior Appropriations Subcommittee.[10] These appearances were accompanied by an intensive lobbying effort aimed at subcommittee members. Clair W. Burgener, the subcommittee's California member, became an early and important supporter. A member of his staff remarked that the issue had not been "on the top of his priority list" and that he would not have been interested had his support not been actively sought. Subcommittee chairman Sidney Yates (D. Ill.) was lobbied by Audubon members in his home district. He received a letter from Representative Robert Dornan (R. Calif.), signed by 19 members of the state delegation representing the full range of political views, urging support. The letter was drafted and circulated by the NAS condor advocate.

Supporting letters also arrived from the leadership of the House and Senate authorizations committees, which heard Audubon testimony in April 1979.[11] Borneman stressed the symbolic importance of the bird. "The Condor has become a symbol to the people of California and to many thousands of other Americans. But, unlike our Washington Monument and our Lincoln Memorial, it can never be rebuilt if it is destroyed." Chairman John Breaux, skeptical of the analogy between the condor and the Washington monument, was nevertheless favorably impressed. "I do have a different opinion of the condor after hearing your testimony than I might have had before."

The thorough lobbying by NAS, the strong support from FWS and highly respected members of the scientific community, and the apparent urgency of the enterprise brought the desired appropriations. Implementation of the recovery plan began. The recovery team was restructured, and its scientific capabilities were bolstered. The California Condor Research Center opened in Ventura, California, staffed by NAS and FWS personnel, and a cooperative agreement was negotiated among the NAS, FWS, U.S. Bureau of Land Management, USFS, and California Department of Fish and Game, in which each pledged certain support and made gestures of cooperation toward the success of the recovery effort.[12]

Those individuals and groups opposed to the captive breeding program had not been able to influence the decision-making process in a significant way to this point, in part because they were locked out by the well orchestrated efforts of NAS and FWS and in part because their opposition was reactive rather than strategic. The nature of the opposition that was to emerge was suggested by Koford's essay "California Condors, Forever Free?" written in response to the FWS draft implementation document and submitted to the House Subcommittee on Fisheries and Wildlife Conservation and the Environment. The essay, primarily a critique of the scientific basis of the recovery program, concludes with the following assessment:

A wild condor is much more than feathers, flesh, and genes. Its behavior results not only from its anatomy and germ plasm but from its long cultural heritage, learned by each bird from previous generations through several years of immature life. A cage-raised bird can never be more than a partial replicate of a wild condor. Aldo Leopold pointed out that the recreational value of wildlife is inversely proportional to its artificiality. . . . Let us keep condors forever free.[13]

Koford's views and the active opposition to the captive breeding program were first promoted by Friends of the Earth (FOE) and especially by David Brower, founder of FOE and its former president and then chairman. FOE's opposition was based on a skepticism that captive breeding would work and on the contention that this "technological" solution relegates the more important, more difficult issues of habitat preservation, pesticide use, and control of hunters to the back burner. As one FOE spokesman remarked, "the longer the plan is considered, the more problematical it becomes." But beyond this, and as suggested by Koford's eloquent plea, some opposition has been based on ethical considerations. Captive breeding denies the species the dignity it is due, and as between extinction and capture, the former may be preferred.

An Audubon staff scientist responded to such sentiments that "deep down inside they just don't want us handling California condors. It is almost a mythical condor that Koford has created. A lot of people are trying to save the mythical bird. Their approach might work for the mythical bird but not for the real blood and guts and feathers bird."[14] But if the debate had been elevated to higher realms of discourse, it was not the work only of recovery plan opponents. Borneman, the NAS condor advocate, remarked that "God has put me in this position. . . . Right now, this is my niche, and I mean to stay in it as long as there's one California condor left in the wild."[15]

The disagreements that surfaced over the captive breeding program questioned process as well as substance. As Brower concluded, "whatever the proper course may be, there is controversy enough to require that the public be heard and that public rights not be overridden."[16] One avenue for opening the decision process to public hearing is offered by the National Environmental Policy Act (NEPA), requiring federal agencies to prepare environmental impact statements for federal actions significantly affecting the quality of the human environment. The FWS, however, issued a Finding of No Significant Impact, rejecting the need to prepare such a statement. The supporting environmental assessment concluded, among other points, that the service "does not regard the notion that the esthetic aspects of the proposed action are objectionable to certain sensibilities as warranting the deletion of actions which might conserve an endangered life form."[17]

Those portions of the recovery plan dependent on capture and handling of birds—for measurement, for sexing (which cannot be done by observing external differences and required, at the time, biochemical analysis of feather or fecal matter or surgical laparoscopy), for fitting with collars for tracking, and ultimately for maintenance in captivity—require federal and state permits under the respective endangered species acts. Thus, developing the program and gaining congressional appropriations, processes successfully dominated by NAS, were to give way to the permit process, where other groups, relying on mobilization of public opinion and possible erosion of scientific support, might assert their influence.[18] It is important to note that the permit process, because it addressed only the hands-on portions of a much broader recovery effort, highlighted policy differences and ignored areas of possible agreement.

The federal permit request, seeking wide-ranging authority to capture, handle, radio tag, and maintain condors in captivity over a 35-year period, was published on May 9, 1980.[19] But opponents of the program looked to the California permit process for their best opportunity to limit captive breeding. State permits are granted by the Fish and Game Commission, an independent body of five appointees, one of whom happened to be a member of the FOE advisory council. (The commission typically delegates permitting authority over fully protected species to the state Fish and Game Department, but for the condor and several other high-profile species, the commission has retained control.) The commission had received dozens of letters from NGOs and individuals on both sides of the issue, indicating strong public concern but suggesting a small likelihood of satisfying all parties. On May 30, 1980, following a review of the correspondence and extensive public hearings, the commission approved the FWS proposal, conditioned by a number of recommendations made by the state Fish and Game Department.[20]

On June 30, 1980, one of two known condor chicks died of heart failure during a routine examination as a part of a nesting study being conducted by FWS and NAS. According to the commission staff, "the permit issued by the Department for that study had not been sanctioned by the Commission."[21] The death of the chick resulted in the revocation of permits authorizing the taking and handling of condors, pending a complete commission review. For opponents of the plan, this event merely confirmed their worst fears and prompted indignation. For proponents it was bad luck of the worst kind, for it delayed the program and cast into doubt its eventual implementation and success.

The death of the condor chick and the delay in the implementation of the recovery plan occasioned by it generated media attention and further public scrutiny of captive breeding. FWS and NAS, backed by prestigious scientific organizations, continued to view captive breeding as the only hope for the species. Indeed, recent field studies on the Andean condor in Peru and the growing success of hands-on recovery programs for the whooping crane, bald eagle, and peregrine falcon, among other species, provided the basis for increased confidence in the plan. Opponents grew more outspoken. FOE even suggested the possibility that the program's minimal emphasis on habitat protection was in service to the environmental politics of the Reagan administration.[22]

The draft environmental assessment of 1981 argued, as had the one before it, that FWS was compelled to take drastic action of the kind proposed to meet in good faith the stipulations of the Endangered Species Act. Habitat protection alone could not be relied upon. Federal acquisition was impractical, and even were funds available, not enough was known to allow identification of critical areas for purchase. The plan to tag and monitor but not breed would run the risk of extinction before enough would be learned to reverse the decline. The assessment recognized that the same factors that limit reproduction in the wild may limit the effectiveness of captive breeding, so that extinction may occur in any event. There is clearly no risk-free path, but the assessment warned against confusing the severity of risk with its visibility. Failure to act would be the greater risk, but it would be less conspicuous because extinction could not be as directly traced to human action. Captive breeding might increase the risk to individual birds but reduce the risk of species extinction. The document concluded that the program was not a major federal action within the meaning of NEPA. On the contrary, for the service "*not* to implement the proposed program could be construed as a major Federal action because that would be tantamount to condemning the species to extinction."[23]

The FWS again applied for federal and state permits in June 1981 to reinstate the hands-on components of the recovery program.[24] The applicants continued to focus on the urgency of the situation. Accordingly, they sought greater latitude in certain areas of action, for example in the possible removal of nestlings and eggs. Following a stormy series of negotiations before the commission, during which the federal government threatened to pull out of the program, permits were granted in August 1981 authorizing the capture of up to five birds through May 1982: two birds to be radio tagged and released, a pair for the breeding program at the San Diego zoo, and a female mate for Topa Topa, the lone captive condor held since 1967 in the Los Angeles zoo.[25]

As the reality of a captive population grew nearer, a new set of organizations—the zoos—emerged as important organizational actors. In 1979 the San Diego zoo had received the captive breeding contract from the FWS because of the zoo's experience in breeding endangered species, despite the fact that Topa Topa resided at the Los Angeles facility. The Los Angeles zoo felt slighted. "But democracy being what it is," remarked Greater Los Angeles Zoo Association

(GLAZA) president Marsha Hobbs, "we knew we would have another chance. When it came, we planned to make sure that people knew they were dealing with an institution that was every bit the equal of San Diego." When the breeding program was shut down following the death of the chick, Hobbs took advantage of political connections high in the Reagan administration to gain a role for her zoo. Following her meetings with Interior Secretary Watt and FWS officials, the service announced its intention to establish a second breeding facility in Los Angeles.[26]

The trapping authorized in August 1981 did not begin until January 1982, when agreement was finally reached on the type of radio transmitters to be attached to released birds. No birds were trapped during the remainder of the first season. New knowledge had been gained, however. The common raven appeared as a major threat to nesting condors. More importantly, breeding pairs had been observed to renest following the loss of their eggs. This suggested that eggs could be taken for captive breeding without jeopardizing the production of wild chicks.

In August 1982, in the face of additional public comment, the commission further restricted the activities of the recovery team. A maximum of three birds could be trapped—an immature female mate for Topa Topa and up to two others for radio tracking, but only if the two for radio tracking were taken first. In addition, the recovery team was permitted to remove a condor chick, claimed to be neglected by its parents, and a single egg for incubation. John G. Rogers, Jr., acting director of the FWS center at Patuxent, complained that the new restrictions "abrogated a three-year agreement which we thought was minimal to start with." John Ogden saw less than a 50-50 chance that NAS would continue to participate under such restrictive conditions. Indeed, NAS president Peterson threatened to pull Audubon out of the program and sought FWS assistance in pressuring the state to relax its restrictions on radio tagging. FWS stated its intention to continue with or without Audubon.[27]

Beginning at about this time, however, the prospects for the condor looked to be markedly improved, and the Fish and Game Commission relaxed its restrictions in response to program successes. The abandoned chick was taken from the nest in August 1982 as planned. The first free-flying condor was captured in October. It was determined to be a male and was released with radio transmitter attached. An immature male, taken December 5, 1982, and scheduled for release, was ultimately retained in captivity.[28] In November NAS withdrew its threat to pull out of the program, and in January 1983 the state commission, basing its decisions on the evidence gathered the previous year suggesting that double-clutching occurred in the wild and that radio tagging did not threaten free-flying birds, authorized the taking of first eggs from active nests, radio tagging of two additional birds, and continued efforts to trap a mate for Topa Topa. In March the commission approved the taking of up to 50 percent of the nestlings and of all nestlings from pairs not represented in the captive flock.[29] By late 1983 the captive population had grown to nine: four chicks hatched from eggs taken from active nests, four immature birds taken from the wild, and Topa Topa. An even more ambitious plan was laid out for 1984. The possibility of triple-clutching had been suggested by a wild pair that hatched its third egg after the first was taken for captive rearing and the second was broken in a domestic squabble.[30]

Spokesmen for the program expressed increasing optimism about its ultimate success. Ogden, not yet confident that the wild population could be restored, did assert that "I think you can now say that we will never lose the condor. . . . We could keep [the wild population] at 20 or 30 birds forever by resupplying [it] from zoos." NAS president Peterson reaffirmed his organization's view that because humans have nearly destroyed the species, it is a human obligation "to do all in our power through *positive* intervention to restore this and other similarly beleaguered species while there is still time." The success of the program was a "cause for rejoicing."[31] But success did not silence program critics. Kenneth Brower argued that the program was

badly out of balance. Its emphasis on captive breeding is fine for the zoos and the biotechnicians of the recovery team, but bad for wild condors. The captive-breeding program . . . threatens the survival of *Gymnogyps Californianus* directly, by its removal of birds and eggs from the wild population and by its harassment of the wild birds left behind. . . . [and] indirectly, by diverting attention and funds from the bird's true problems and from components of the larger program aimed at solving those problems.[32]

Such criticism did little to dampen the renewed optimism over the recovery effort, optimism that had influenced the revised recovery plan, issued in July 1984. The plan, summarizing research findings and outlining projected recovery efforts, suggested that "with reasonably good survival of the remaining wild pairs, continued multiple-clutching and annual-nesting may allow establishment of a viable captive population and initiation of a release program of captives within a few years." The plan called for a captive flock including a minimum of five progeny from each of five known breeding pairs, a criterion already met for two pairs. The captive flock would ultimately include 32 breeding adults, but this goal would be subordinate to the maintenance of a wild population through releases.[33]

The recovery plan attended in considerable detail to the question of habitat needs. Whereas ignorance about behavior and foraging patterns had, for some advocates, justified decisions to postpone habitat acquisitions in the past, new knowledge gained from radio-tracking studies identified previously unknown critical habitat. A prime forage area was discovered to exist on private ranch land that had recently been sold for potential second-home development. This Hudson Ranch property was costly, however, and the need ran head-on into the Reagan Administration's freeze on land acquisitions. No funds were requested by FWS, but at the urging of NAS and other interests, the appropriations committees nonetheless earmarked a total of $8.9 million in fiscal 1984 and 1985 for the purchase of Hudson Ranch.

The turning point for the recovery effort came in the spring of 1985 with the realization that the winter had taken a disastrous toll: six of fifteen known birds, representing four of five breeding pairs, had been lost. Three of the remaining birds were already scheduled to be taken into captivity. Pressure was clearly building to bring in the remaining birds. The state commission resolved to take that action at its April meeting, contrary advice from the director of the condor research center notwithstanding.[34] The FWS argued before the commission in May that this action would not be in the best interest of the condor. Instead, Wildlife research chief Jan Riffe proposed to capture two adult females and one adult male (excluding the Santa Barbara pair, the only known breeding pair in the wild, and IC-9, an immature male) and release three immature females from the captive flock. He argued that while FWS supported the growth of the captive population of 32 breeding adults, as described in the recovery plan, captive breeding must remain subordinate to the maintenance of a wild population. Removal of all the birds, furthermore, would make difficult the preservation of those lands not already identified as "critical" under the Endangered Species Act. The release of birds would boost the research component of the program but also be "a shot in the arm" for the program's public support. Of all the groups testifying, only the Zoological Society of San Diego offered unqualified support for the commission's position.[35]

In June the commission voted to bring in all the birds. For Jesse Grantham, an NAS biologist, "when you bring all the birds in you have essentially brought to the end the culture of a species which has taken thousands of years to develop." For Kent Smith, Coordinator for the California Fish and Game Department's Endangered Birds and Mammals Program, "with all the knowledge and all the experts, it's still a best guess and you hope to hell that you are right."[36] In July a female condor was taken into captivity under existing permits.

The FWS came to the August 30 meeting of the Fish and Game Commission prepared to present a compromise plan to capture all birds except the Santa Barbara pair and IC-9 and to release three immature females in the spring of 1986. Despite disagreement on the commission and among those representing interested organizations, the plan was accepted, contingent however on the willingness of the Interior Department to acquire the Hudson Ranch. Despite the fact that the commission held written assurances of Interior's intention to purchase the property, purchase seemed unlikely. Indeed, the Office of Management and Budget had already issued a draft decision paper arguing for delay in acquisition. The Interior Department's hesitation, according to one source, stemmed from "a growing belief . . . that the condor is a lost cause." In October, Interior announced that further purchase efforts would be contingent on the actual release of three captive birds as proposed, and suggested that a lease or some other option to buy agreement be signed to protect the government's interest.[37]

During the late summer and fall of 1985, two more birds were taken into captivity under previously existing permits. Six remained. On October 31, 1985, the acting director of the FWS, F. Eugene Hester, issued a "Summary of Fish and Wildlife Service Decisions Regarding California Condor Recovery Activities," clarifying official policy in the face of what he called "polarized positions" and "a considerable amount of misunderstanding among all parties." The document continued to support the maintenance of a wild population of condor and certified that the primary use of birds produced and/or raised in captivity would be release to bolster the wild population.[38] Of critical importance was that wild birds would serve as guides, introducing new releases to the learned behavior of the species.

On the same date, an addendum to the recently approved October 21 environmental assessment was filed, identifying a new preferred action. An inspection of zoo facilities conducted October 28–29 revealed that "due to a failure to maintain an appropriate isolation regime for captive condors at the zoos, there are presently no birds suitable for release in the spring of 1986."[39] Various charges and countercharges were levied concerning the circumstances leading to this failure at the Los Angeles zoo. At best there had been poor communication and cooperation among program participants.[40] The new preferred alternative continued to support the capture of three birds but made the spring 1986 release contingent on availability of at least three suitable birds. Release would otherwise be postponed until fall 1986 or spring 1987. The trapping effort to bring in three birds commenced pursuant to October permits, but it was clear that FWS was under a great deal of pressure to bring in all of the birds. The lone breeding female (of the Santa Barbara pair) was trapped in November and found to have an elevated blood lead level. Not among those birds to be retained, it was released.

In mid-December the service again recommended a change in policy. Richard Smith, Associate Director, Research and Development, announced that the "wild population will have to be sacrificed temporarily in order to ensure sufficient numbers of birds and genetic representation for a successful captive propagation program."[41] Three new pieces of information made this change necessary. First, AC-8, a female that was to have been captured and paired with AC-5, a male genetically important to the captive flock, was showing courtship behavior with IC-9, a male thought to be too young for breeding that was to be left in the wild. The pair should not be broken up. Second, because it was unlikely that any birds would be suited for spring 1986 release, birds left in the wild would have to survive at least 16 months, subject to uncontrolled mortality, before they could serve as guide birds; this was judged to be an unacceptable risk. Third, AC-3, the Santa Barbara female, which was scheduled to be left in the wild, was judged to require further evaluation and possible treatment for lead poisoning.

This decision was reached following a great deal of high-level consultation in the Interior Department, possibly involving the President and probably involving his close advisors, probably responding to more or less subtle pressures from GLAZA but with virtually no consultation outside of the department, in particular with NAS or with the field staff operating the recovery effort. Amos Eno, representing NAS, met with Interior undersecretary Ann Dore McLaughlin and FWS director Hester on December 20 to lay out his concerns. Eno registered his strong opposition to the plan, and he expressed his concern that NAS and other cooperators had not been involved in the decision. He mentioned the possibility of legal action and of congressional inquiry.[42]

By December 23, 1985, the supporting documentation had been prepared and approved, and trapping commenced. On January 2, 1986, the Santa Barbara female was captured. Despite extensive treatment for lead poisoning at the San Diego zoo, the bird died two weeks later. On January 7, FWS associate director Smith initiated a dialogue among interested parties in search of a new administrative structure for the condor recovery effort. His proposal, which would have relegated NGOs to an advisory role, was predictably unpopular with NAS and other interests.[43] Meanwhile, attention had shifted to the courtroom.

On January 9, 1986, U.S. District Court Judge Barrington Parker temporarily enjoined the trapping of the remaining five condors. In its trial brief, Audubon argued that the new circumstances cited by FWS in support of its December change of policy had already been known when the agency made its previous decision to leave three birds in the wild. Furthermore, the change had been made without consulting interested parties when "a few isolated Washington bureaucrats did a flip-flop." NAS cited FWS's continued support for maintaining a wild flock, as well as the service's failure to consider certain impacts of the change, such as on habitat protection, release schedules, and possible injury to breeding females; nor had the service considered other alternatives, for example working to further reduce field mortality or allowing the new pair, AC-8 and IC-9, to remain in the wild.[44]

The service, for its part, recognized Audubon's legitimate apprehension that land preservation would be more difficult without condors in the field, but contended that

the imminent high risk of losing some or all of the last wild birds far outweighs any possible longer-term worry about maintenance of the habitat needed by a reintroduced, hopefully expanded, wild flock. We must deal with first things first. . . . This case is really just a clash (emotionally, politically, and philosophically charged) over the best strategy for securing the recovery of the California condor. . . . Audubon is virtually alone in its stubborn opposition to a plainly prudent course of action. We submit that this Court should uphold the FWS determination as to how to protect the condor.

Further, the plaintiff's challenge to the decision "represents the attempt to engage this Court in second-guessing the wildlife agency on the relative weight to accord competing expert opinions."[45] The court was willing to be engaged, however, and granted a preliminary injunction on February 3.[46]

Over the next several months, formal and informal negotiations continued among various organizations at various levels, in good faith efforts to get the program back on track. Other groups, notably the Los Angeles Zoo and its affiliated Greater Los Angeles Zoo Association (GLAZA), took their cases to the public. The association issued a lengthy document in February 1986, charting a future course for the recovery effort.[47] The proposal challenged the Hudson Ranch feeding program because of wide foraging patterns among condor that seem resistant to change and that would subject birds to continued and uncontrolled hazards, despite the provision of safe carcasses. The crux of the zoo proposal, which supported the decision to remove all of the wild birds and which obviated the need to acquire the Hudson Ranch, was to create new foraging traditions among the released birds so that they would stay close to release sites wholly within existing, and therefore protected, federal lands. Accordingly, retaining wild birds to serve as guides for new releases would be not only unnecessary but destructive.

The zoo association held a March press conference announcing that, together with the Zoological Society of San Diego, legal action would be taken "to save the lives of the five remaining wild California condors."[48] Los Angeles mayor Tom Bradley presented GLAZA president Marcia Hobbs with a proclamation supporting GLAZA's effort to save the condor and urged that the voices of the People of California "not be silenced by Washington, D.C.," a view echoed by the presidents of the City Council and the Fish and Game Commission. Hobbs lashed out at NAS, threatening that "the blood of these [wild condors] will be on Audubon's hands." Audubon, rejecting both the style and substance of GLAZA's strategy, did agree with the zoo association's assertion that decision making for the program must be moved back to California from Washington. "We couldn't agree more. In fact, we filed suit to stop just that kind of arbitrary, Washington-based thinking from dominating the condor program."[49]

Continuing discussions on the restructuring of the recovery effort led, by May, to a consensus that a new recovery team should be constituted in place of the interagency review committee promoted by FWS associate director Smith. The creation of this new team would be accompanied by a shift in control over the program from Washington to FWS Region 1, including the condor's California habitat. All discussants agreed that the first order of business would be to revise the recovery plan.[50]

On another front, recovery personnel remained active in the field. On February 13, by agreement between NAS and FWS, the injunction was modified to allow the capture of an unpaired male condor (AC-6) not genetically represented in the captive flock. The bird was taken on April 21. In June the injunction was again modified to permit the taking of AC-8, a female that was to have been taken under previous permits but that had recently paired with IC-9 (now AC-9 in view of its sexual maturity) and had produced one viable egg in the wild earlier in the year that had been hatched in captivity. The decision to bring in this bird, about which there was disagreement within Audubon, would seem to have strengthened the case for bringing in its mate, AC-9, a bird not originally intended for the captive flock. Three birds remained, all males.

Congress also began to take notice of the disharmony within the recovery program. The appropriations committees had originally responded to the NAS call for recovery program funding, had continued to provide add-on funding for the condor, and had appropriated monies for the acquisition of the Hudson Ranch and adjacent lands. These committees now reasonably became concerned that their confidence had been misplaced. Representative Vic Fazio, California member of the House Interior Appropriations Subcommittee, requested language in the subcommittee's report on fiscal year 1987 appropriations expressing concern over the conduct of the recovery program. FWS was asked to account for the alleged mishandling of birds to have been released from the Los Angeles Zoo, the discrepancies between "the current conduct of the condor recovery program and the advice from its own professional service biologists," and the plans to establish a new timetable for reestablishment of birds in the wild.[51]

The FWS appeal of the injunction on captures was argued on May 30, 1986, and the decision, overturning the district court opinion, was announced June 10. The appeals court, in its September 5 written opinion, found that the "decision to capture the remaining wild condors was manifestly defensible." There is no particular significance to be attached to the specific date that factual information reaches an official or agency, because it takes time for information to reach appropriate decision makers and for decision makers to analyze information. Precisely how "new" the new information was that FWS used to justify its change in preferred action is not relevant. But beyond this, agencies may alter their policies with or without new information if they satisfactorily explain why they have done so. The court found that FWS had met this standard.[52]

NAS interest in pursuing legal avenues diminished as the likelihood increased that its main concerns would otherwise be addressed: prevention of trapping during the breeding season, restoration of field-based biological decision making under the regional director, and acquisition of Hudson Ranch. The delay itself addressed the first concern. Some of the desired movement in other regards was facilitated by the March 1986 appointment of Frank Dunkle as FWS director. He implemented a significant change in organizational structure by decentralizing the agency through delegation of responsibility to the regional directors. Immediately following the appeals court decision, Rolf L. Wallenstrom, the newly appointed director of Region 1, announced his intention to disband the existing recovery team and constitute a new one. Recovery team recommendations would thereafter be transmitted to the California Fish and Game Commission and to the regional director, who would discuss them with members of the coordinating committee that represented interested parties.[53] The director of research and development, now designated regional director of Region 8, would continue to supervise the Condor Research Center, a program of the Patuxent Wildlife Research Center. Nominations for recovery team membership were solicited from various program cooperators on June 11; the recovery team was constituted by the regional director in July; and it met in August.[54]

The shift of control to the regional director also coincided with more rapid movement on the Hudson Ranch acquisition, negotiations for which had been stalled for many months. Indeed, immediately following the decision to bring in all of the birds, the Interior Department had withdrawn its offer to obtain a short-term lease or easement on the property, an offer that had been made in lieu of purchase. A departmental position on purchase had not yet emerged by April.[55] FWS reappraised the property at $3.2 million, well below the $8.9 million authorized by Congress but also below the owner's asking price. Despite generally declining property values in the region, the developers who had bought the land from the Hudson brothers sought a price consistent with their expected gain from development. As one FWS spokesman commented, however, the agency does not understand its function to include bailing investors out of bad business decisions. Through foreclosure the land eventually returned to the Hudson brothers, whose lower financial stake permitted more realistic discussions on purchase. The new regional director, now with unified control over the condor recovery, undertook to engage in extensive face-to-face bargaining with the landowners, ultimately reaching a December 1986 deal for $3.5 million. This property constitutes the vast majority of the Bitter Creek National Wildlife Refuge.[56]

The new recovery team met for the first time in August 1986. At that meeting, although a core of members continued to favor the maintenance of a wild flock, the team agreed to bring in all birds contingent on the prompt development of a release protocol and the vigorous pursuit of habitat preservation. The team also addressed the interests of the Chumash Indian tribe, the members of which claim spiritual links to the condor.[57] The second meeting, in October, was devoted primarily to discussion of the experimental release of Andean condor in the California range and the protocol for the ultimate release of California birds. The Andean birds would be used to test the suitability of two potential release sites, to fine-tune release methods, and to train staff. Birds of a single sex would be radio tagged and recovered prior to the release of California birds. The team recommended that all California condor presently in captivity remain a part of the breeding population. Their progeny would be released as fledglings under conditions that would be met most optimistically by 1990.[58]

Despite the apparent harmony and trust that characterize the reconstituted recovery effort, a number of difficult issues remain on the horizon. The Andean condor release plan, not having been fully implemented as of fall 1988, generated the kind of controversy that program participants have come to expect at every turn. The financial burden of the program (on the order of $10 million to date) will continue far into the future and will shift in the direction of the zoos. It is not at all clear how program expenses will be met. A 1986, 3-year appropriations measure passed by the California legislature was vetoed by the governor. A San Diego zoo spokesman observed that because of the high profile of the program, the public believes that the condor has sufficient financial resources, but fund raising is difficult. The zoos consequently may feel pressure to exhibit the birds to raise revenues and generate public support, the merits of which have already been discussed by the recovery team.[59]

In addition, individuals and groups long opposed to the captive breeding program continue to make their views known. FOE interest in the program has resurfaced, following that group's traumatic reorganization and move to Washington, D.C., at the Earth Island Institute. Earth Island, together with Earth First! and Alternative Environmental and Social Action, oppose the release of Andean condor and seek the scheduled release of captive birds and the protection of vast habitat. According to these groups, condors need friends "willing to take direct action if necessary" by demonstrating against or boycotting participating zoos. The groups subsequently have sponsored demonstrations at the Los Angeles Zoo and at the research center in Ventura.[60]

Finally, while there are disagreements, there are also uncertainties. It is not known whether the initial captive breeding success can be replicated or whether released birds will adapt and survive. Nor is it known, should the condor again fly free, whether the success will be judged worthy of the resources it will have required.

NOTES

1. Cass Peterson, "California Condors Vanishing Despite Long, Expensive Effort," Washington *Post*, February 10, 1986, p. A3.

2. In general, see Sanford R. Wilbur, *The California Condor, 1966-1976: A Look at Its Past and Future.* U.S. Fish and Wildlife Service, North American Fauna No. 72 (Washington, D.C.: Government Printing Office, 1978); Faith McNulty, "The Last Days of the Condor," *Audubon*, March 1978, pp. 53-87, and May 1978, pp. 78-100; and David Phillips and Hugh Nash, eds., *The Condor Question: Captive or Forever Free?* (San Francisco: Friends of the Earth, 1981).

3. The sanctuary was enlarged to 53,000 acres in 1951, and several critical inholdings have since been acquired.

4. The committee included the NAS president, the director of the University of California's Museum of Vertebrate Zoology, and the assistant regional forester.

In 1951 a part-time patrolman was assigned to the sanctuary, his salary shared by NAS and USFS.

5. McNulty, "Last Days of the Condor," p. 74.

6. *Federal Register* 40 (December 16, 1975): 58308; *Federal Register* 41 (September 24, 1976): 41914.

7. Robert E. Ricklefs, ed., *Report of the Advisory Panel on the California Condor*, Audubon Conservation Report No. 6 (New York: National Audubon Society, 1978), p. 14.

8. Ibid., pp. 5–7; 15–24.

9. U.S. Department of the Interior, Fish and Wildlife Service, *Recommendations for Implementing the California Condor Contingency Plan*, 1979, and U.S. Department of the Interior, Fish and Wildlife Service, *California Condor Recovery Plan*, January 1980.

10. Submitted testimony of Elvis J. Stahr to U.S. Congress, House, Committee on Appropriations, *Department of the Interior and Related Agencies Appropriations for 1980, Hearings*, 96th Cong., 1st sess., Part 3, pp. 203–204. Testimony of Lynn A. Greenwalt, ibid., Part 4, p. 700.

11. U.S. Congress, House, Subcommittee on Fisheries and Wildlife Conservation and the Environment of the Committee on Merchant Marine, *Endangered Species: Hearings on Endangered Species Authorization and Oversight–H.R. 2218*, April 6, 1979, 96th Cong., 1st sess., Serial No. 96–12, pp. 38–46, and U.S. Congress, Senate, Subcommittee on Resource Protection of the Committee on Environment and Public Works, *Reauthorization of the Endangered Species Act of 1973, Hearing*, April 3, 1979, 96th Cong., 1st sess., Serial No. 96–H11, pp. 44–47; 51–52.

12. Agreement dated December 12, 1979.

13. U.S. Congress, House, *Endangered Species*, Serial No. 96–12, p. 65.

14. John Ogden, quoted in Constance Holden, "Condor Flap in California," *Science* 209 (August 8, 1980): 670–72. See also the remarks of FWS biologist Noel Snyder, Los Angeles *Times*, August 4, 1981, p. V:1.

15. Quoted in John Peer Nugent, "Is the California Condor Worth Saving?" *National Wildlife*, August–September 1981, p. 29. In fact, Borneman left the position shortly thereafter, although he remains affiliated with NAS in Southern California.

16. *Not Man Apart*, February 1980, p. 9. A FWS spokesperson perceived the position of FOE as "based on the notion that the recovery plan is unpopular with large elements of the public" and that the plan should, on that ground alone, be open to public scrutiny. The Sierra Club, which like FOE, is based in California and has a solid and historic claim to legitimacy, became the third national environmental organization to enter the debate. See Sierra Club, *Report of the Sierra Club California Condor Advisory Committee*, August 1980.

17. U.S. Department of the Interior, Fish and Wildlife Service, "Finding of No Significant Impact," November 30, 1979; U.S. Department of the Interior,

Fish and Wildlife Service, *Final Environmental Assessment: Conservation of the California Condor by Trapping and Captive Propagation*, December 1979, p. 12.

18. One FWS respondent remarked that "Friends of the Earth can't even get in the door of half the offices on the hill, whereas Audubon can go to just about any hill office."

19. Permit application dated April 25, 1980. *Federal Register* 45 (May 9, 1980): 30996-97.

20. California Fish and Game Commission, minutes of the meeting of May 29-30, 1980, p. 17.

21. Letter from A. Petrovich, Jr., Assistant Executive Secretary, California Fish and Game Commission, July 7, 1980.

22. *Not Man Apart*, July 1981, p. 18, and August 1981, p. 12; see also Paul Erlich and Anne Erlich, *Extinction: The Causes and Consequences of the Disappearance of Species.* (New York: Random House, 1981), pp. 215-18.

23. U.S. Department of the Interior, Fish and Wildlife Service, *Draft Environmental Assessment: Conservation of the California Condor by Trapping and Captive Propagation*, 1981, pp. 23-24, 31, 37-41.

24. *Federal Register* 46 (June 3, 1981): 29918-20.

25. California Fish and Game Commission, minutes of the meetings of July 28-29, 1981, pp. 26-48, and August 6-7, 1981, pp. 35-44; Los Angeles *Times*, July 29, 1981, p. I:3, and August 1, 1981, p. 1; New York *Times*, July 29, 1981, p. A12.

26. Aiding the zoo's claim was a $230,000 fund, already set aside, that would make requests for federal funds unnecessary. Los Angeles *Times*, August 5, 1981, p. I:3.

27. New York *Times*, August 8, 1982, p. 22; Los Angeles *Times*, August 7, 1982, p. II:1; September 2, 1982, p. II:1.

28. Los Angeles *Times*, October 14, 1982, p. II:1; October 15, 1982, p. II:1; October 16, 1982, p. I:25; November 6, 1982, p. II:1; December 16, 1982, p. 3; December 29, 1982, p. I:3; New York *Times*, October 14, 1982, p. A20.

29. California Fish and Game Commission, minutes of the meetings of January 7, 1983, pp. 31-37, and March 3, 1983, pp. 3-15; Los Angeles *Times*, January 9, 1983, p. I:27.

30. *Endangered Species Technical Bulletin* 8 (January 1983): 3; 8 (April 1983): 3; 8 (June 1983): 7; 8 (July 1983): 8.

31. Los Angeles *Times*, July 10, 1983, p. 1; *Audubon*, January 1984, p. 4.

32. Kenneth Brower, "The Naked Vulture and the Thinking Ape," *Atlantic*, October 1983, 87-88.

33. U.S. Department of the Interior, Fish and Wildlife Service; *California Condor Recovery Plan* (Portland, Oreg.: U.S. Fish and Wildlife Service, July 31, 1984, pp. 11, 59).

34. California Fish and Game Commission, policy statement regarding Cali-

fornia condor, draft, April 26, 1985, and California Fish and Game Commission, minutes of the meeting of April 26, 1985, pp. 5–8.

35. California Fish and Game Commission, minutes of the meeting of May 16, 1985, pp. 2–10.

36. Los Angeles *Times*, June 8, 1985, p. II:1.

37. Mark Crawford, "The Last Days of the Wild Condor?" *Science* 229 (August 30, 1985), 845. The department did, however, make an unaccepted offer of $5.3 million. Los Angeles *Times*, September 4, 1985, p. I:3; September 23, 1985, p. I:3; October 18, 1985, p. I:3. See also letter from Senator Alan Cranston (D. Calif.) to Interior Secretary Donald Hodel (July 30, 1985) urging the purchase.

38. U.S. Department of the Interior, Fish and Wildlife Service, "Summary of Fish and Wildlife Service Decisions Regarding California Condor Recovery Activities," approved by F. Eugene Hester, Acting Director, October 31, 1985.

39. U.S. Department of the Interior, Fish and Wildlife Service, "Addendum to the Environmental Assessment and Findings of No Significant Impact Approved October 21," October 31, 1985.

40. See letter from David Trauger, Patuxent Wildlife Research Center, to Dr. Warren D. Thomas, Director of the Los Angeles Zoo, December 5, 1985. This debate is now moot, since the recovery team has recommended that no birds presently alive be released. See New York *Times*, May 6, 1986, A23, and Los Angeles *Times*, December 2, 1985, p. I:3.

41. U.S. Department of the Interior, Fish and Wildlife Service, memorandum to Assistant Secretary for Fish, Wildlife and Parks, through Deputy Director, Fish and Wildlife Service, from Associate Director, Research and Development, December 16, 1985.

42. U.S. Department of the Interior, Fish and Wildlife Service, memo from F. Eugene Hester, Acting Director, to Ron Lambertson, Acting Deputy Director, and Richard Smith, Associate Director, Research and Development, December 20, 1985.

43. U.S. Department of the Interior, Fish and Wildlife Service, letter from Richard Smith, January 7, 1986, and proposal, "United States Department of Agriculture, U.S. Department of the Interior and State of California Memorandum of Agreement to Establish an Interagency California Condor Committee," January 10, 1986, distributed to representatives of eight participating organizations, and National Audubon Society, letter from Amos Eno to Richard Smith, January 14, 1986.

44. National Audubon Society v. Hester, Civil Action No. 86–0053, D.D.C. February 8, 1986, plaintiff's memorandum in support of its motion for a preliminary injunction and summary judgment.

45. National Audubon Society v. Hester, memorandum in support of defendants' cross motion for summary judgment, pp. 3–4, 21.

46. National Audubon Society v. Hester. See also *Environmental Law Review* 16: 20445, June 1986, and Los Angeles *Times*, February 4, 1986, p. I:3.

47. Greater Los Angeles Zoo Association, "The California Condor Program: A Proposal for the Next Essential Steps," February 14, 1986. The proposal "represents a consensus of discussions" among 13 persons affiliated with the zoos, the FWS, and other groups and including several members of the recovery team. For an NAS review, see memo from Linda Blum to John Ogden and Amos Eno, February 27, 1986.

48. GLAZA news release, March 13, 1986. GLAZA had been granted *amicus curiae* status in the appeal proceedings.

49. Peter A. A. Berle, "The Condor and Endangered Species Protection," remarks to the Western Regional Conference of the National Audubon Society, March 22, 1986.

50. U.S. Department of the Interior, Fish and Wildlife Service, memorandum from Associate Director, Research and Development, to Regional Director, Region 1, May 23, 1986.

51. U.S. Congress, House, Committee on Appropriations, *Department of the Interior and Related Agencies Appropriation Bill, 1987. Report to Accompany H.R. 5234.*, 99th Cong., 2d sess., July 24, 1986, Report 99-714, p. 20.

52. 801 F. 2d 405 (D.C. Cir., 1986).

53. Letter to members of the condor coordinating group from Rolf L. Wallenstrom, Director, Region 1, June 11, 1986. See also letters from FWS director Frank Dunkle to directors, Regions 1 and 8 (formerly Associate Director, Research and Development), clarifying roles and responsibilities, July 15, 1986.

54. The team members were Richard Olendorff (U.S. Bureau of Land Management), Ronald Jurek (California Department of Fish and Game), Lloyd Kiff (Western Foundation of Vertebrate Zoology), John Ogden (National Audubon Society), Jared Verner (U.S. Forest Service), Oliver Pattee (Project Leader, Condor Research Center), Michael E. Soulé (geneticist, University of Michigan), Bill Toone (Zoological Society of San Diego), Michael Wallace (Los Angeles Zoo), Cathleen Cox (Los Angeles Zoo), and James Carpenter (U.S. Fish and Wildlife Service, Patuxent Wildlife Research Center). The first five also were members of the previous recovery team, while the last two were late additions, made in recognition of the need for additional expertise in captive breeding. (One critic suggested that the additions resulted from political pressure exerted by GLAZA.)

55. U.S. Department of the Interior, Fish and Wildlife Service, memo from Associate Director, Federal Assistance, to Director, April 10, 1986.

56. Interior Secretary Hodel subsequently complained that, while the department had responded to environmentalist pressures to acquire the property, "not a single one of those constituencies . . . has ever acknowledged that we did it and we saved $5 million." Rochelle L. Stanfield, "Tilting on Development," *National Journal*, February 7, 1987, pp. 314-15.

57. California Condor Recovery Team, minutes, general session, August 19, 1986, pp. 4-5; minutes, executive session, August 19, 1986, pp. 2-3; minutes, open session, October 15, 1986, pp. 2-3; minutes, January 13, 1987, p. 2.

58. California Condor Recovery Team, recommendations, October 16, 1986. See also minutes, closed session, October 15, 1986, pp. 1-6.

59. California Condor Recovery Team, minutes, January 13, 1987, pp. 7-9; March 11, 1987, pp. 8-9.

60. R. C. Leyland, "Last Flight of the Condor," *Whole Life Monthly*, July 1986, p. 30. The recovery team took note that 35-40 vocal demonstrators had presented a list of demands at the condor research center just prior to its fourth meeting. Although concern was expressed over the demonstrators' implied threats to free the captive birds, the consensus was that the demands should not be acknowledged. Minutes, March 10, 1987, p. 3.

4

The Bobcat

On March 3, 1973, "Recognizing that wild fauna and flora in their many beautiful and varied forms are an irreplaceable part of the natural systems of the earth which must be protected for this and the generations to come . . . and Recognizing . . . that international cooperation is essential for the protection of certain species of wild fauna and flora against over-exploitation through international trade," over 80 nations concluded the Convention on International Trade in Endangered Species of Wild Fauna and Flora (CITES). In January 1974, the United States was the first nation to ratify the convention, and on July 1, 1975, following ratification by the tenth nation, the agreement entered into force. There are, at this writing, 96 signatories.[1]

The convention protects three categories of species threatened by trade. Appendix I of the convention lists those species "threatened with extinction which are or may be affected by trade," which require both export and import permits; Appendix II(a) lists species that may become threatened with extinction unless trade is strictly regulated; and II(b) lists "look-alike" species that must also be regulated to support the effective regulation of Appendix II(a) species. Appendix II species require export permits only. Appendix III of the agreement lists species identified by individual signatories as requiring protection in support of domestic regulation. Each party is to name a management authority to issue permits and perform record-keeping tasks and a scientific authority to provide independent judgment on the merits of particular permit requests.

Article VII of the convention creates an explicit and potentially influential role for NGOs. All international organizations (governmental or nongovernmental), all national governmental agencies or bodies, and all national nongovernmental agencies or bodies that have been approved by the state in which they are based, may participate fully (but not vote) if they are "technically qualified in protection, conservation, or management of wild fauna and flora." Consequently, NGOs have two opportunities to influence CITES affairs, first, as the parties formulate their individual positions prior to the meetings and, second, as the delegates debate proposals over cocktails and on the floor. NGOs have exercised this influence with considerable success, perhaps most notably at the second meeting of the parties in March 1979 at San José, Costa Rica. This success, in turn, spawned domestic controversies over the proper role of NGOs in meeting U.S. treaty obligations and over the management of the bobcat. These controversies were the subjects of congressional hearings, and they led ultimately to 1979 and 1982 amendments to the Endangered Species Act.

The entire sequence of events may be traced to a U.S. proposal to modify the criteria, agreed to at the first meeting of the parties in Berne, for listing and delisting protected species. Under the criteria, deletion or transfer of species from Appendix I to Appendix II requires "positive scientific evidence that the plant or animal can withstand the exploitation resulting from the removal of protection."[2] The United States argued that some species listed prior to the adoption of the Berne criteria, could not have been listed under those criteria for lack of information, yet they could not be delisted for lack of similar information. A U.S. proposal in 1979 would have suspended temporarily the delisting criteria to allow the removal of "improperly" listed species. The proposal failed, at least in part because of organized NGO opposition. This proposal would never have emerged were it not that the bobcat, lynx, and river otter are listed on Appendix II. Listing jeopardized the trade opportunities of U.S. trappers and threatened the states, which resented federal encroachment on their traditional authority to manage resident wildlife. Thus an international convention became the vehicle for the airing of a jurisdictional dispute between the states and the federal government, and NGOs were the primary contestants.

Prior to the mid-1970s, the bobcat was in little demand for its fur. Few states actively managed the species, and several had granted no agency the authority to do so. Indeed, the bobcat was even the object of federal predator control measures. When several species of foreign spotted cats received Appendix I protection, bobcat prices rose dramatically, and the harvest for export intensified. At the 1976 meeting of the parties, the United Kingdom, arguing that "all cats are potentially involved in the fur trade," proposed that spotted cats not already protected by Appendix I, including the bobcat, be listed in Appendix II. The proposal, supported by the U.S. delegation, was adopted.[3]

At that time the administration of the convention was barely underway, and some observers had little confidence that the bobcat would be materially aided by such listing. For Defenders of Wildlife, the major opponent of U.S. policy on this issue, Appendix II was a "paper tiger."[4] Beyond this, it was not clear to what extent export controls would reduce harvest intensity, since the species could still be taken for domestic use under terms dictated by individual states. Thus, in January 1977, Defenders petitioned the Interior Department for a status review of the bobcat to determine its suitability for protection under the Endangered Species Act. The selection of species for review among those proposed was, at that time, based on stated but very broad criteria, and Defenders, hoping to influence the process, urged its members to make their views known to the appropriate authorities.[5] FWS announced its decision to conduct a status review in July 1977.[6]

The states responded quickly to this proposal. Not only would listing threaten state control of a species they did not regard as endangered, but listing would also prohibit the use of nonselective predator control measures by the federal government on leased public grazing lands in the West. Stockmen, formerly opposed to state management plans in any form, now encouraged the development of such plans with the hope that they would weaken the case for listing. Nearly 20 states adopted new regulations or tightened existing ones.[7]

Meanwhile, Defenders and other groups turned their attention toward the administration of CITES and the enforcement of controls over Appendix II species. The Endangered Species Scientific Authority (ESSA), the U.S. scientific authority designated under the convention, sought advice and comment from the public and the states on the development of procedures and criteria for evaluating the impact of harvest for export. ESSA executive secretary William Brown announced a review of data on the bobcat, lynx, river otter, and ginseng root, and he reported a possible ban on the further export of bobcat pelts. "It's important to remember that these species can be exported only if ESSA is able to find that it won't hinder their survival—and has data to back up that finding."[8] In August, based on a lack of data rather than on positive evidence of declining populations, ESSA issued a preliminary finding prohibiting the export of bobcat taken on or after August 30, 1977.[9]

The scientific authority empaneled 12 scientists to review the status of the bobcat, lynx, and river otter. The report of this "working group" significantly influenced, or at least provided reputable justification for, ESSA practices. But the members "felt extremely uncomfortable about their charge. This discomfort arose from the feeling that the bobcat, lynx, and river otter had been placed on Appendix II for political rather than biological reasons." The working group thus recommended that the management authority reevaluate the inclusion of these species on Appendix II and that, in future listing actions, the U.S. seek adequate consultation with states and other agencies. The group also recommended a set of state management practices that, if implemented, should allow ESSA to approve all exports from complying states.[10]

While this report was in preparation, ESSA, following a review of emerging state management plans, published export quotas of 79,000 pelts for the 1977–78 season, representing an estimated 25 percent reduction in harvest.[11] Distressed by this apparent reversal, and learning that the FWS endangered species review of the bobcat was making its way to the bottom of the agency's agenda, Defenders undertook its own analysis of bobcat populations. Treating separately nine subspecies, Defenders concluded that six were threatened or endangered and that the data on the remaining three were so unreliable as to "preclude reasonable anlaysis." Defenders submitted this data to ESSA and FWS, asked for an emergency listing, and sought support from its members in achieving these ends.[12]

In April 1978, following the submission of the working group report, ESSA issued guidelines for bobcat export for the 1978–79 season. The findings, made final in September, permitted all exports from the Navajo Nation and from 32 states that had met the minimum information requirements defined by the working group or supplied other information deemed sufficient for a "no detriment" finding. Export quotas were set for two other states.

The states, although not generally constrained by the ESSA rules, deeply resented the federal interference and the diversion of resources that compliance demanded. Individually, and through the International Association of Fish and Wildlife Agencies (IAFWA), they prevailed upon the federal government to propose a delisting of the bobcat at the 1979 meeting of the parties to CITES.[13] Such a proposal, which did not appear in a preliminary list of changes published on May 3, 1978, nor in the management authority's "Review of Native Species" of September 11, did appear in the revised list published in November, which was forwarded to the CITES secretariat for distribution to the parties to meet an October deadline.

According to Defenders, staff members of the permit office and other FWS officials had met with state representatives to explain the inadequacies of the existing data and had given the states until October 10 to submit the additional information required to make the case for delisting. Because the data requirements appeared large and the time remaining to gather it short, Defenders and others saw little threat to CITES protection.[14] When the change was announced, Defenders sought an explanation. The explanation was that new information allowed an estimate of a bobcat population of 750,000 to 1,000,000 and the consequent determination that the species was not threatened by international trade. Further inquiries were rebuffed.

In cooperation with the Natural Resources Defense Council (NRDC), Defenders sought a more complete response through the Freedom of Information Act and pressed for the withdrawal of this and other "secret" proposals directly and through the Council on Environmental Quality (CEQ).[15] FWS reopened the public comment period. Defenders learned that the "new data" had been promised by the states but that little had actually been received at the time the proposal was submitted to CITES; in any event, when it finally arrived there was little new information. Both ESSA and CEQ favored retention of Appendix II protection for the bobcat, and Defenders was prepared to go to court. The FWS appeared willing to concede that the available data did not support delisting. This concession was made official when the final proposals were published in February 1979, but pending a suit by Louisiana and Wisconsin challenging the legality of withdrawing a proposal formally submitted to the secretariat, the United States had not formally withdrawn the proposal.[16]

The strict application of the Berne criteria thus led to the position that the bobcat must be retained in Appendix II, but it called into question the propriety of the criteria themselves. At a public hearing to discuss U.S. and foreign proposals, U.S. delegates revealed that a proposal to modify the criteria was being developed. Because the details of such a proposal had not been worked out, discussion at the hearing was general and touched on a variety of issues; it considered not only the delisting of nonthreatened species but the listing of threatened species for which individual nations, particularly with low incomes and limited scientific resources, could not amass adequate data.[17] In due course, a U.S. proposal to suspend the Berne criteria emerged.

The March 1979 meeting in Costa Rica was attended by 34 of the 51 nations then parties, observers from 16 nonparty nations and several international governmental organizations, and 56 NGOs representing state government, commercial, and conservation interests. The influence of the conservation community was evident and decisive. A coalition of approximately 25 U.S., foreign national, and international groups was headed by Russell E. Train, then president of the World Wildlife Fund–U.S. (WWF–US) and head of the U.S. delegation to the session at which the convention was originally negotiated, and Lee Talbot, a World Wildlife Fund–International scientist. Michael J. Bean of EDF served as legal counsel and occasional spokesman. According to Train, "the NGOs met each day before and after the formal CITES sessions, worked out positions on issues, communicated these by memorandum to the official delegations and lobbied the latter during breaks and in the evening."[18]

The well organized coalition lobbied hard on several issues but particularly in opposition to the U.S. proposal to suspend the Berne criteria. The key step in the NGO success was in gaining the support of the British delegation. Following the presentation of the U.S. case and expressions of support by Switzerland and Canada, the United Kingdom offered a series of amendments, the primary of which undercut the U.S. proposal by asserting that deletion proposals must meet the existing criteria for deletion. NGOs offered public support, and other party nations followed suit. At the request of the United States, the United Kingdom explained that under its amendment, "the absence of sufficient data to support the original listing should be taken into account when the Parties decide whether a deletion has met the appropriate criteria." The U.S. delegation elected to accept the amendment with this clarification because "it would preserve all the preambular language which recognized that certain listings were supported with little or no information." The amendment was adopted 16 to 12.[19]

The impact of NGOs was disputed neither by NGOs nor by other observers. A newspaper account reported that "many delegates and officials of the conference said that an unusual aspect of the convention was the influence of unofficial, nongovernmental observers."[20] WWF–US wrote to its members that "the coalition of conservation groups effectively blocked two moves which would otherwise have weakened the intent of the Convention."[21] A U.S. congressman, John Breaux, lamented that "NGO strength at the convention, I think, was one of the major reasons why our position on this particular issue [the Berne criteria] was defeated."[22] Indeed, as Bean observed in hearings before the House Subcommittee on International Organizations,

in a sense, this convention owes its very existence to the conservation efforts of nongovernmental conservation organizations around the world. Their constant efforts to persuade the governments of the world of the gravity of the problem of endangered wildlife and the channeling of their efforts through the nongovernmental International Union for the Conservation of Nature and Natural Resources are the real origins of this convention.[23]

The congressional airing of the NGO role at Costa Rica resulted from the interplay of at least three factors. First, the fur industry and state fish and game departments, individually and as represented by IAFWA, were disappointed by their defeat and angered by NGO influence.

Second, Breaux, the chairman of the House Subcommittee on Fisheries and Wildlife and a representative from the alligator state of Louisiana, had arrived in Costa Rica the day after the U.S. defeat on the Berne Criteria, as a congressional observer and to oversee convention action on the U.S. proposal to shift the American alligator from Appendix I to Appendix II. At a meeting of NGOs convened at Breaux's request, he reminded conservationists that his subcommittee would shortly take up the reauthorization of the Endangered Species Act and suggested the impropriety of contesting the relisting of the alligator. There was no contest.[24] Despite his success here, Breaux, a guardian of states' rights in the management of wildlife, was distressed by what he saw and heard about the role of NGOs.

Third, Don Bonker (D. Wash.) had recently assumed the chair of the House Subcommittee on International Organizations. His environmental interest led the committee to explore its jurisdiction and establish a record on matters of international environmental concern. The recent CITES meeting helped to identify this convention as the initial topic.

Although the committee had not intended to review the NGO role in particular, Breaux's testimony focused the committee's attention on that issue. Breaux addressed the "very serious problem" that occurs when NGOs, outnumbering national delegations, assume positions "in opposition to many of the strategically important positions that we as a nation have adopted." The NGOs were "very well equipped, and our official delegation was completely out-lobbied and completely out-manned in the beginning, out supplied. . . . By far, the NGOs were the single most influential group present in Costa Rica." He observed that "many of the nations complained to me and complained to our official delegates that they didn't know what the actual U.S. position was on a particular issue." He pointed to rumors that NGOs were in touch with the CEQ and White House and that "the two were able to pressure the delegation at the bidding of the NGOs." He suggested that international organizations such as WWF and the International Union for the Conservation of Nature and Natural Resources (IUCN) had acquired influence over third-world delegations by providing financial assistance to certain nations.[25]

John Gottschalk, legislative counsel of IAFWA, amplified Breaux's remarks, noting in particular the influence of organizations opposed to trapping and hunting. Breaux and Gottschalk proposed remedies that included amending the convention to limit the role of NGOs, unilaterally limiting the number of NGOs approved for participation, and limiting NGOs "to those which have a legitimate international interest or responsibility and which are constituted, organized, and governed in such a way that the positions taken by such organizations represent the authorized positions of their memberships."[26]

Representative Bonker suggested that the topic of NGO participation in international wildlife management, although not raised as a problem by the federal government officials who had testified earlier, might be the subject of future hearings. But such hearings have not been held. Interview data supplies additional insights. An NGO spokesman failed to see how the confusion claimed by Breaux as to the identity of NGO representatives might have occurred. All printed material was clearly identified with the names of supporting NGOs, and all formal remarks were made from behind the proper name/affiliation plaques. "I never heard anyone claim that any NGO member represented himself as a member of the U.S. delegation." Further, NGOs can hardly be faulted for their own superior organization nor for the failure of the U.S. delegation to secure the support services it might expect to need in conducting its business. A spokesman for the management authority stated that all eligible NGOs would continue to be admitted and saw neither reason nor basis for a change. At the same time, he argued for a reduction in social gatherings, because they had become informal continuations of convention business when delegates need a break after a full day of concentrated effort. Finally, he was not displeased to admit the possibility that the location of the 1981 meeting in New Delhi might discourage attendance by NGOs, although this possibility had in no way led to the selection of that distant city.

It seemed inevitable, given Breaux's interest in the administration of CITES, that these issues would surface in the congressional re-authorization of the Endangered Species Act. The House Subcommittee on Fisheries and Wildlife Conservation and the Environment, which Breaux chaired, devoted a day to oversight hearings on ESSA, leading to Breaux's proposed amendment stripping the agency of its independent status, a modification of which was accepted by the conference committee reconciling House and Senate versions of the bill.[27]

But while ESSA had been an ally of Defenders and other NGOs in their efforts to protect the bobcat from CITES delisting, the authority nonetheless recommended virtually open export of bobcat pelts. Indeed, as has been noted, ESSA essentially had authorized the export of all pelts legally taken during the 1978–79 season, and it proposed the same approach for the following season.[28] In November 1979 Defenders filed suit in federal district court to halt the export of bobcat skins taken during the 1979–80 season, challenging the ESSA finding that exports would not be detrimental to the species. Following the issuance of a temporary restraining order barring exports, the court ruled in December that exports might continue from all but seven states, where partial or total bans would remain in effect. Defenders appealed, and on February 3, 1981, the U.S. Court of Appeals for the District of Columbia, although rejecting most of Defenders' claims, ruled that the treaty language must be taken literally with respect to the no-detriment findings. In remanding the case to the lower court, the appeals court determined that "any doubt whether the killing of a particular number of bobcat will adversely affect the survival of the species must be resolved in favor of protecting the animals and not in favor of approving the export of their pelts." The court ruled, further, that no-detriment findings must be based on a "(1) a reliable estimate of the number of bobcats and (2) information concerning the number of animals to be killed in the particular season." Although the court would allow the scientific authority "considerable discretion to determine the method by which that [population] estimate may be made and in evaluating its reliability," the authority could not avoid its responsibility under the convention to make a no-detriment finding "by deferring to the limits upon killing the states have imposed."[29]

The district court subsequently issued a permanent injunction on the export of bobcat taken after July 1, 1981, until such time as the "federal defendants promulgate guidelines consistent with the Court of Appeals decision and make findings on the basis of those guidelines."[30] For its part, FWS found that the "court's requirements are obviously a departure from wildlife management as it has traditionally been practiced in almost all states."[31] Pending resolution of the issues, the service undertook to respond to the court's standards.[32] Reluctant to abandon traditional management practices, however, the service made only slow progress and was unable to satisfy the court.[33]

The resolution of this controversy was to come, not through development of regulations satisfactory to the court, but through an amendment to the Endangered Species Act undermining the court requirement that export findings be based on population estimates. The International Association of Fish and Wildlife Agencies (IAFWA) convened its 72nd annual convention just as the ESA reauthorization was going to the House floor. IAFWA legislative counsel Wesley Hayden was pleased to report that the proposed measure addressed "essentially all of the IAFWA's primary needs and interest—due largely to the fact we were able in advance discussions with committee staff people and representatives of other organizations to eliminate controversial issues." IAFWA legal counsel Paul Lenzini emphasized the influence of IAFWA. Although the appeals court "gave us a pretty bad decision," and the Supreme Court chose not to hear the case, the IAFWA had other options. "When you're working for an ordinary client, your only remedy then as a lawyer is to go down to the bar and curse the judges. But when you're working for an outfit with clout like this you can go to Congress, and you can ask them to change the law."[34]

Although congressional action did not result from such a simple application of influence, some congressional response to the problem seemed likely from the early stages of the reauthorization process. The resolution was slow in coming, however, and failure to reach a compromise on this issue with states and user groups threatened resolution of other endangered species issues generally believed by the conservation community to be more important. In Senate oversight hearings of December 1981, representatives of several key groups opposed to the court ruling took the opportunity to express their concern about the implications of the ruling and their hope for some kind of legislative solution. Stephen S. Boynton, counsel for the American Fur Resources Institute, saw grave implications for the fur industry. "It is not an idle belief that various antihunting and antitrapping groups will attempt to utilize this decision to further attempt to block annual harvests of various species."[35]

William S. Huey, chairman of the IAFWA legislative committee, urged Congress to amend the act to "provide that where a state exercises management authority over a species listed in Appendix II of CITES the determination by the state agency respecting harvest shall constitute the 'no detriment' finding under Article IV of CITES."[36] Covington and Burling, a law firm serving as counsel to Defenders, argued that such a proposal "goes so far in eliminating federal responsibility for controlling the export of listed species as to constitute a de facto, unilateral amendment of Article IV of CITES. As such, it would violate the treaty."[37] The Wildlife Legislative Fund of America (WLFA) proposed an alternative approach, suggestive of the language finally adopted, retaining federal control but establishing that population estimates would not be a necessary element in a no-detriment finding.[38]

It was increasingly clear that bobcat policy had become a divisive issue within the conservation community. Defenders and also the Humane Society of the U.S. (HSUS), with an expanded wildlife and environment program that was now headed by John Grandy, recently departed from Defenders, stood alone as outspoken critics of congressional action. Bean of EDF and Kenneth Berlin of Audubon, representing a newly organized coalition of environmental groups (including Defenders and HSUS) seeking to "secure the reauthorization of a strong and effective endangered species Act in 1982," did not mention the issue in their congressional testimony other than in an obscure reference to the fact that groups were individually considering their responses to amendments offered by IAFWA.[39] It was not until March 1982, in the fourth issue of the coalition bulletin, that the bobcat was even mentioned, and the position taken therein was that, while extreme amendments would be opposed, a compromise seemed likely.[40] Only the National Wildlife Federation (NWF), not a member of the coalition, publicly supported the need for a legislative solution.[41]

The initial version of ESA reauthorization legislation appeared as S.2309 on March 30, 1982. With respect to CITES administration, the bill proposed that the secretary's no-detriment findings shall be "based on the best available biological information derived from reliable wildlife management practices," but that he shall not be required to use population estimates when "such estimates are not the best available biological information derived from reliable wildlife management practices." Spirited debate followed during subsequent Senate hearings. Chairman John Chafee responded to expressed concerns about international treaty obligations that the State Department had cleared the proposed legislation in that regard. But Grandy, of HSUS, alleged additional international ramifications. Other nations would see "that our Congress has been begged and indeed pushed and indeed shoved into providing an unwise legislative fix for a rational court decision. I don't see how any nation can view that but as a step backward in terms of this Nation's international obligations."[42]

Other NGOs, notably the reauthorization coalition, remained on the sidelines. Only Patrick Parenteau, on behalf of NWF, supported the amendment. He offered the further observation that because the amendment language requires the secretary to use the best available information, he would therefore be "*required* to use estimates of population size when those estimates *are* the best available biological information."[43]

The amendment, finally adopted by Congress and signed into law on October 13, 1982, appeared to give the secretary somewhat more flexibility, but the congressional reports accompanying the legislation preserve the stronger language: "If population estimates are available for a particular species, such information shall be considered with other data in making export decisions."[44] According to Defenders' staff, this language was pushed in negotiation by the coalition as it became increasingly clear that Defenders' long term commitment to this issue represented a substantive environmental concern rather than a parochial antitrapping crusade. Others suggested that the whole process had been handled as expediently as possible so as to get on to other, more important concerns, particularly the collapse of the listing process in the first two years of the Reagan administration.[45]

Following congressional action, the District Court, on December 23, 1982, dismissed the suit brought against FWS by Defenders and vacated the injunction against bobcat exports. The service determined that its existing rule, published October 14, 1981, was consistent with the terms of the ESA amendment, and it made that rule effective February 3, 1983.[46] The 1982–83 guidelines, however, which were developed in response to the court's requirements and published August 20, 1982, were now superfluous. The service proposed to return to the guidelines developed in 1979 by the ESSA working group which "represent professionally accepted wildlife management practices."

During the course of the ESA reauthorization cycle in 1981–82, the United States participated in the third meeting of the parties to CITES in New Delhi (February 25–March 8, 1981). The U.S. delegation declined to renew its effort to delete the bobcat from Appendix II at New Delhi despite continued encouragement from the IAFWA and several states. The Berne criteria simply could not be satisfied. Similarly, based on the defeat at Costa Rica, reconsideration of the Berne criteria was rejected.[47]

As the fourth meeting of the parties approached, the United States once again developed a proposal to delist the bobcat.[48] The proposal met with opposition from importing countries in Europe because of a look-alike problem between these animals and other species.

However, most parties felt that none of the populations or species addressed by the proposals are, on the whole, potentially threatened with extinction. The Parties and the CITES Secretariat indicated that the United States had the latitude and competence to treat bobcats . . . as lookalikes. . . . Given the consensus of the Parties on these points, the U.S. delegation withdrew these proposals [and issued a statement, jointly with Canada, affirming this interpretation] .[49]

The FWS subsequently announced that the United States regarded the bobcat as listed on Appendix II as a look-alike species under Article II(2)(b) rather than as a species which is itself threatened by trade under Article II(2)(a). The United States interpreted this to mean that different criteria would apply to a finding of no detriment. The *Federal Register* notice asserted that this change in purpose permits a much less vigilant control over export. The previous seven years of export findings, combined with state management programs in place as a result, and the current healthy status of the population, allow the service "to project findings on those species for an unlimited period of time into the future." While change is unlikely, the service will continue to monitor information on the species and exercise the option of revising the findings if new information shows they are no longer appropriate.[50]

While the parties to CITES and other observers accepted the U.S. right to regard the bobcat and other species as listed in Appendix II for look-alike reasons, they did not necessarily agree that the regulatory burden is thereby lessened. Article IV(2) states that an export permit may only be granted when the scientific authority has advised "that the export will not be detrimental to the survival of *that* species."[51] Defenders of Wildlife submitted comments in response to the *Federal Register* notice on this and other points. In its final rule making, issued January 5, 1984, the service rejected Defenders' view but argued that the actual procedures followed in arriving at the export findings in fact do permit the conclusion that "the species or geographically separate populations addressed here are not potentially threatened with extinction because of international trade."[52]

In retrospect it seems clear that the threat to state control posed by ESSA regulation and Defenders' legal action soured the IAFWA and other key allies on U.S. participation in international wildlife agreements. A case in point is the Convention on the Conservation of Migratory Species of Wild Animals, negotiated at Bonn, West Germany, in June 1979, which the United States declined to sign. Breaux and others expressed concern over language describing the role of NGOs that was modeled after CITES. IAFWA, on behalf of the states, strongly opposed U.S. participation because the broad range of species that would be subject to international control might seriously threaten state control, as had occurred with the bobcat.[53] Indeed, the states and IAFWA remain fundamentally leary of U.S. involvement in CITES and other international wildlife activity. A House staffer identified this alienation as a substantial negative effect of the bobcat controversy.

One Defenders staffer concluded that Defenders had been "right on the issue but wrong on the politics" of the bobcat affair. The organization became something of an outcast within the environmental community, which was otherwise well organized on the issues surrounding the reauthorization of the Endangered Species Act in 1982. Defenders has since sought to remedy this condition and has, indeed, become one of the central groups in subsequent efforts to oversee and amend the act. Another Defenders staffer remains convinced that this was an important issue, which not only deserved to be pursued vigorously, the political consequences notwithstanding, but which also achieved substantive results in creating a meaningful management regime for the bobcat, which was indeed threatened by harvest. Several congressional committee staffers pointed as well to the very real achievements for the bobcat.

A recent assessment by FWS, embedded in a series of press releases commemorating the fiftieth anniversary of the Pittman-Robertson program and its impact on wildlife management, confuses the history and hardly notes the controversy. The growth in trade in bobcat pelts and the subsequent increase in prices had

alarmed the wildlife conservation community in the United States, which pushed for controls on bobcat trapping. In response, Congress in 1982 required the U.S. Fish and Wildlife Service to monitor bobcat population levels and annual harvests. The Service, in turn, encouraged the States to launch extensive research on bobcats. . . . Prior to the 1970's, little scientific research had been conducted on bobcats. Now, more needed to be known about how many bobcats there are, whether their populations are rising or falling, the effects of trapping and hunting on their numbers, and what environmental factors influence bobcat population levels. The first step has been to find ways to count bobcats.[54]

This "first step" more or less returns us to the beginning of the story.

The cases discussed in this and the preceding chapter reveal a rich texture of NGO involvement in the complex fabric of wildlife policy making, a fabric largely of NGO construction. Specific policy issues are addressed: the restoration of the condor and the conditions under which the bobcat may be exported. The difficulties in narrowly circumscribing cases such as these should be evident: the structure of the problem, the relevant interests and alliances, and the realms of activity have evolved as the cases have unfolded. Connections to other issues and actions may be seen in every direction. In the former case, a nonprofit organization initiated a new program for the recovery of the condor in the belief that existing government activity was inadequate, and it committed financial and scientific resources to implement it. In the latter case, a nonprofit organization challenged the export of bobcat in the belief that such export would violate an international agreement to which the United States was a party. In each case, NGOs brought substantial expertise and tremendous energy to the policy process. In the condor case in particular, NGOs also brought significant financial resources to bear on the design and implementation of the recovery effort. In each case, NGO initiative invited NGO opposition; in one case, allies became adversaries. NGOs served to channel various expressions of the public interest into the policy process. NGOs also served to legitimate the views of individuals who spoke through them.

Each case turned on the shared jurisdiction between the state and federal governments. In the condor case, shared jurisdiction over an endangered species residing in California required a concurrence on recovery plans, not only between the state and federal governments, but among several decision centers at each level. Participating NGOs quite logically directed their attention toward what they believed to be the most responsive constituencies, in or out of government. In the bobcat case, a federal agency was asked to challenge the standard operating procedure of states in order to enforce an international agreement. Opposing groups simultaneously sought to pressure the agency for a favorable ruling. At the same time, these groups moved into the international arena to defend or challenge the treaty language itself. In both cases, the courts were asked to interpret federal obligations. In the bobcat case, NGOs developed congressional support that undermined the judicial action.

Of the two cases, the management of the condor more closely approximates the analyst's view of the policy process: a problem was identified; the Endangered Species Act mandated that a solution be found; the National Audubon Society, in conjunction with the U.S. Fish and Wildlife Service, produced a solution that was judged to be appropriate, and it was implemented. Any series of decisions such as this is made within an institutional context created by previous legislation and programs, including recovery efforts for other species. The larger policy questions, the answers to which are presumed in the analyst's approach—Is condor recovery the best use of wildlife protection dollars? Is wildlife protection the best use of environmental protection dollars?—cannot be reconsidered in every instance and indeed may never have been explicitly asked. NGO and public participation in the policy process, which in the condor case, at least, has been informed by media attention to the innovative, hands-on recovery effort, may raise these broader questions and push them onto the policy agenda. The condor case in particular reflects a tension between scientific and nonscientific decision making. Many questions that flow from these cases are questions not of fact but of value. NGO and public participation serve to monitor the boundary between these two decision realms and to assert the broader public interest in the realm of values.

NOTES

1. 27 U.S.T. 1087. In general, see Simon Lyster, *International Wildlife Law* (Cambridge: Grotius, 1985), Chapter 12 and Appendix 8, and Michael J. Bean, *The Evolution of National Wildlife Law*, rev. ed. (New York: Praeger, 1983), pp. 324-29, 380-83.

2. Reproduced in *Federal Register* 46 (September 14, 1981): 45652.

3. *Federal Register*, 46 (September 14, 1981): 45652.

4. *Defenders*, February 1977, p. 46.

5. Ibid.

6. *Endangered Species Technical Bulletin* 2 (August 1977): 4.

7. Hank Fischer, "Bobcats: Battle Won but War Still Raging," *Defenders*, April 1978, pp. 116-19.

8. *Endangered Species Technical Bulletin* 2 (July 1977): 2.

9. *Endangered Species Technical Bulletin* 2 (September 1977): 3. The prohibition was later postponed until November 30, 1977.

10. "Draft Report to the ESSA by the Working Group on Bobcat, Lynx, and River Otter," reprinted in U.S. Congress, Senate, Subcommittee on Resource Protection of the Committee on Environment and Public Works, *Amending the Endangered Species Act of 1973, Hearings on S.2899.*, April 13 and 14, 1978, 95th Cong., 2nd sess., Serial No. 95-H60, pp. 316-24.

11. *Federal Register* 43 (March 16, 1978): 11082-93; *Endangered Species Technical Bulletin* 3 (April 1978): 7.

12. *Defenders*, October 1978, p. 296.

13. International Association of Fish and Wildlife Agencies, *Proceedings of the Sixty-eighth Convention*, September 10-13, 1978, Resolution No. 2, pp. 122-23.

14. Ginger Merchant, "Thwarting the Effort to 'Unlist' Bobcats," *Defenders*, April 1979, pp. 119-20.

15. Letters from John Grandy, Executive Vice President of Defenders, to Cecil Andrus, Secretary of the Interior, November 8, 1978, summarizing the irregularities of the process, and from Jane Yarn, member of the CEQ, to Robert L. Herbst, Assistant Secretary of the Interior for Fish, Wildlife, and Parks, November 15, 1978, offering a point-by-point rebuttal of the FWS's scientific justification.

16. FWS's inability to withdraw the proposal resulted from an earlier legal settlement that had made specific reference to delisting the bobcat. A new settlement was reached that permitted withdrawal, but it committed the United States instead to propose suspension of the Berne criteria. Letter from Ginger Merchant, Defenders of Wildlife, February 26, 1981.

17. U.S. Department of the Interior, Fish and Wildlife Service, *Public Meeting on U.S. Proposals to Amend the Appendices and to Discuss Foreign Proposals*, transcript of proceedings, February 1, 1979, pp. 51-134.

18. *Focus*, Summer 1979, p. 6. Bean attended at the invitation of the American Committee for International Conservation, a coalition of major U.S. conservation organizations. *EDF Letter*, March-April 1979, p. 4.

19. *Report of the U.S. Delegation to the Second Meeting of the Conference of the Parties to the Convention on International Trade in Endangered Species of Wild Fauna and Flora*, San José, Costa Rica, March 19-30, 1979, pp. 24-26.

20. Bayard Webster, "Protection is Given Wildlife in Danger," New York *Times*, April 2, 1979, p. D10.

21. *Focus*, Summer 1979, p. 6. The second issue concerned the U.K. proposal to limit enforcement of the treaty to a minimum list of animal parts and derivatives rather than the "readily recognizable part or derivative" stipulated by the treaty.

22. U.S. Congress, House, Subcommittee on International Organizations of the Committee on Foreign Affairs, *Review of Recent Efforts to Protect Endangered Species, Hearings, Convention on International Trade in Endangered Species (CITES), Part I*, May 15 and 24, 1979, p. 35. See also Richard K. Yancey, "Implications of International Conventions on Management of Living Resources," in *Transactions of the Forty-fifth North American Wildlife and Natural Resources Conference* (Washington, D.C.: Wildlife Management Institute, 1980). "It was obvious that persuasions by protectionist-oriented nongovernmental organizations had a profound effect on decisions by the Conference of the Parties." P. 39.

23. U.S. Congress, House, Subcommittee on International Organizations, *Review of Recent Efforts*, p. 26. It is important to note that NGOs may join together in a single position for very different reasons. In the debate over the Berne criteria, for example, some groups were primarily concerned with the well-being of the bobcat for humane reasons, others because they genuinely believed

the species to be endangered by trade, and still others because of the implications that criteria revision would have for a host of other species.

24. On the relisting of the alligator, see *Endangered Species Technical Bulletin* 3 (November 1978): 1; 4 (April 1979): 1; 4 (June 1979): 6; 4 (July 1979): 1; 4 (October 1979): 1.

25. U.S. Congress, House, Subcommittee on International Organizations, *Review of Recent Efforts*, pp. 31-39.

26. Ibid., pp. 31-39; 61-63.

27. U.S. Congress, House, Subcommittee on Fisheries and Wildlife Conservation and the Environment of the Committee on Merchant Marine, *Endangered Species: Hearings, Endangered Species Scientific Authority Oversight*, July 16, 1979, 96th Cong., 1st sess. Serial No. 96-12. The amendments designate the secretary of the interior as the scientific authority under CITES. The seven-member panel that formerly constituted the independent ESSA became the International Convention Advisory Commission (ICAC). Should the secretary reject the recommendations of ICAC, the reasons for rejection must be published in the *Federal Register*. ICAC was itself dissolved by the 1982 amendments to the act.

28. *Federal Register* 43 (September 1, 1978): 39309; *Federal Register* 44 (April 30, 1979): 25385.

29. Defenders of Wildlife, Inc. v. Endangered Species Scientific Authority, 659 F. 2d 168 (D.C. Cir., 1981), cert. denied, 454 U.S. 963 (1981). See Bean, *Evolution of National Wildlife Law*, pp. 380-81, and Ginger Merchant, "Defenders and Bobcats Win Appeals Court Decision," *Defenders*, June 1981, pp. 46-47. For commentary on the case, see Gregory A. Chaimov and James E. Durr, "*Defenders of Wildlife Inc. v. Endangered Species Scientific Authority*: The Court as Biologist," *Environmental Law* 12 (1982), who argue that "the court of appeals erred in substituting its judgment of proper wildlife management practices for that of ESSA's biologists." P. 774.

30. Order filed April 23, 1981, Civil Action No. 79-3060. Defenders agreed that pelts already harvested could be exported.

31. *Federal Register* 46 (May 26, 1981): 28193.

32. *Federal Register* 46 (May 26, 1981): 28192; (September 10, 1981): 45172; (October 14, 1981): 50774; 47 (January 12, 1982): 1294.

33. *Federal Register* 47 (April 5, 1982): 14664; (July 15, 1982): 30788; (August 20, 1982): 36457.

34. International Association of Fish and Wildlife Agencies, *Proceedings of the Seventy-second Convention*, September 19-22, 1982, pp. 52, 61.

35. U.S. Congress, Senate, Subcommittee on Environmental Pollution of the Committee on Environment and Public Works, *Endangered Species Act Oversight, Hearings*, December 8 and 10, 1981, 97th Cong., 1st sess., Serial No. 97-H34, pp. 34-35.

36. Ibid., p. 160.

37. U.S. Congress, House, Subcommittee on Fisheries and Wildlife Conservation and the Environment of the Committee on Merchant Marine and Fisheries, *Endangered Species Act: Hearings on Endangered Species Act Reauthorization and Oversight*, February 22, March 8, 1982, 97th Cong., 2d sess., Serial No. 97-32, pp. 71-73.

38. Ibid., p. 178.

39. U.S. Congress, Senate, Subcommittee on Environment and Public Works, December 8 and 10, 1981, *Endangered Species Act Oversight*, Serial 97-H34, pp. 341-65.

40. *Endangered Species Act Reauthorization Bulletin*, No. 4, March 8, 1982, pp. 3-4.

41. U.S. Congress, House, *Endangered Species Act*, Serial No. 97-32, pp. 422-25.

42. U.S. Congress, Senate, Subcommittee on Environmental Pollution of the Committee on Environment and Public Works, *Endangered Species Act Amendments of 1982, Hearing on S. 2309.*, April 19 and 22, 1982, 97th Cong., 2nd sess., Serial No. 97-H46, pp. 32-37. See also testimony of Christine Stevens, representing the Society for Animal Protective Legislation, ibid.

43. Ibid., p. 253.

44. Endangered Species Act Amendments of 1982, P.L. 97-304; U.S. Congress, Senate, Committee on Environment and Public Works, *Endangered Species Act Amendments of 1982: Report to Accompany S. 2309*, May 26, 1982, 99th Cong., 2d sess., Sen Rept. 97-418, p. 22; U.S. Congress, House, Committee on Merchant Marine, *Endangered Species Act Amendments: Report to Accompany HR 6133*, May 17, 1982, 99th Cong., 2d sess., House Rept. 97-567, Part 1, p. 29; U.S. Congress, House, Committee on Merchant Marine, *Endangered Species Act Amendments of 1982: Conference Report to Accompany HR 6133*, September 17, 1982, 99th Cong., 2d sess., House Rept. 97-835, p. 29.

45. Two related amendments were included in the legislation. The first struck down the International Convention Advisory Commission (ICAC), created in 1979 to advise the Secretary of the Interior "on all matters pertaining to the responsibilities of the Scientific Authority under the terms of the Convention." At the time of the 1982 reauthorization hearings, the commission had already been zero-funded, and although there was some initial opposition to its elimination, it was not a hotly argued concern. The second convention amendment instructed the Secretary of State to explain to the appropriate congressional committees any failure of the United States to enter a reservation under the terms of the convention for any species placed on Appendices I or II against U.S. vote.

46. *Federal Register* 48 (February 3, 1983): 4795. On the subsequent development of the regulations, see *Federal Register* 48 (February 23, 1983): 7604, and 48 (April 18, 1983): 16494.

47. *Federal Register* 45 (April 4, 1980): 23370, and (July 21, 1980): 48830. Following the 1981 meetings, Breaux held brief oversight hearings during which

he apparently satisfied himself that the treaty was no longer being used to impede legal trade in species not threatened by trade and that NGOs were no longer a threat to the orderly conduct of convention business. U.S. Congress, House, Subcommittee on Fisheries and Wildlife Conservation of the Committee on Merchant Marine and Fisheries, *Fish and Wildlife Miscellaneous: Part 1, Hearings, Convention on International Trade in Endangered Species (CITES) Briefing*, March 19, 1981, 97th Cong., 1st sess., Serial No. 97-5, p. 357. The issue was to arise again in conjunction with the efforts of the Cayman Turtle Farm to import its products to the United States. At the fifth meeting of the parties in 1985, several technical proposals that would have aided the farm's cause were defeated, due in significant measure to NGO influence. The CITES representatives of the farm, Stephen Boynton, who was also the counsel to the American Fur Resources Institute, and Richard Parsons, formerly head of the Wildlife Permit Office of the FWS (the CITES management authority), sought Breaux's assistance in determining whether NGO financial aid to the delegations of developing countries might have come in exchange for certain votes. In lieu of a requested hearing, Breaux asked for an audit by the U.S. General Accounting Office, which showed no evidence in support of the charge. *Report of the U.S. Delegation to the Fifth Meeting of the Conference of the Parties to the Convention on International Trade in Endangered Species of Wild Fauna and Flora (CITES)*, Buenos Aires, Argentina, April 22–May 3, 1985, pp. 8-9, 43; *Endangered Species Technical Bulletin* 11 (January 1986): 8-9; Lyster, *International Wildlife Law*, pp. 260-61; and U.S. General Accounting Office, *International Organizations—Private Funding of Delegate Travel*, GAO/RCED-87-22, October 1986.

48. IAFWA Resolution No. 11. *Proceedings of the Seventy-second Convention*, September 19-22, 1982, pp. 191-92. See *Federal Register* 48 (July 5, 1983): 30732, noting withdrawal of the proposal.

49. *Federal Register* 48 (August 18, 1983): 37494.

50. Ibid. See also Lyster, *International Wildlife Law*, pp. 253-55.

51. Lyster, *International Wildlife Law*, p. 254.

52. *Federal Register* 49 (January 5, 1984): 590. Public concerns over management practices are now likely to be aired at the state level. Citizen challenges to state harvest practices have surfaced in Nevada, Arizona, and Georgia, resulting in minor management changes.

53. See correspondence in U.S. Department of State, *Appendices to the Draft Environmental Impact Statement concerning the Convention on the Conservation of Migratory Species of Wild Animals Proposed by the Federal Republic of Germany*, Vol. 2. See also Yancey, "Implications of International Conventions." Strong opposition was also maintained by commercial fishing interests.

54. U.S. Department of the Interior, Fish and Wildlife Service, press release, Feature Release Series No. 8, "Restoring America's Wildlife—The Bobcat," 1986. See also Ted Williams, "The Fur Still Flies," *Audubon*, January 1984, pp. 28-31, and the response from John Breaux, *Audubon*, May 1984, pp. 121-22. For a re-

cent review of these events and their implications for bobcat management, see Ernest A. Gluesing, S. Douglas Miller, and Richard M. Mitchell, "Management of the North American Bobcat: Information Needs for Nondetriment Findings," *Transactions of the Fifty-first North American Wildlife and Natural Resources Conference* (Washington, D.C.: Wildlife Management Institute, 1986), pp. 183–92.

5

Wildlife Ends
and Means

The condor and bobcat case studies reveal a wide range of NGO tactics. Organizations lobby Congress, assist in drafting legislation, monitor agency performance, testify at congressional and administrative hearings, sue, commission research and publicize findings, produce educational materials, mobilize citizen involvement, and organize public demonstrations. This chapter constitutes a selective review of these and other activities, considering, first, direct communication between organizations and governments; second, indirect influence through public participation, education, and political action; and third, market transactions designed to meet organizational goals outside the political process.[1] These activities are often facilitated, indeed perhaps legitimized, by organizational nonprofit status. The privileges and responsibilities of nonprofit NGOs are investigated briefly at the conclusion of the chapter. The focus here is on the individual organization and the activities it elects to pursue. The broader context, questioning not only the coherence of individual organizational strategies but also the interaction among organizations as they contribute to collective performance, is addressed in Chapter 6.

CONGRESS

Although the executive and judicial branches wield exceptional powers in the environmental arena, it is the legislative branch that attracts the broadest attention of the wildlife industry. The administrative agencies and their programs are created by Congress, and once created, they must look to Congress for approbation and funding. Agencies derive much of their discretionary power from congressional reluctance to wade deeply into the administrative details of legislated programs. But Congress is not reluctant to change or refine its control under pressure from constituents. Even the courts, in their findings of procedural failure, often invite congressional reconsideration. Thus, Congress amended the Endangered Species Act in 1982 to reverse a court's requirement that bobcat export permits be based on population data, and Congress overrode the Supreme Court's refusal to permit completion of the Tellico Dam because of its threat to the snail darter, first by creating an administrative review procedure to weigh federal projects against endangered species and then, when that procedure failed to save the dam, by legislating a specific exemption allowing construction to continue without regard for the risk to the endangered fish.

The promotion of the California condor recovery program by the National Audubon Society (NAS) is a classic example of successful lobbying, one which was frequently cited by informants in discussions of NGO influence. The campaign combined testimony before the authorizations and appropriations committees of both houses and systematic efforts to gain the support of the California house delegation and of other key members of Congress; the strong support of the United States Fish and Wildlife Service was enlisted, as well as the backing of influential members of the scientific community. Yet this success cannot be widely emulated because it represents a commitment of organizational resources that the NGO community can seldom afford. Audubon's long-term financial interest in, and substantive involvement with the condor is likely to stand as an exception among advocacy groups.[2]

The critical nature of the appropriations process, highlighted in the condor recovery program, may be overlooked by reviewers of the NGO role in the legislative cycle and by NGOs themselves. Appropriations are often less visible and dramatic than authorizations and oversight, in part because the process has been largely intragovernmental as agencies have made and defended budget requests. However, whereas the appropriations committees were inclined to guard the public purse in the 1960s and 1970s, when federal environmental programs were rapidly expanding, they are as likely now to preserve the integrity of existing programs by appropriating funds in excess of administration requests. Constituency support for these efforts, as focused through NGO participation, is an essential ingredient in this process. But the appropriations committees are not limited to modifying the size of existing programs; they can substantively alter the direction of wildlife policy by reordering funding priorities, and they can design and implement innovations in program funding. An instance of the latter practice occurred when the Interior Appropriations Subcommittee under Senator James McClure (R. Idaho), in response to an NGO proposal, attached a matching-funds requirement to an increased fiscal 1985 Bureau of Land Management appropriation for bighorn sheep restoration. This approach, drawing private resources into public ventures, has seen limited application in other wildlife management programs.[3]

A particular focus for NGO attention is the Land and Water Conservation Fund (LWCF), appropriations from which have been used to acquire properties for the National Wildlife Refuge System. The Reagan administration budgets reflect dramatic reductions in acquisitions under the fund. The NGO community has responded by preparing unified annual proposals that rank desired acquisitions and document their importance. For example, *The Land and Water Conservation Fund—The Conservation Alternative for Fiscal Year 1986*, prepared by twelve national NGOs concerned with public lands, reported the precipitous decline in administration requests for funds, from a high of $649.4 million in fiscal 1979 to $15 million in fiscal 1986. It observed that $900 million from offshore oil and gas leases and other sources is credited annually to the fund (the balance in which then exceeded $4 billion), and requested appropriation of $335.6 million in fiscal 1986 to fund specific projects detailed in a 63-page analysis.[4] Congress provided half of the monies, adding to a five-year total appropriation under the program exceeding administration requests by more than $800 million.

The reductions in LWCF budget requests placed a particular burden on the Nature Conservancy, which had been acquiring lands in anticipation of their transfer to the federal government. It was this issue, perhaps more than any, that encouraged the conservancy to adopt a more aggressive approach to conservation politics. Conservancy president William Blair came before the House Interior Appropriations Subcommittee in March 1982 to protest drastic reductions in LWCF budget requests. Although sympathetic to the need for cuts in government programs, he argued that cuts here would threaten the cooperation between government and private sectors on which the administration pinned great hopes for a reduced federal government profile. Blair reminded the committee of the benefits of past coopera-tion but observed that, in the absence of increased appropriations, the government would not be able to take title to $4 million of lands then held for transfer by the conservancy. He spoke to the federal government's "moral obligation to help us by fulfilling its end of the bargain—repurchasing the land—as promptly as possible." He asked for, and received, half of the outstanding $4 million in fiscal 1983. (The balance was provided the following year.) In support of con-tinued grants to states for the natural heritage program, Blair cited then-presidential-adviser Edwin Meese's praise of the conservancy-pioneered program, which "is a wonderful example of private initia-tive and government-private cooperation. We hold a strong belief that the private sector initiatives are a strong and very desirable means to protecting . . . [natural] resources of value."[5]

Another illustration of NGO attention to appropriations may be found in the evolution of NAS concern. In its fiscal 1980 testimony before appropriations committees, the society had limited its remarks on endangered species funding to an expression of support for the administration by FWS of the act and to a summary assessment that "funding appears to be adequate." In its fiscal 1987 testimony, Audubon submitted a detailed appraisal, specifying needed improve-ments and their estimated costs, for example $75,000 to allow the scheduled release of four mated pairs of red wolves; $700,000 and 14 full-time-equivalent staff positions to insure adequate consultation under Section 7 of the Endangered Species Act; and $4,400,000 for state cooperative grants, naming 14 state programs as examples of those that would have to be terminated without this source of fund-ing.[6]

The NAS review did not attend only to programs deserving of increased funding; it supported the service's continuing efforts to reduce federal spending for the peregrine falcon in view of the suc-cess of the Peregrine Fund in generating private and nonservice gov-ernment funds. According to NAS, the Peregrine Fund had received $3,297,000 from the service over a ten-year period, whereas only $1,477,000 had been appropriated by Congress. This had necessi-tated the transfer of other FWS monies and jeopardized the recovery of other species. "The National Audubon Society applauds the efforts of the Peregrine Fund, but we think that in this era of fiscal constraint, a program that has plenty of private financial support should not receive precious federal dollars."[7] Tom J. Cade, testifying for the fund, observed that the eastern peregrine restoration program was among the few species recovery efforts actually on schedule and argued for continued add-on appropriations. That the program was close to completion should give it a higher, not a lower, congressional priority. Furthermore, the federal support "is a powerful inducement for other agencies and organizations to provide the balance of funds needed."[8] The appropriations committees agreed, and the peregrine received the full $300,000 requested.

In these instances, appropriations committees mediate differences between NGOs and agencies. Alternatively, agency and NGO interests combine to challenge committee priorities. The efforts of FWS to implement steel shot regulations where waterfowl populations had been damaged by lead poisoning were frustrated, despite necessary authorizations, by the Senate appropriations committee, which, under pressure from certain hunting constituencies, directed the service to gain state approval before designating steel shot zones within each state. Such approval could not always be obtained. Lynn A. Greenwalt, then director of the service, came before IAFWA to request passage of a resolution

not to endorse steel shot, but to . . . decry this approach to resolving what are fundamentally, fish and wildlife management problems; . . . I fear . . . less for the future of the steel shot program than I do for the precedent established by . . . the introduction of prohibitive . . . language which pre-empts the opportunity for the professional level agencies to deal with a resource decision in a rational sort of way.

Resolution No. 3, adopted by the association, recognizes that the decision

to implement or not to implement non-toxic shot requirements in the United States is a biological decision . . . [and] strongly urges that the 1979 Interior and Related Agencies Appropriation Act not contain language that would restrict the Fish and Wildlife Service in its overall administration of the non-toxic shot program.[9]

Despite this intervention, the committee renewed, and has continued to renew, the 1978 directive by Senator Ted Stevens (R. Alaska). It was not until 1985, under pressure and ultimately a lawsuit from the National Wildlife Federation (NWF), that the service took action under the Endangered Species Act and the Migratory Bird Treaty Act to circumvent this restriction. The former law obligates the service to protect the bald eagle and other endangered species from the hazards of lead shot, and the latter empowers the service to protect migratory birds by closing certain areas to hunting if necessary.[10]

The more commonly noted opportunity for NGO influence is presented by the authorization and oversight processes. The number of hearings in the wildlife issue area is considerable, in part because of overlapping jurisdictions and in part because of the high level of public interest in wildlife issues. The 1973 Endangered Species Act, for example, was the subject of 21 days of hearings before House and Senate subcommittees between 1977 and 1979; their records fill 3,200 pages. The extensive 1978 House hearings brought one or more appearances or statements from each of some 35 NGOs, often on behalf of yet other groups. But hearings are widely regarded by NGOs and committee staffs alike as playing a small role in policy making. Four respondents described such hearings as "dog and pony shows," carefully orchestrated by committee staffs. Nonetheless, virtually all groups participate. Of Berry's sample of public interest groups, testifying at congressional hearings was the most common tactic of advocacy, used by 88 percent of groups. Of Schlozman and Tierney's broader sample of interest groups, 99 percent offered testimony. But of Berry's groups that used and could evaluate the effectiveness of testimony, only 26 percent regarded the activity as effective or very effective, while 54 percent thought the activity was not effective.[11]

The direct impact of the hearing process on NGO goals appears to be small. One congressional staffer suggested that a competent performance will generally have little impact on the legislative outcome, but a poor showing can be detrimental to a group's standing. Another argued that any result would be greater in the House than in the Senate. Larger Senate staffs permit better in-house information capabilities, whereas more specialized House members must accept information from outside interests. A House committee staff member suggested that "an impression can be made at a hearing which will make or break an issue." Testimony previously described in the condor case genuinely seemed to have aided in gaining funding for the recovery effort. Another house staffer identified the 1985 testimony of David Attenborough in support of a strong Endangered Species Act as having decidedly influenced the views of subcommittee chairman John Breaux regarding not only the importance of maintaining biological diversity but also the importance of sustaining the U.S. role model in the international conservation community.[12] All in all, the staffer continued, the conservation community in general and certain individuals in particular account for the prevailing ethic that supports the act and related legislation. One hears many fewer disparaging remarks in Congress about the leverage that "insignificant" species exercise over material prosperity. This ethic notwithstanding, the reauthorization of the act was stalled in the Senate from 1985 to 1988 by members who placed holds on the legislation out of concern for the development implications of protecting the Bruno Hot Springs snail and the cui-ui fish, among other species.

The minimal and uncertain impact of hearings would hardly justify the resources all sides devote to the process. Committees hold hearings to stake jurisdictional claims, to establish a record of committee interest, to set agendas for future action, and, especially for field hearings, to create good will among constituents, present and prospective. NGOs participate to establish public positions on policy issues and to build and solidify working relationships with other NGOs and with the committee members and staff.

The highly ritualized congressional hearing is overshadowed in strategic importance by less structured opportunities for NGO influence. NGO and congressional staff members frequently meet, in formal and informal settings, on matters that range from the development of legislative language, to the discussion of scientific data, to the articulation of committee or floor strategies. The effectiveness of NGO lobbyists is constrained by their reputations and the reputations of the organizations they represent. Committee and agency staff members expressed strong opinions in this regard, and they willingly identified particular individuals and organizations who had earned their respect and others who had failed to do so. These opinions are based on positions as well as on style, but whatever their basis, they circulate widely among individuals within the wildlife issue area. This is especially noted among several cliques of mid level professional staff members.

In the course of interviews for this book, congressional committee staff members ventured numerous opinions about NGO influence in Congress. A selection of these opinions follows (1980 or 1986 interviews as indicated). One must bear in mind that while staff acceptance may promote access, congressional access is not the only key to organizational effectiveness.[13]

- The criteria for NGO effectiveness are age, visibility, and worth of information, thus making Audubon, Sierra Club, Wilderness Society, NWF, and Nature Conservancy the most influential groups. But, this Senate staffer added, the stature of the individual lobbyist is critical, and one who regularly meets members of Congress in social settings or is a major campaign contributor can be very influential (1980).

- A House committee staff member reported that environmental groups "arrive at the eleventh hour, throw a stack of information on the desk, and say 'Bonker has got to do something about this.' They call up in crisis and, when all is quiet, they fade away." Human rights groups, on the other hand, maintain constant pressure and involvement, perhaps because committee jurisdiction is more narrowly focused than in the environmental arena (1980).

- A Senate staff member observed that there is "a lot of flim-flam going on—squeaky wheels who raise a lot of hell and get press coverage but represent few. . . . Lots of people in the movement have self-centered perspectives and overblown visions of their impact" (1980).

- A House committee staffer reported that the IAFWA was the most effective group, at least in part because its states' rights and consumptive use orientation corresponded more closely to committee leadership's position than did the federal rights and nonconsumptive use orientation of other large groups. Effective also were NAS and NWF. He remarked, however, that even the most "protectionist" groups have their own successes. Overall, groups see things only in black-and-white terms, and to them, those who disagree have "sold out." This is especially true of "leftist" groups. Nonetheless, the groups represent a "tremendous interest" in wildlife on the part of the public, perhaps more interest than for other "more important" issues (1980).

- A Senate staff person criticized one organization for publishing her "opinion" on upcoming legislation and urging other groups to lobby her without first having directly sought out her (somewhat different) views (1980).

- A House committee staff member reported that, at staff level, the committee will talk to anyone in its search for ideas. As the legislation develops, the staff considers the merits first and then whether it can achieve its goals without involving interest groups. If not, then the groups have influence. But the impact of groups is clearly issue specific and member specific. In general, however, the groups "do poor research and rely on the strength of their memberships." They offer emotional arguments that represent a failure to understand political and scientific reality. He criticized groups for taking "over my dead body" positions that prevent creative bargaining and raise the stakes too high. Espepecially effective, however, are the NAS, NWF, IAFWA, Wildlife Management Institute (WMI), and Sierra Club (1980).

- The environmental community is aging; it is more corporate/bureaucratic in salaries and structure; it has lost its leanness. On the other hand, this House staffer observed, personal contacts built up over a long period are paying off. EDF's "Mike Bean doesn't have to file a lawsuit to have an impact" (1986).

- A Senate staffer reported that what makes groups effective is the information and expertise, the quality, reliability, and judgment that individual lobbyists possess. "Mike Bean has more influence than anyone. . . . If I can get EDF, National Wildlife, and Audubon on board, I am pretty well covered and the boss is pretty well covered" (1986).

- A House staffer reported that the most effective groups were the NWF, EDF, Center for Environmental Education, and Defenders. He would have listed NAS as the most effective group but for the recent departure of an influential wildlife lobbyist. Fading organizations included HSUS, the Sierra Club, FOE, and Greenpeace, in part because they rely on confrontational techniques (1986).

- The Senate leaders (Robert T. Stafford and John Chafee), because of their personal views and their New England liberal constituencies, need not worry much about groups such as IAFWA and NRA. But the fact that wildlife issues are not that contentious in committee does not mean that legislation makes its way easily through the Senate. Indeed, reauthorization of the Endangered Species Act has not made it to the Senate floor owing to several holds. In the House, on the other hand, the bill had been shepherded by Breaux, whose alliances with user groups had already forged a consensus bill in committee (1986).

It seems clear that legislators and their staffs feel comfortable with, and rank as effective, "conventional" lobbying strategies that provide facts and opinions and that offer creative solutions to differences that always arise in legislative disputes. They do not appreciate what they consider to be unprofessional behavior—*ad hominem* attacks, claims based on "emotion," or unforgiving or uncompromising attitudes. As Harmon Ziegler and Michael Baer conclude, "In lobbying, as in all human communication, the best technique is to minimize hostility."[14] In this view, the specific conflict occurs within the context of a larger battle, and long-term victory requires the maintenance of a dialogue that legitimizes continued interaction. Those who fail to play by the rules do not appreciate the larger struggle. One lobbyist remarked that "congressmen respect you if you fight clean and hard," but it was he who was most often mentioned by committee staff members as an example of a lobbyist who failed to do so. A contrary view is that the long-term struggle is merely a collection of short-term skirmishes, that the outcome of each weighs in the final tally, and that strategies must be evaluated according to their effectiveness, not their popularity. Deep personal and emotional involvement is itself a strategy that shows commitment and gains support.

An instructive case study in lobbying and NGO tactics may be found in the 1978 debate over the reauthorization of the Endangered Species Act.[15] The act had gained a certain notoriety in providing constituencies opposed to the completion of the Tellico Dam a vehicle for halting its construction. A stretch of the Little Tennessee River, which would have been (and now has been) flooded by the dam's completion, had been designated a critical habitat for the endangered snail darter; Section 7 of the act protected, without exception, the critical habitats of endangered species. The challenge to the act arose in part out of fear among development interests that the snail darter was but the first of many "insignificant" species that would halt major public works projects, and in part out of Senator Howard Baker's commitment to save the project in his home state.

In the House hearings of February 1978, Section 7 and its alleged weaknesses did not play a prominent role. According to one Senate committee staffer, subcommittee chairman Robert L. Leggett regarded Tellico as Baker's problem. (Leggett's attitude was to change. By the time the House took up the legislation on the floor, FWS had listed four endangered beetles that threatened a port project in Leggett's California district.) Public-interest NGO testimony focused on inadequate funding, but several spokespeople warned that threats to the integrity of Section 7 would "be met with an unparalleled public outcry" and that "the conservation and humane movements, across their entire spectrum, are for once united on an issue and determined to fight as hard, and as long, and as vindictively as may be necessary to defend Section 7."[16] At the same hearing other interest groups, allied with development industries, aired their already well known objections to the act. In a joint statement, the National Cattlemen's Association, the Public Lands Council, and the National Wool Growers' Association called for "extensive review and revision" of the act. Pointing to the adverse effects of the act on the use of federal lands and the potential for infringement on private property rights, the statement concluded that "if enforced to its limit, the Endangered Species Act could halt national growth and development."[17]

Senate hearings in mid-April were preceded by the development of a subcommittee bill, the Culver/Baker bill, featuring the creation of a high-level committee (affectionately known as the God Squad) to evaluate conflicts between federal actions and endangered species that could not be resolved through good-faith consultations and to recommend for or against an exemption for the project in each case. This bill offered Baker what he thought would be a certain exemption for the Tellico Dam, and it offered Senator John C. Culver a way to protect the essential features of the law from the severe attack he felt would follow a proposal for simple reauthorization. The committee had convened a meeting with representatives of several NGOs to explain the evolving legislation and to solicit comments. Later there was to be some disagreement as to what had been said at that meeting and as to what its significance was for the support of the environmental community. According to one staff person, the NGO representatives were "trying to find out what was going on," as there had been to that date little indication of the committee's thinking. The NGOs expressed satisfaction that the committee was working on the legislation and that NGOs were involved in the early stages. Although the NGOs clearly opposed any change that would weaken the existing law, they indicated modifications in the committee proposals that they regarded as improvements. Some changes were made, but the general structure of the committee bill was unaltered. Culver, perhaps more than his staff, read more NGO support into the committee "compromise" than did the environmental community.

Prior to Senate floor debate, environmental NGOs communicated widely with their members in an effort to generate pressure on Congress for preservation of the act. NGOs favoring no change found an ally in Senator Gaylord Nelson, a long-time advocate of strong environmental legislation, who offered to serve as a rallying point for NGO activity. The environmental constituency in the Senate, such as it was, was split, and the NGOs, while opposing Culver's position, could not afford to alienate him and his usually supportive allies. The NGOs agreed that, in their opposition to the Culver position, they would avoid personal attacks on the senator.

The position of the conservation community resulted from both substantive and strategic considerations. The consensus was that the act was working well in its present form and should not be changed. Even those groups that might have accepted the Culver/Baker amendments felt that only an extreme position could effectively stave off amendments such as that of Senator John Stennis exempting any project authorized before the act was passed in 1973. The committee bill would then appear as a reasonable compromise. (A Senate aide told an NGO lobbyist, "Listen, you guys have got to be on the lunatic fringe. We love you out there. It is the only way we can ever get anything good accomplished."[18] A spokesman for Nelson claimed that the senator's position and the support it gathered had indeed prevented the passage of the Stennis amendment or something like it. (The amendment was defeated 76–22). A former Senate staffer claimed that Nelson's willingness to adopt the extreme position resulted from his view that Tellico was the only issue at stake and that the committee bill was a Baker power play. Others argued that the NGOs had been forced into their extreme position by previous organizational and individual commitments. A Senate staffer identified one advocate whose "entire reputation was staked on this one." A House staffer asserted that extreme strategies are generally counterproductive and represent a failure to recognize political and scientific reality. If groups begin with "extreme positions, they tend to get written off. . . . [They] get cut out of the action."

The unified NGO public stance in support of Nelson's amendment obscured gradual shifts in the thinking of particular lobbyists and the groups they represented. Audubon, in a last-minute action that other groups say caught them by surprise, offered public support for the Culver/Baker position in a letter to Culver that spoke to the need "to still our rhetoric and to ask ourselves how to most effectively protect species from extinction." Citing the timidity of the listing agency and of the NGO community in encouraging full implementation of the present act for fear of backlash, and tempered by a request for several strengthening amendments, Audubon offered its support for change. "We are aware of some of the heavy pressures that have been brought upon you from both sides and we want to commend you for your statesmanship and courage in trying to achieve a resolution that protects all aspects of the national interest."[19]

Culver referred to the letter in his remarks on the floor in opposition to Nelson's amendment to strike Culver/Baker in its entirety.

We have had a number of environmental groups privately come in and whisper and wink and nod that this is what they want, . . . but they know if they are going to get their dues every year they have to keep demagoging to their constituency. . . . I am sick and tired of that kind of politics. . . . I would like them, if they are worthy of representing these outstanding groups, to have the integrity to tell them the same thing they tell me. . . . We do have some letters that have come in today from the National Audubon Society, for one, praising the statesmanship of this committee. That is one group that has put their money where their mouth is. They put their mouths where their constituency's money is. They have been honest and responsive, and they follow the political climate.[20]

Nelson withdrew his amendment.

There is disagreement about the impact of the split on the legislative outcome. According to one Senate staffer, Nelson "got taken by the environmental groups." His amendment "never had a dog's chance in hell." For the Society For Animal Protective Legislation, "there is little doubt that this stab in the back played an important role in the outcome of the Senate vote."[21] For Friends of the Earth, "public support of the Culver/Baker amendment by an environmental group . . . left us very little leverage to pry concessions from Culver on our strengthening language."[22] Culver, in an appreciative letter to NAS president Stahr, noted "that the support of the Audubon Society contributed significantly to the successful adoption by the Senate of this legislation."[23]

The NAS view was that, even if the act could have been preserved in 1978, it would have been under more severe attack in 1979. It was preferable therefore to gain support for a relatively modest weakening before even that was impossible. In addition, even though the House leadership had early indicated a preference for an unchanged act, Audubon saw a serious attack ahead and thought it wise to create a solid Senate position that would moderate weakening House amendments at the conference committee. Indeed, House leaders gave in to Representative Robin L. Beard, who withdrew 682 proposed amendments (one to delete funding for each endangered and threatened species then listed) in exchange for an open floor debate on the act.[24] In a letter to regional representatives, chapter presidents, and others, the Audubon lobbyist commended senators Culver and Malcolm Wallop for fighting off "attacks to seriously weaken the Culver/Baker Amendment . . . during three days of brilliantly controlled debate."[25] It should not be surprising that, in a profile of the Washington staff of the Audubon Society published in *Audubon* some two years later, Culver would be mentioned as the cosponsor of the "controversial amendment that saved the Endangered Species Act during the 1978 Tellico Dam–snail darter debate."[26] Somewhat more surprising is that Culver, with a League of Conservation Voters score among the highest in the Senate, was, in his 1980 reelection bid, receiving the unqualified support of the environmental community for, among other virtues, defending the National Environmental Policy Act and the Endangered Species Act "against their many detractors."[27]

While the legislative impact of the split within the environmental community may have been limited, the impact on the community itself was substantial.[28] Some Audubon members felt betrayed. One member wrote that "support for Culver/Baker was a tactical blunder of the first magnitude." In response to what he regarded as an unsatisfactory reply from the Washington office, he concluded that "Audubon, once in the vanguard of the conservation movement, has now become fat, complacent and ineffective."[29] In a letter to the Audubon president, a Defenders of Wildlife staff member wrote,

I am fairly inured, after years in Washington, to divisiveness and backstabbing within the conservation movement, . . . but I was nonetheless absolutely shocked at your sudden decision to sign and place into Culver's hands a letter which completely undercut Senator Nelson's effort . . . to strengthen Culver/Baker on the floor, and which was absolutely contrary to Audubon's previous, publicly stated position on the issue. The effect of your action has been to erode the credibility of the entire conservation movement. We are exposed as being divided and irresolute, susceptible to manipulation and co-optation; of being feeble opponents and untrustworthy friends.[30]

The 1978 and 1979 amendments to the Endangered Species Act, including those supported by Culver to gain support for his 1978 proposal, clearly weakened the act.[31] It is difficult to ascertain whether the act would today be stronger or weaker had the united front of the conservation lobby been maintained throughout. The 1982 reauthorization, initially thought by observers representing a wide range of constituencies to pose a serious threat to the act's remaining integrity, resulted in a somewhat stronger act. The community of environmentalists maintained an active, unified, and well informed presence throughout the reauthorization process.[32]

THE AGENCIES

The extreme complexity of environmental management and the disinclination of Congress to specify regulatory details of wildlife and environmental programs have resulted in extensive bureaucratic decision making in this as in many other realms of federal policy making.

Environmental NGOs are foremost among those that have pushed for, and taken advantage of, increased access to administrative proceedings.

Among the more notable aspects of public participation in environmental decision making has been NGO and citizen monitoring of agency compliance with the National Environmental Policy Act of 1969 (NEPA). The act, which constituted a declaration of national environmental policy, directed all federal agencies to prepare environmental impact statements (EIS) for federal actions "significantly affecting the quality of the human environment." But the act and the subsequent implementation guidelines left unanswered numerous procedural and substantive questions that were to be addressed by the courts. The notoriety of NEPA and its associated environmental impact statement derive largely from NGO-initiated legal actions that have followed alleged agency failure to comply with the provisions of the act as interpreted by the Council on Environmental Quality (CEQ). Such legal action has been initiated not only by NGOs alleging that agencies ignore their responsibilities toward environmental quality, but also by competing NGOs alleging that agencies are overresponsive to the pressures exerted by the first group, thereby hindering responsible and legal economic activity.[33]

Of equal importance to these court challenges has been the extraordinary commitment of resources that agencies and NGOs have made to the preparation and review of environmental impact statements. During the years 1970–75 federal agencies filed nearly 7,000 draft environmental impact statements. The number of assessments prepared to determine the need for the more elaborate analysis was many times greater. The Army Corps of Engineers, for example, produced an estimated 10,000 assessments in 1975 but only 273 statements.[34] Although the numbers have declined in more recent years, time devoted by agencies and NGOs to the EIS remains substantial. In 1984, for example, agencies filed 577 draft and final statements.[35] In a recent instance, 45 NGOs, ranging from Greenpeace USA to the Pacific Legal Foundation and from the Alaska Oil and Gas Association to the Wilderness Society, submitted 481 pages of detailed commentary to the Interior Department in response to department's draft recommendation to Congress proposing oil and gas leasing in the coastal plain of the Arctic National Wildlife Refuge. FWS, in addition, received opinions and information from numerous government agencies, corporations, and private individuals, bringing total correspondence to 11,361 pieces.[36]

Meaningful participation in agency proceedings requires knowledge of opportunities for involvement. Such knowledge is generated through personal and organizational networks and through perusal of the *Federal Register*. One of the functions of the Monitor Consortium is identification of *Federal Register* notices that may merit comment or action by member organizations. At one weekly meeting of the consortium, members were apprised of the following four permit applications: to capture five beached or stranded California sea lions for export to a Hong Kong aquarium, to import a wild-caught jaguarundi from a Mexican zoo to an Arizona museum; to purchase, in interstate commerce, two Brazilian tapirs from a Pennsylvania animal farm by a Kansas zoo; and to import a Canadian polar bear to a Minnesota zoo. It was determined that two letters would be drafted for member signatures, one seeking controls on the conditions of display of the sea lions and another questioning the quality of the Minnesota zoo and noting a glut of bears already within the United States. Other notices brought before the members were status reviews under the Endangered Species Act for the Uncompahgre Fritillary butterfly (estimated adult population less than 200) and a regional population of the Bell's vireo; a proposed rule making to declare an emergency manatee refuge in Florida, where swimmers and divers harass the species; and the announcement of final rules describing the procedures by which applicants seek exemption from the Endangered Species Act. In addition, the members discussed draft letters to the deputy assistant secretary of agriculture opposing transfer within the department of enforcement of the Animal Welfare Act, to the governor of Florida questioning the impact of water hyacinth control measures on manatees, and to a California senate committee in support of a proposed four-year ban on the taking of bobcat. Finally, members were informed of upcoming meetings and hearings on international environmental issues (at NRDC), on the Ocean Decade (at the Library of Congress), on "the general image and public relations perceptions of the National Wildlife Refuge System" (at the Interior Department), and on acid rain (at the House Commerce Oversight and Investigations Subcommittee). Considerable discussion took place on the U.S. District Court of Appeals reversal of the ban on the aerial hunting of wolves on federal lands in Alaska. This was seen to represent backsliding by Interior toward states' rights.[37]

This matter of state versus federal jurisdiction over wildlife has been shown to be of great import in the two case studies and elsewhere. NGOs devote resources to political activity within existing divisions of responsibility, but they also seek to modify the boundary line to expand access or achieve favorable outcomes. Two examples illustrate this point and suggest the tensions that exist in the wildlife issue area.

In November 1979 the Department of the Interior produced a draft National Fish and Wildlife Policy, a section of which sought to clarify the nature of the shared state-federal jurisdiction over wildlife. The section, prepared by Jay D. Hair, then of North Carolina State University and now executive vice-president of NWF, would appear to have sought the prevention of further erosion of state control. It began with the clear recognition of shared jurisdiction but went on to describe the state authority as more, and the federal authority as less, inclusive than current statutes and court rulings suggested. Following on the heels of the bobcat/CITES controversy, the document noted in particular that "the United States will not become a party to international treaties or conventions that jeopardize the jurisdictional responsibilities of the states or territories over fish and resident wildlife."[38]

The Council on Environmental Quality (CEQ), at the time regarded by state agencies and environmental NGOs as supportive of an enlarged federal role in environmental affairs, recommended important changes in its extensive review of the document for the Secretary of the Interior. CEQ reminded the secretary of the President's exclusive authority to enter into international agreements, noting, however, that consultation with affected states would be appropriate.[39] Robert L. Herbst, then Assistant Secretary of the Interior for Fish, Wildlife and Parks, addressed the 45th North American Wildlife and Natural Resources Conference in March 1980 to offer his views on the importance of the policy and to announce the forthcoming second draft statement. He observed that "wildlife policy has never been chipped in stone" and must recognize the increasing importance of nonconsumptive wildlife values. But wildlife constituencies are "weakened by internal warfare, by hostility and distrust, by the inordinate desire to protect our own turf." Speaking to the issue of state-federal jurisdiction, Herbst sought "a *national* fish and wildlife policy, *not a federal* fish and wildlife policy."[40]

The new draft policy included small but important changes limiting the authority of states and expanding the authority of the federal government.[41] This draft was unacceptable to the International Association of Fish and Wildlife Agencies (IAFWA), however, and in October 1980 the organization notified Interior Secretary Cecil Andrus to that effect. The change in federal administration effectively halted further development in this policy direction. In July 1981 assistant secretary Ray Arnett indicated his interest in renewing work on Interior's policy.[42] Meanwhile, the IAFWA was exploring a more aggressive approach to shoring up states' rights to wildlife through its Ad Hoc States' Rights Committee. The committee, arguing that the political climate had never been more favorable, urged an omnibus legislative approach, while others at IAFWA, concerned that Congress would not be receptive, argued for a piecemeal approach through modification of existing federal legislation.[43] The decision was made to postpone further action until the department's policy was available for review.[44]

The draft policy produced in October 1982 was considerably more to the liking of the states. "It is the purpose of the Departmental Fish and Wildlife Policy to reaffirm the role of the States in this area by restating succinctly the Federal and the State authorities." The document generally emphasized state authority and noted the historical reluctance of congress to limit this authority despite available constitutional powers. Accordingly, the Interior Department would encourage public use of federal lands for hunting, fishing, and trapping and recommend U.S. participation in international agreements only if they are "supportive of effective state programs designed to insure the perpetuation of fish and wildlife populations."[45] Once again public comment led to moderations in the policy, but the final version remains supportive of states' rights.[46]

Throughout this period FWS was in other ways exploring its jurisdiction. The service funded an extensive survey research project by Stephen R. Kellert, designed to assess public attitudes, knowledge, and behaviors toward wildlife.[47] Early in the development of the project, the service created an external advisory board with members who represented such constituencies as the Environmental Defense Fund (EDF), Humane Society of the United States (HSUS), National Wildlife Federation (NWF), New York Zoological Society (NYZS), International Council for Bird Protection, IAFWA, League of Women Voters, National Association for the Advancement of Colored People, and the AFL-CIO. FWS received considerable mail addressing the composition of the committee, some of it questioning the right of certain "nonhunting" constituencies to influence the agency's policies. The National Rifle Association (NRA) viewed the committee as "pretty urban oriented, non-wildlife oriented, and anti-hunting oriented." The association's "Reports from Washington" quoted Senator James McClure as saying,

This bizarre action by an agency that has traditionally served the nation's 20 million hunters should be viewed as a dire warning of things to come—of a change in direction toward a heavy interest in urban ecology. It does not bode well when a major policy review power is handed to people who have literally no footing or interest in wildlife management or who are either anti-gun or who are opposed to hunting.[48]

Richard Starnes, writing in *Outdoor Life*, observed that "we all know surveys and polls prove whatever they're intended to prove." What if the study is the "subtle opening gun in a long-range campaign to switch the emphasis on the use of our land and game away from hunting and into birdwatching, hiking, and other saintly, non-noisy enterprises?" His inside source at FWS reported that for "the last couple of years there has been a shift in emphasis toward accommodating the twitty-bird crowd."[49]

FWS by no means denied that its mission and constituency was evolving. The service press officer reported that "we can tell by the letters, comments, and the way the press treats us, it's changing. We're seeking out new people in our constituency, even if they don't know they're part of our constituency." Service director Greenwalt asserted that the "results of this investigation will help us to promote greater citizen participation in the decision-making process and in our future plans to manage wildlife for the benefit of all Americans."[50]

The volume of concern, coupled with the specific attention given the matter by several members of the Senate, led to the creation of committee slots for NRA and the American Farm Bureau. In the end, the controversial committee met only once and played a small role in the development of the project. The study findings were sufficiently broad and detailed to provide supporting data for even the most severe critics. Starnes' first review, making no reference to his earlier diatribe, carries the title "Exploding the Anti-Hunting Myth" and concludes that the study "will provide the ammunition to answer many of the unthinking attacks that are leveled against our chosen recreation."[51] At the same time, the humane movement could find support in the results that only 18 percent of respondents "see nothing wrong with using steel traps to capture wild animals," and

65 percent "would rather pay a higher price for tuna fish than see the tuna industry continue to kill porpoises in their nets."[52]

While the broad scope of agency mission evolves in response to and in cooperation with constituency groups, the agency is also, given its present legislative and regulatory mandate, implementing the law. Because the charge to any agency exceeds its capacity to meet that charge fully, the agency must select particular actions from among a set of all possible actions. NGOs are clearly important in this selection process. Participation may be invited by statute, as in the Endangered Species Act, which solicits petitions to aid in the identification of endangered and threatened species. Among proposed species, groups champion their favorites. A biologist formerly with the Office of Endangered Species estimated that "at least 50 percent of all post-1973 listings resulted from the presence of a visible constituency." NGOs may also "legitimize the role of internal advocates. Basically, if no one knows what is right, they listen to what the loudest group wants."[53] Several agency respondents volunteered that they were responsive to NGO pressures. The proposal to lift a ban on the importation of kangaroo products was probably delayed because of the active opposition of certain advocates, one of whom, referred to as "our lady of the kangaroo," could "get forty congressional signatures in no time."[54]

An important change in agency-NGO relationships is marked by initiatives taken to preclude the legal challenges that often result from traditional rule makings, a process that requires agencies to solicit public opinion, digest that opinion internally, and promulgate regulations. In efforts that parallel mediated dispute resolution (addressed below), predispute negotiations among government, NGO, and industry groups have, in a few instances, produced regulations for agency implementation. Two 1987 examples include the woodstove pollution control regulations negotiated among the NRDC, U.S. Environmental Protection Agency (EPA), woodstove manufacturers, and states and the sea turtle protection proposals negotiated among NGOs, the National Marine Fisheries Service, and representatives of the Gulf of Mexico and South Atlantic shrimp industry.[55] In the former case, NRDC reports that the "negotiated standard is far better than what we could have expected from EPA following normal procedures."[56] In the latter case, implementation was threatened by Gulf Coast shrimpers who sought court delays and enlisted congressional support for their claims that the mandated turtle excluder devices (TEDs) would prove economically burdensome.[57] The matter was resolved with a controversial amendment to the 1988 Endangered Species Act reauthorization delaying required offshore use of TEDs until May 1, 1989, and delaying instore use until May 1, 1990. Incentives for participation in such proceedings vary. Agencies may be relieved of substantial burden through a process that has co-opted the important parties and largely precludes subsequent litigation. Industry may prefer to aggressively negotiate federal regulations rather than risk independent regulation by a number of states. NGOs may be able to build on their reputations as constructive policy makers rather than as obstructionists and may be rewarded with more favorable regulations at lower organizational cost.[58]

Thus NGOs may monitor agency behavior, seek to modify agency jurisdictions, and assist agencies in selecting among a range of possible actions. NGOs may also fill organizational niches apparently left vacant in agency structure—that is, NGOs may assume responsibilities that might be seen to fall logically within an expanded agency agenda. Rather than confront agencies over alleged failure to fulfill their mandates or confront Congress over failure to appropriate adequate funding, the private sector may marshall comparable energies toward the formation of new organizations. TRAFFIC—Trade Records Analysis of Flora and Fauna in Commerce—was created in London under the Species Survival Commission of the International Union for the Conservation of Nature and Natural Resources (IUCN). With the opening of the U.S. office of TRAFFIC in 1978, funded entirely by annual grants from WWF–US, the London office has become the international, under which national offices operate in several major wildlife trading nations. TRAFFIC (USA) monitors international trade in wild plants and animals, prepares investigative reports—for example on trade in sea turtle products, macaws, and orchids—and offers testimony on its findings.[59] The organizational niche filled by TRAFFIC had been left vacant by a curious division of responsibilities among five federal agencies that share jurisdiction over trade in wild plants and animals. This division explained, or at least offered a reasonable excuse for, several years of inaction on petitions to protect sea turtles, as the departments of Interior and Commerce debated jurisdiction over species that spend part of their lives on land and part in the sea.[60]

By combining figures produced in scattered offices at home and abroad, TRAFFIC has uncovered inconsistent and incomplete record keeping as well as patterns of trade that had escaped observers with access to limited data. Prompted by the obvious concern within the environmental community for the seemingly unchecked volume of illegal trade in wildlife products, in part as documented by TRAFFIC, President Carter, in his 1979 environmental message, directed the several departments to attend to their enforcement responsibilities. In October the Wildlife Section of the Justice Department was created to organize prosecutions. Early in 1980 the agencies joined in the Wildlife Law Enforcement Coordinating Committee, which sponsored task forces to attack particular enforcement problems. Since this new effort has begun, several major smuggling rings have been broken and considerable publicity has been generated. Illegal trade continues apace, however.[61]

Although the most dramatic threats to protected wildlife result from black-market commercial activity, private citizens purchasing souvenirs abroad represent a significant cumulative, if unintentional, threat. Much of this illegal merchandise is confiscated by customs agents, but the toll on foreign wildlife cannot be undone. TRAFFIC (USA) developed a public education campaign, which it proposed for joint sponsorship with FWS. The program, partially funded and facilitated by the National Fish and Wildlife Foundation, consists of print advertising and the distribution of "Buyer Beware," a colorful and informative brochure aimed at U.S. tourists. The program has also gained the support of the American Society of Travel Agents, the 13,000 member agencies of which may request brochures for distribution to clients. By the end of 1986 approximately 250,000 brochures had been distributed. This complex joint venture, involving industry, public interest, and government nonprofits, as well as FWS, represents a promising model for future cooperative efforts.[62]

The aforementioned National Fish and Wildlife Foundation, chartered by Congress in 1984, exemplifies the government creation of nonprofit organizations to fill perceived empty niches. The foundation is modeled after a similar organization serving the National Park System, and as noted in a Senate committee report, "is designed to be a structure through which the Fish and Wildlife Service will work with the leaders of the private sector on a continuing basis in an atmosphere of mutual respect."[63] In 1986, its first full year of operation, the foundation generated nearly $1,000,000 in revenues, including $250,000 in congressional appropriations and $650,000 in corporate and individual contributions. Since 1987 the foundation has benefited from the sale of conservation stamps and prints. In addition to its support of the Buyer Beware campaign, the organization has funded bald eagle restoration programs, wetlands preservation, and waterfowl banding, among other wildlife conservation projects.[64]

The partnership between agencies and NGOs is nowhere more clear than in the realm of land acquisition, where NGOs such as the Nature Conservancy frequently intermediate between private and public owners. A major example is the Great Dismal Swamp Wildlife Refuge, consisting of 71,507 acres transferred to the service by the conservancy, which in turn had assembled an 89,055-acre sanctuary from major gifts of the Union Camp and Weyerhauser Corporations, combined with other purchases. Transfers of this magnitude may suggest an NGO role in determining federal acquisitions. Lynn A. Greenwalt, director of FWS at the time of the transfer, asserted that "the Conservancy does not establish the Service's priorities for land acquisition, but rather acts at the request of Fish and Wildlife and carries out programs initiated by the agency."[65]

This relationship was broadly confirmed by GAO in its 1981 study prepared at the request of Senator Ted Stevens. The report, while dismissing "substantial" NGO influence on agency purchases, noted that "agencies do prefer to negotiate with a 'willing seller.' Consequently, once a nonprofit organization has acquired a tract of land, the agency has a willing seller situation, which influences when the agency will acquire the property."[66] At the same time, the report noted distinct advantages of the NGO link. "Nonprofit organizations are able to obtain bargain sales and donations more readily than the federal agencies primarily because of their ability to be more flexible and because they promote the tax benefits more aggressively."[67] Between 1965 and 1980, land transfers from NGOs, representing 4.5 percent of the cost of all lands acquired, saved agencies $50 million of an estimated fair market value of $162 million.[68] In sum, GAO noted five services that NGOs provide to the government: "avoiding the need to condemn land, solving complex title problems, moving quickly on a transaction, holding properties at reduced prices in rapidly appreciating markets, and acquiring land where there is antipathy toward the Government."[69]

An equally close relationship has been established by a 1984 memorandum of understanding between Ducks Unlimited, Inc. (DU) and FWS, the Bureau of Land Management, and the Forest Service, in which DU is to restore agency wetlands and increase their waterfowl productivity. The organization, which had previously limited its activities to projects in Canada and Mexico, has, according to then Secretary of the Interior William Clark, joined in "the most ambitious cooperative public and private effort to improve wildlife habitat in U.S. conservation history." Under the program, DU will review high-priority proposals from federal and state agencies that the agencies cannot themselves fund.[70] On the occasion of the organization's 50th anniversary, Interior Secretary Donald Hodel saluted DU, noting that it had long ago realized "that conservationists cannot and should not wait around for government to bear the entire responsibility of sound resource management. The private sector must lend a hand, and Ducks Unlimited has."[71]

NGOs constitute repositories of expertise that can be tapped to fill positions in agencies or on U.S. delegations to international commissions or treaty sessions. Staff movement between agencies and NGOs has been extensive and an important source of continuity and shared values in the issue area. This expertise can also be tapped through contractual relationships to undertake specific tasks for individual agencies. This practice not only permits a narrower match between NGO and agency but may circumvent personnel ceilings that would otherwise limit agency activity. The EPA contracted with the Center for Environmental Education, for example, to review the agency's compliance with the Endangered Species Act. The center, in its 1986 report to EPA, concluded that the agency has failed to take action to protect endangered species from pesticides and herbicides in about one-third of the 40 cases where FWS had warned EPA of threats requiring mitigation.[72] Agencies with international wildlife and environmental responsibilities are often more dependent on NGOs than are those with largely domestic agendas. The State Department's Office of Food and Natural Resources of the Bureau of Oceans and International Environmental and Scientific Affairs "maintains very close contact with the U.S. NGO community, in view of its large pool of expertise, contacts, and potential conservation funds," an assertion validated in part by the fact that the report on international wildlife resources in which it appears was prepared by the World Resources Institute under contract to FWS.[73]

A similar agency partnership has emerged with the corporate sector. Corporate support for the bald eagle recovery program has already been noted. According to FWS, such projects are mutually beneficial.

The corporations benefit from 'institutional' advertising and the positive publicity generated about their conservation contributions. The government benefits by receiving free literature at a significant savings to taxpayers, from the free advertising, and also by being able to reach entirely new audiences that it would not reach through traditional means.[74]

The service reports that corporate involvement has no effect on the agenda of the agency. "We propose a number of projects that corporations might support, and they are free to select those that interest them." It would seem, however, that once a donor has identified a species, total resource commitment toward, and public awareness (which then generates demands for further commitments of resources) of, that species is likely to be larger than in the absence of corporate support. A DuPont spokesman observed that "if the agency had come to us with a three-legged creeper they wanted us to save, probably we couldn't have helped them." On the other hand, a spokesman for the service noted that corporate support for "attractive" species means more agency money is available for others. "Every dollar we save on the eagle means there is a dollar we can spend on the fringe-toed lizard."[75]

THE COURTS

The rapid growth of administrative decision making, combined with constraints imposed on agencies by the National Environmental Policy Act, the Administrative Procedures Act, and the Freedom of Information Act, have fostered a corresponding growth in environmental litigation. William Ruckleshaus observed, in another environmental arena, that as many as 80 percent of EPA rules are challenged in court, and 30 percent are substantially modified as a result.[76] NGOs turn to the courts, as described in the condor and bobcat case studies, and numerous other instances of wildlife litigation have been identified.[77] Environmental law NGOs initiate the majority of court challenges, but several other organizations attend closely to administrative proceedings and actively pursue legal options through staff members or consulting attorneys. Of particular interest is the increasing prominence of development-oriented NGOs such as the Mountain States and Pacific Legal foundations, which are the oldest in a network of regional organizations that now represent development interests nationwide.

The size and substance of the NGO judicial impact on the disposition of wildlife resources has come to depend directly on the evolution of the rules governing standing. Standing was traditionally limited to those aggrieved persons suffering "injury in fact," generally regarded as a material or economic injury. Alternatively, Congress may grant standing by statute to certain persons or groups. The Endangered Species Act of 1973, for example, provides that "any person may commence a civil suit on his own behalf" to enjoin any person, including the U.S. government, alleged to be in violation of any provisions of the act.[78]

During the 1970s the courts substantially broadened the notion of standing, allowing that injuries need not be economic but may be "aesthetic, conservational or recreational."[79] In Sierra Club *v.* Morton, in which the Sierra Club challenged the legality of a proposed ski resort on federal land in Mineral King Valley, the court elaborated on injuries to noneconomic interests. Because the club failed to assert that it or its members would be affected by the development, the court found the club to lack standing. The court allowed, however, that "an organization whose members are injured may represent those members in a proceeding for judicial review" and thereby invited the club to amend its complaint to assert a more direct injury.[80] Although the courts have not uniformly supported the broadest possible interpretations of standing under these and related decisions, organizations have generally been granted standing on behalf of their constituents.

Environmental litigation rarely represents a direct confrontation between environmental and development interests. Rather, government action or inaction prompts challenge by interested parties. Thus, in the condor case, the National Audubon Society (NAS) challenged the decision of FWS to bring the remaining wild birds into captivity; in the bobcat case, Defenders of Wildlife challenged the finding of the Endangered Species Scientific Authority (ESSA) that the export of bobcat pelts would not jeopardize the health of bobcat populations. In each instance, the government was supported by other wildlife NGOs. A recent survey of federal environmental law cases decided between 1970 and 1980 shows that 50 percent of district court cases were of this type; another 18 percent represented business challenges to government action; 14 percent of the cases saw government challenge commercial interests, and in 13 percent, government challenged government. In only 4 percent of the cases did environmentalists directly challenge business interests, and in only a single case did business challenge environmental interests. The distribution changes dramatically in the Appeals Court, where the percentage of business-initiated cases doubles, almost entirely at the expense of environmentalist cases. At the Supreme Court, environmental NGOs initiated only 9 percent of the cases, while business initiated 31 percent and government 59 percent. The proportion of business-initiated cases increased over the decade as environmentalist procedural challenges under NEPA slowed, as business challenges to the implementation of regulations grew, and as business-initiated appeals were readied. Overall, government agencies were more successful as litigants than were business or environmental groups, an advantage that increased at the Appeals and Supreme Court levels. Among environmental groups, national organizations enjoyed greater success than did ad hoc plaintiffs.[81]

There is a wide range of opinion as to the efficacy of litigation in the environmental arena. Among Berry's sample of public interest groups, just over half had turned to the judiciary, and 63 percent of those who could evaluate litigation had found it an effective or very effective strategy.[82] Goetz and Brady concluded, in 1975, that "it is difficult to escape the conclusion that litigation was far and away the most efficacious activity carried on by environmentalist [NGOs] during the past decade."[83] Robert J. Golton, then representing the NWF, reported his "discovery" that, to the contrary, "trial by fire (i.e., litigation) is the most costly, the most time consuming, and generally the least effective way to solve an environmental problem and most others, as well."[84] It would appear that the success of litigation depends critically on the clarity of congressional language.[85] Even under the most favorable conditions, the courts "rarely devise permanent solutions to environmental problems, but their capacity to delay the implementation of political decisions until the equity of the situation can be established sometimes reverses the outcome of an earlier decision."[86] As has been shown, however, the most impressive court victory may but temporarily derail an outcome that is directed by larger forces. Thus the U.S. Supreme Court's decision in Hill *v.* TVA, prohibiting completion of the Tellico Dam in the interest of the endangered snail darter, led first to congressional weakening of the Endangered Species Act and later to an outright congressional exemption for the dam. Likewise, the lengthy controversy over export of the bobcat was settled in part by congressional determination of wildlife management practices.

Concern about the resources consumed in litigation, as compared to the often meager results, and consideration of the costly adversarial relationships thereby created have fostered a search for alternative modes of environmental dispute resolution. Mediation in particular appears to hold great promise. NGOs might logically embrace mediation in a hostile political environment.[87] Mediation offers to replace the high-stakes, winner-take-all confrontation with a process that divides efficiency gains among disputing parties. But this approach is limited to certain disputes and certain views of politics. Issues that reflect deeply held constituency values are less likely to be successfully mediated than are disputes of degree. Contesting interests might reach agreement on the proportion of roadless areas to be designated in a national forest or on the timetable for reducing the number of porpoises taken incidental to the tuna fishery, but they are less likely to find common ground on gun control or the merits of leghold traps.

Thus, despite some successes and the emergence of a network of mediation centers across the nation, the technique has been only cautiously embraced. Environmental public interest groups may risk a loss of support if their constituencies view submission to mediation as a sign of weakness. On the other hand, a developer, even with the best of intentions, may not be able to identify and bring together all of the interests whose concurrence would lend legitimacy to the mediated outcome. Groups that do participate may have no authority to make concessions, and local affiliates that have a strong stake in the outcome may disagree with their national organizations. A former executive director of the Sierra Club didn't "think any of the dialogues have had any effect." An NWF attorney observed that it is "premature to say whether we are wholeheartedly in support of negotiation. The bottom line is results, and we measure results in concrete benefits to wildlife."[88]

A careful review of 161 disputes mediated since 1973, conducted by Gail Bingham for the Conservation Foundation, presents a mixed picture. Most of the disputes were site specific and neither raised nor resolved broad policy questions; about half concerned land use decisions. Environmental NGOs and private business confronted each other in about one case in five. Government agencies were represented in 82 percent of cases. Overall agreement was reached in 78 percent of the cases and, of these, implementation was successful for 80 percent of site-specific and 41 percent of policy-level cases. The generally high success rate can be explained, however, by premediation assessments that may have screened out difficult cases and by voluntary participation. There is little evidence to support the claim that mediation is cheaper than litigation. Although environmental disputes have the potential to become long and costly court battles, few lawsuits actually go to trial. Furthermore, the cost of preparing for negotiation can be as great as the cost of preparing for litigation. Nor is it clear when to begin counting the costs. Previous interactions among the parties, including litigation or the threat of litigation, may explain a willingness to negotiate and must be included in any cost accounting. In addition, the costs may not be comparable, since the outcomes are likely to differ. Initial mediation may lower the cost of future confrontation to the extent that learning occurs and trust is established; it may raise the cost to the extent that the hope for a more favorable outcome encourages more costly preparation.[89] Innovations in dispute resolution, especially insofar as they permit voluntary participation, would increase the number of options available to disputing parties and would allow a better match between the dispute and the technique for resolving it. This self-selection will no doubt leave most disputes, particularly the more contentious ones, to the courts.

PUBLIC PARTICIPATION

The substantial NGO involvements in the Congress, the bureaus, and the courts are complemented and even legitimized by the broad public participation that has accompanied the environmental and social movements of the 1960s and 1970s. NGOs not only welcome but actively encourage a variety of forms of participation—from lobbying Senators to lobbying foreign heads of state, from educating neighbors to organizing boycotts.[90] Bulk mailings, often centered on a specific policy issue, invite citizen action as well as membership or financial support. Newspaper and other media advertising solicit a similar mix of funding and citizen action. Regular NGO newsletters and periodicals urge action on specific issues. Many NGOs mail special alerts to activist members. Maintenance of computerized mailing lists permits the larger organizations to target these alerts by issue interest or by state, region, or congressional district.

NGOs also seek media coverage through press conferences, political action, personal appearances, publication of research reports, and placement of articles, essays, op-ed pieces, and letters to the editor. The notable increase in NGO-sponsored research has occurred, first, because many organizations have systematically developed their expertise to improve their legitimacy and stature in the policy arena and, second, because reductions in federal initiatives have called forth an unprecedented round of criticism and a spate of substitute environmental agendas.[91] Some of the policy debates in which NGOs interest themselves are "news," and organizations may benefit from coverage by the proprietary sector. This coverage is often informed by press releases that NGOs regularly issue and enhanced by the public stature of organizational representatives. When Bob Barker refuses to give away furs on "The Price Is Right," or when Brigitte Bardot auctions her collected memorabilia to support animal welfare, the media take notice.[92] But newsworthy wildlife issues are by no means the ones of greatest interest to NGOs, nor is the news angle necessarily consistent with NGO interests. The press coverage accorded the battle over the Tellico dam often pitted "tiny fish against giant dam," highlighting the alleged absurdity of the Endangered Species Act and obscuring important issues revealed by the conflict.[93] On the other hand, a *Parade* magazine report on the decline of the eastern bluebird generated 75,000 letters to the North American Bluebird Society offering help.[94] The snail darter did not muster such a flurry of activity. In addition to the fact that people may care more about the bluebird than about the snail darter, in this instance individuals could offer direct aid to particular birds by building nesting boxes; the snail darter did not hold out the same kind of involvement.

Notice must be paid, finally, to the roles of organizations of all types in fostering a public interest in wildlife through books, films, and nature tours, among other products. Jacques Cousteau, whose oceanographic explorations and environmental advocacy have been supported by grants from NGOs including his own Cousteau Society, and government grants, undertook an eleven-month, $4 million exploration of the Amazon River basin "financed by television networks around the world." The networks were to receive copies of all film taken, in exchange for their financial support.[95] In a somewhat different vein, the fourth edition of Roger Tory Peterson's *Field Guide to the Birds East of the Rockies*, "sponsored by the National Audubon Society and National Wildlife Federation" but published by the proprietary sector, begins with a "Conservation Note" recommending that readers support NAS, NWF, Defenders of Wildlife, local Audubon or natural history societies, and the World Wildlife Fund (WWF). "The observation of birds leads inevitably to environmental awareness."[96]

Electioneering among environmental groups is of modest but growing importance as compared to other strategies of influence. The candidate rating system of the League of Conservation Voters (LCV) and Environmental Action's "Dirty Dozen" list of candidates most closely allied with major polluters have attracted media attention—and have served as models for the more ambitious efforts of other, politically conservative, political action committees (PACs). LCV does not assess its impact other than to calculate the percentage of supported candidates who were victorious in a given election. The 1986 election was "the most successful" for the environmental movement "in its 16 years of involvement in electoral politics." In the Senate, eight of ten league-supported candidates in priority races were successful; in the House, every league-endorsed incumbent and half of the challengers and open seat candidates won.[97]

The LCV presence has grown dramatically, its budget increasing nearly 30-fold to $4 million between the 1977–78 and 1985–86 election cycles. The most recent complete data from the Federal Election Commission for all PACs covers the years 1983–84. In that period, 4,374 nonparty PACs raised $294.5 million, of which 38 percent was contributed to candidates, 7 percent spent on behalf of candidates, and 1 percent spent against opposing candidates. The remaining 54 percent of receipts cover fund-raising costs and overhead expenses. Fund-raising efficiency (the percentage of funds raised that is dispersed in direct efforts to influence electoral outcomes) is generally higher for PACs affiliated with existing organizations than for independent PACs since, in the former case, varying amounts of overhead can be charged against the parent organization. In 1983–84, 757 membership PACs distributed 50 percent of receipts, whereas 1,146 independent PACs distributed only 33 percent of receipts.

These differences are broadly confirmed for environmental and wildlife PACs, which account for less than 1 percent of total PAC funds. The independent LCV distributed 24 percent of its $1.77 million—43 percent of that to 77 candidates, 32 percent for use against candidates, and the balance on behalf of candidates. The Sierra Club Committee on Political Education distributed 75 percent of its $335,000 to 189 candidates. Among other groups, FOEPAC (Friends of the Earth) distributed 33 percent of $169,000; ENACTPAC (Environmental Action) distributed 29 percent of $79,000; and ANPAC, or the Animal Political Action Committee, seeking to elect members of Congress who support animal protective legislation, raised $15,673 and distributed none.[98]

The expansion of electoral activity by NGOs has been accompanied since 1980 by a general politicization of the environmental policy arena. Conservation NGOs grew increasingly outspoken in their attacks, first on Secretary of the Interior Watt, then on Anne Gorsuch Burford, administrator of EPA, and finally on President Reagan himself. NWF, in an uncharacteristic action, called for Watt's resignation. Other organizations had already collected 1 million signatures in support of the same demand.[99] Friends of the Earth attacked the administration in full-page newspaper advertisements. "Our president is taking apart nearly every institution that protects planetary and human health. His actions and his rhetoric are consistent: Destructive, disdainful and uncomprehending of environmental values."[100] Ten national NGOs joined together to prepare *Indictment: The Case against the Reagan Environmental Record*, which documents "hundreds of actions that endanger the quality of life of all Americans. These separate actions add up to the Reagan environmental record. It is difficult to read that record without sorrow, anger, and a real concern for our future."[101] NGO efforts to establish a dialogue with the administration were generally unsuccessful.[102]

It has been observed elsewhere that some NGOs have fared well in organizational terms under the Reagan presidency. While no case will be made that groups prefer organizational health in a hostile environment to organizational weakness in a benevolent one, it must be recognized that such a trade-off exists. The executive director of the Wilderness Society reported that while his group was "spending a lot of money to cope with Watt, . . . he is building up our membership base and energizing people to defend the environment." An Audubon Society vice-president expressed similar ambiguity: "Sure our membership is up, but Watt and Gorsuch are a heavy price to pay." A New York *Times* observer concluded that "Mr. Watt and the environmentalists seem joined in a mutually beneficial symbiosis of the sort that keeps Washington lively."[103] This tension likewise characterizes the positions of certain elected officials. Representative Morris Udall was said to have responded to the Sierra Club's petition to recall James Watt, "Tear it up immediately—that man is my ticket to reelection."[104] With the departure of Watt and Gorsuch, the controversial personalities were gone, but the politics of the administration were little altered.

Environmental politics as usual may offer a comfortable, interactive forum for mainstream participants, but neither the Reagan administration's environmental critics nor its ideological allies are likely to be satisfied. Critics, Republicans and Democrats alike, continue to press aggressively in traditional arenas for a more responsive approach to a wide range of environmental concerns. Direct action, having gained a new visibility when the French government sank Greenpeace's Rainbow Warrior in a New Zealand harbor, promises to play an increasing role in environmental politics. Animal rights activists in particular have explored such tactics as disrupting sport hunting and releasing captive wild and laboratory animals. Ecological sabotage, ranging from the sinking of whaling ships to the spiking of trees, is occasionally practiced. At the other extreme, the administration's allies have expressed disappointment in the government's failure to implement more aggressively a privatization program that would transfer to the voluntary sector those resource management tasks that federal agencies are alleged to perform inefficiently. Yet as the following pages make clear, voluntary exchange and market transactions already play a critical role in the wildlife issue area.

THE MARKET

The emphasis on political activity must not obscure the critical importance of market and exchange activities undertaken by NGOs in pursuit of their organizational goals. Most of these represent intermediate transactions for staff services, educational materials, membership mailings, research grants, and campaign contributions. It may be difficult to distinguish intermediate from final organizational goals and equally difficult, therefore, to allocate activities and expenses accordingly. Insofar as the provision of private goods to members is simply the price the organization must pay to gain control over member resources, or insofar as such goods contribute to the production of educated members who in turn become more effective and involved advocates, expenditures are intermediate. Insofar as the goals of the

organization include the creation of an educated constituency, however, the expenditures may be regarded as final. From the perspective
of the industry as a whole, this is a distinction created in part by
organizational boundaries. More outputs are intermediate to the industry as a whole than to individual organizations. Similarly, the
larger the number of organizations and the more specialized they are,
given total industry size, the higher the proportion of final to intermediate production, since each organization defines its activities in
terms of final goals.

Easier to categorize are certain commercial ventures of NGOs designed to raise revenues for the organizations' charitable purposes.
Examples include the sale of advertising space in NGO publications,
wilderness outings and natural history tours, and the sale or distribution of NGO merchandise such as shirts and books.[105] It is a fine
line, however, that divides the NGO that supports itself with the
profits from merchandise sales, from the proprietary concern that
contributes a portion of its profits to a wildlife or environmental
cause. Interested persons may purchase Special Friends endangered
species stuffed animals to benefit the Nature Conservancy, Ralph
Lauren panda ties to benefit WWF, Paolo Soleri Care for the Wildlife wind bells to benefit HSUS, and Heritage Series wildlife prints
to benefit WLFA.[106] These arrangements can be quite lucrative.
WWF–US, for example, earned $245,000 in royalty income in 1983.
(The amount declined to just under $100,000 in 1985.) But they
also can generate controversy that makes for-profit partners wary.
Mattel Toys' Snuggles the Seal campaign to benefit HSUS ran up
against hunter-trapper opposition orchestrated by WLFA. (Mattel
had apparently considered, but rejected as too controversial, an
alliance with Greenpeace.) Mattel, in response to letters of opposition from individuals and organizations, reexamined the promotion.
"The bottom line is whether Mattel makes money on the deal." The
prospects looked bleak enough that the promotion was canceled. Another toy company subsequently agreed to produce the dolls but
withdrew, according to WLFA, following protest from the sporting
community.[107]

Cause-related marketing, given notoriety by the American Express
Corporation's sponsorship of the Statue of Liberty restoration, has
emerged throughout the environmental issue area, albeit in a limited
way. Numerous banking corporations have marketed credit cards in
the names of major environmental NGOs, benefiting the groups

through enrollment fees and use royalties. Nor is the strategy limited to the benefit of NGOs. General Foods promoted its new recipe for raisin bran with the Post Natural Raisin Bran National Park Pledge, urging consumers to aid the park system through cereal purchases. The company promised to donate up to $250,000 to the National Park Foundation at the rate of 50 cents for each proof of purchase submitted. Park Service director William Penn Mott praised the "creative and innovative partnership" and noted that the service was discussing similar arrangements with other corporations. Mott asserted that such programs would enhance rather than threaten public funding for the parks by demonstrating the high regard in which businesses and individuals hold these natural resources.[108]

A separable category of transactions includes the direct purchase of outcomes. Wildlife habitat can be protected through political action leading to the acquisition of lands by government agencies, to a modification in management regimes for existing government holdings, or to increased restrictions on private owners. Habitat can also be protected by private purchase in the marketplace. The long history of major acquisitions by the Nature Conservancy and Ducks Unlimited, among other organizations, illustrate well the importance of these techniques. Although large portions of these acquisitions are transferred to governments, an extensive network of private holdings protects important habitats throughout the nation. Nor is private wildlife and habitat protection the particular domain of nonprofit organizations. Commercial sporting grounds and sanctuaries that market access to wildlife for consumptive or nonconsumptive uses have in some cases proven to generate higher returns than from other uses that would destroy wildlife values.[109]

A second major form of commercial activity depends on ownership of the wildlife itself and is practiced by zoos, circuses, wild animal parks, and private dealers who breed, raise, buy, sell, trade, and display plants and animals. Since, in the United States, wildlife is held as common property that may be reduced to private possession only under conditions defined by the state and federal governments, political action may be required to establish the viability of private control. Debate over the impact of the commercial aspects of falconry on the well-being of the peregrine and other raptors has been a regular feature of Endangered Species Act oversight. In some instances, markets can be effectively developed. Destruction of sea turtle eggs on Caribbean beaches is difficult to regulate even when protective legislation exists; if NGOs make known their willingness to outbid local consumers, however, they can acquire eggs that may be relocated on protected beaches.[110]

Wildlife entrepreneurs and market-oriented theorists argue not only that commercial wildlife activities are legitimate business forms, but also that these activities accomplish efficiently what government at great expense and in the face of some resentment struggles to achieve. Where wildlife is not endangered and is managed strictly for harvest, and where species lend themselves to ranching or semido-mestication, prices and markets may well contribute to efficient resource use. Where the species is endangered, the cover that commercial activity provides for illegal wild harvest may undermine efficiency gains. Where important categories of wildlife benefits (for example, existence value) would elude the entrepreneur, private rights could lead to substantial misallocation of resources. Whatever the virtues of creating private rights, the strength of the common property heritage, in which wildlife is collectively managed in the public interest, must not be underestimated.[111]

But it is not only proprietary concerns that offer competition to the nonprofit enterprise. Government is searching aggressively for sources of funds independent of appropriations from general revenues. In 1985 FWS received congressional authorization to license the duck stamp image for commercial use. Approximately 10 percent of retail sales from such uses are returned to the Migratory Bird Conservation Fund. The service director, noting that licensees can increase sales by promoting the contribution, sees this as a "unique marketing feature for an increasingly conservation-minded public."[112] User fees are a well accepted application of the principle that the beneficiaries of government programs should pay for them. The duck stamp, state sporting licenses, and the taxes on hunting and fishing equipment that underwrite the Pittman-Robertson and Dingell-Johnson state aid programs offer long-standing and important examples in the wildlife arena. The discussion of funding the Fish and Wildlife Conservation Act of 1980, providing state support for nongame programs, similarly centers on taxing the sale of items associated with the enjoyment of nongame wildlife resources.[113]

But beyond this, government agencies are seeking to raise funds through donation and in ways that compete more directly with the efforts of NGOs. To attract donations, governments have created earmarked funds, quasi-public organizations, and other hybrid forms.[114]

Some nonhunters, for example, purchase the annual duck stamp for its philatelic value or as a means to channel donations directly to the acquisition of waterfowl habitat, a practice promoted by FWS.[115] The creation of the National Fish and Wildlife Foundation and the matching-fund requirements of certain congressional wildlife appropriations have already been noted. In a related way, many states, with support from NGOs and from state fish and game departments, the existing revenues of which derive from the sale of sporting licenses, have enacted legislation permitting taxpayers to earmark donations (from tax refunds or otherwise) for nongame wildlife programs. The success of such legislation has attracted the attention of other special interest groups that covet officially sanctioned private philanthropy of this kind. The nongame program in California, in fact, was predated by voluntary checkoffs for political parties, prevention of child abuse, the 1984 Olympics, and the Senior Legislature, a lobby for the elderly.[116] Pennsylvania advocates, fearing that competition from other causes would erode support for wildlife or even lead to a ban on all such choices, engineered a rider prohibiting additional checkoffs on the state income tax form. The amounts collected are substantial in comparison to existing state nongame program budgets, but they are dwarfed by revenues from the licenses that have long been sold to sportsmen. The 1981 nongame programs in 12 states derived $3.75 million, about 3 percent of the sporting license receipts in those same states. In 1983 taxpayers in 31 states donated nearly $9 million, but more recently, owing perhaps to an increase in competing checkoffs and to erosion of the novelty value, these revenues appear to be waning.[117]

If donations replace charitable gifts that otherwise would have supported nongame programs, the growth of direct finance might threaten the incomes of NGOs that depend on public support. The success of tax checkoffs might also weaken pressures to appropriate state funds out of general revenues or through the creation of special taxes. On the other hand, the improved security of nongame programs at the state level may provide for increased government staff, permitting the creation of closer and more permanent links between agencies and advocacy groups. NGOs may even benefit from contract work generated by the growing state programs.[118]

These matters of interorganizational resource flow caution us against a parochial view of nonprofit organizations in which their own health and success is measured only in terms of the resources that pass through their boundaries. This chapter has focused on the nonprofit organization in relative isolation, but it should be clear that a broader structure, one that encompasses the entire industry, is appropriate and necessary.

ORGANIZATIONAL FORMS

The organizations that provide the center of interest for this book are, for both historical and logical reasons, nonprofit organizations, and few share their realms with competing organizational forms. Among organizations that exhibit a high degree of commercialism and entrepreneurial control,[119] there is the greatest degree of competition. Thus the municipal zoological park, the proprietary circus and roadside zoo, and the nonprofit zoological society exist side by side, and the nonprofit *Natural History* and *Smithsonian* share the science market with *GEO* and *Discover*. At the same time, TRAFFIC–USA might logically find a home within the U.S. Department of the Interior, but a historical division of labor among several agencies (and the accompanying vested interests) has belied the logic. Nonetheless, the force of the logic opens extensive boundaries between government and nonprofit organizations and symbiotic, if not explicitly cooperative, effort is both common and important.

However, the proprietary analog of Defenders of Wildlife is unlikely to emerge.[120] Although Defenders offers some private goods to contributors, its fundamental product shares significant attributes with the pure public good. The resources it directs to the protection of the black-footed ferret or the small whorled pogonia do not promise harvestable populations to be shared by a group of hunters but a set of highly uncertain benefits that are difficult to measure and impossible to appropriate. Among these is the knowledge and the satisfaction that accompanies it, that the protection effort has been made and/or that it has been successful. Members may derive disproportionate satisfaction from this knowledge, but they cannot keep from nonmembers whatever satisfaction they might derive (short of carefully controlling the flow of information). Because those who benefit but do not voluntarily pay cannot be excluded, a proprietary organization would be unlikely to survive in the marketplace. Were it to survive, it would surely provide a smaller quantity of public good than that for which the society collectively would be willing to pay.[121] But even were excludability not a problem, contributors to a proprietary Defenders would have great difficulty judging the quality and quantity of output per dollar of income. The proprietary manager could easily limit both for personal gain. A distinguishing feature of the nonprofit organization is the nondistribution constraint, requiring that net revenues be devoted to charitable purposes rather than paid as dividends to stockholders or as bonuses to managers. As Henry Hansmann has argued, the nondistribution constraint engenders trustworthiness by removing the most obvious incentives for managerial deceit.[122] On the other hand, the trustworthiness created by the class of nonprofit organizations may provide the opportunity for the proliferation of organizations and the consequent dissipation of efficiency gains. That is, organizations may trade on the attributes of a class of organizations to which they belong.

Nonprofit status holds out certain competitive advantages. Virtually all nonprofit organizations are exempt from payment of taxes on net income. Although organizations on balance have little difficulty spending what they receive, annual budget surpluses arise from time to time as the result of extraordinary gifts or unexpected fund-raising success. This provision, then, becomes a significant benefit. NGOs may opt out of participation in social security and unemployment insurance programs, although organizations that might select these options are likely to be benefiting from a high degree of volunteerism and a salary schedule already below that for comparable jobs in other organizations. NGOs receive heavily subsidized bulk-mailing rates, a benefit that appears to skew the allocation of organizational resources significantly. Finally, those NGOs qualifying as 501(c)(3) charitable organizations may receive foundation grants and tax deductible gifts.

The importance of this charitable deduction is suggested both by econometric studies[123] and by the interest that NGOs take in proposed changes in the tax law. NGOs, acting singly and in concert, for example through Independent Sector, Inc., lobbied long and hard for full deductibility of charitable donations even for those individual donors who do not itemize. NWF, for example, in a special "Action Alert" accompanying the February 1980 *Conservation Report*, urged active member involvement in seeking the passage of then-pending legislation that would have achieved this goal.[124] The 1981 Economic Recovery Tax Act initiated changes that permitted increasing amounts of deductions year by year, but the possible boost that this gave to charitable gifts may have been offset by a reduction in the maximum tax rate that raised the cost of charitable giving by high income donors. The impact of the 1986 tax reform act, substantially lowering marginal rates for high income donors but leaving some taxpayers with higher after-tax income, remains to be assessed.

The restrictions on charitable organizations are few, and other than the aforementioned nondistribution constraint, they relate primarily to lobbying and political action. Prior to 1976, exempt organizations could devote "no substantial part" of their expenditures to "carrying on propaganda or otherwise attempting to influence legislation."[125] Charles J. Goetz and Gordon Brady, in a 1975 assessment, argue that these restrictions are minor because lobbying groups create interlocking foundations to receive tax-deductible gifts, because of a division of labor within the movement, because the Internal Revenue Service had not been vigorously enforcing the vague restrictions, and because lobbying does not generally represent the highest-valued use of organizational resources.[126] While these arguments seem fundamentally correct, they are belied to the extent that NGOs have taken very seriously any regulatory threats to their freedom of action. In 1966 the IRS stripped the Sierra Club of its 501(c)(3) status for spending "substantial" resources on grass-roots lobbying in opposition to a proposed Grand Canyon dam.[127] There seems little doubt that this action delayed for a decade the more active political involvement of established, relatively wealthy groups reluctant to jeopardize their exempt status. The disadvantage at which this put charitable organizations was made clear by Russell E. Train, then chairman of the CEQ, before the House Ways and Means Committee.

It is clear that both business and administrative agencies have open access to the legislature. Thus, the present situation has the practical effect of discriminating against section 501(c)(3) organizations. So long as there is a threat hanging over our public charitable bodies that they will lose their favored tax status if they present their case on issues related to their purposes to the legislature, the legislature is not getting the full picture.[128]

The need for more liberal, and better articulated, lobbying provisions led Elvis J. Stahr, then president of the National Audubon Society (NAS) and others to organize the Coalition of Concerned Charities. The coalition, with the active support of New York governor Nelson Rockefeller and the congressional leadership of Barber Conable, saw many of its proposals included in the Tax Reform Act

of 1976. The act permitted 501 (c)(3) organizations to elect to replace the previous vague standard with a sliding-scale limitation on
lobbying activities based on total expenditures. Of the first $.5 million
of exempt-purpose expenditures, 20 percent could be so utilized, with
the percentage falling until a maximum of $1 million is allocated for
lobbying purposes.[129] More restrictive standards limit grass-roots
lobbying. These clearer standards have raised few complaints, but it
was not until the fall of 1986 that the IRS proposed regulations interpreting the 1976 law—regulations that would greatly expand the range
of activities to be included within the scope of lobbying. Furthermore, the proposed rules would be retroactive to 1977, offering a
potential threat to the financial health of numerous organizations.
In particular, the costs of fund raising appeals and advertising would
be charged entirely to grass-roots lobbying if any parts constitute
grass-roots lobbying, and dissemination of the results of nonpartisan
analysis would be considered grass-roots lobbying "if the method of
distribution favors those persons interested solely in one side of a
particular issue," as for example might occur in a magazine or news-
letter mailed to members. The proposed rules would similarly jeopardize the tax status of foundations making grants to organizations
that concern themselves with public policy making, broadly defined.
Following intensive NGO lobbying and the resulting congressional
pressure, however, the IRS announced that it would revise the proposals, but, by mid-1988, revisions had not appeared.[130]

A second restriction on the behavior of exempt organizations
concerns the aforementioned nondistribution constraint, which
eliminates stockholders' equity as a source of organizational capital.
Hansmann has argued, in fact, that the desirability of offsetting this
constraint may offer the most satisfying justification for the income
tax exemption allowed nonprofit organizations.[131]

The value of these privileges and restrictions taken individually is
debated, but the proliferation of nonprofit organizations leaves little
doubt that, taken together, they offer net gains to individual organizations as compared to other organizational forms that might be
utilized to achieve the same ends. (On the other hand, most organizations are not nonprofits, suggesting that the competitive advantage of
this form is narrowly limited.) The outputs of these organizations
represent in part public subsidies of meritorious activities and in part
efficiency gains through the exploitation of new organizational forms.
A growing literature explores the provision of incremental quantities

of public goods, the establishment of entrepreneural niches not otherwise available, and the creativity that emerges from a decentralized and idiosyncratic third sector.[132]

NOTES

1. Description and analysis of NGO strategies and tactics may be found in Jeffrey M. Berry, *Lobbying for the People: The Political Behavior of Public Interest Groups* (Princeton, N.J.: Princeton University Press, 1977); David P. Forsythe, "Humanizing American Foreign Policy: Non-Profit Lobbying and Human Rights," Program on Non-Profit Organizations, Yale University, Working Paper No. 12, 1980; Elvis J. Stahr and Charles H. Callison, "The Role of Private Organizations," in Council on Environmental Quality, *Wildlife and America, Contributions to an Understanding of American Wildlife and Its Conservation*, edited by Howard P. Brokaw (Washington, D.C.: Government Printing Office, 1978), pp. 498–511; Andrew S. McFarland, *Common Cause: Lobbying in the Public Interest* (Chatham, N.J.: Chatham House, 1984); and Kay Lehman Schlozman and John T. Tierney, "More of the Same: Washington Pressure Group Activity in a Decade of Change," *Journal of Politics* 45 (1983): 351–77.

2. Single-species groups often sustain a similarly focused interest but, due to resource limitations, rarely make such a mark.

3. *Outdoor News Bulletin*, October 18, 1985, p. 4. See Allen Y. Cooperrider, "BLM's Desert Bighorn Sheep Program," in *Transactions of the Fifty-first North American Wildlife and Natural Resources Conference* (Washington, D.C.: Wildlife Management Institute, 1986), pp. 45–51. The largest such program is the $1.5 million Fish and Wildlife Challenge Grant Program in the forest service. See U.S. Congress, Senate, *Department of the Interior and Related Agencies Appropriation Bill, 1987. Report to Accompany H.R. 5234*, 99th Cong., 2d sess., Rept. 99–397, pp. 67–68.

4. The participating groups are the American Hiking Society, American Rivers Conservation Council, Defenders of Wildlife, Friends of the Earth, Izaak Walton League, National Audubon Society, National Parks and Conservation Association, National Recreation and Parks Association, National Wildlife Federation, Sierra Club, Trust for Public Land, and the Wilderness Society. See U.S. Congress, House, Committee on Appropriations, *Department of the Interior and Related Agencies Appropriations for 1986, Hearings*, 99th Cong., 1st sess., Part 4, pp. 168–231.

5. U.S. Congress, House, Committee on Appropriations. *Department of the Interior and Related Agencies Appropriations for 1983, Hearings*, 97th Cong., 2d. sess., Part 5, pp. 1392–1401; U.S. Congress, House, Committee on Appropriations, *Department of the Interior and Related Agencies Appropriations for 1984, Hearings*, 98th Cong., 1st sess., Part 5, pp. 381–91.

6. U.S. Congress, House, Committee on Appropriations, *Department of the Interior and Related Agencies Appropriations for 1980, Hearings*, 96th Cong., 1st sess., Part 3, p. 161; U.S. Congress, House, Committee on Appropriations, *Department of the Interior and Related Agencies Appropriations for 1987, Hearings*, 99th Cong., 2d. sess., Part 4, pp. 555-58.

7. U.S. Congress, House, Committee on Appropriations, *Department of the Interior Appropriations for 1987*, p. 556. The justification of the fish and wildlife service budget estimate may be found in ibid., Part 1, p. 532.

8. Ibid., Part 4, pp. 1052-54.

9. International Association of Fish and Wildlife Agencies, *Proceedings of the Sixty-eighth Convention*, September 10-13, 1978, pp. 113, 123.

10. William J. Chandler, "Migratory Bird Protection and Management," in *Audubon Wildlife Report 1986*, (New York: National Audubon Society, 1986), pp. 236-40; See National Wildlife Federation *v.* Hodel, 23 E.R.C. 1089 (August 26, 1985). See also U.S. Department of the Interior, news releases, February 21, 1985 and August 29, 1985. Subsequently, the federation petitioned the service to impose, within 30 days, a ban on all use of lead shot for waterfowl hunting in the lower 48 states. The service instead adopted an IAFWA-proposed phaseout by 1991. The federation's challenge to this plan was dismissed in federal district court. See U.S. Department of the Interior, news release, June 25, 1986, and *Outdoor News Bulletin*, July 18, 1986, p. 1.

11. Berry, *Lobbying for the People*, pp. 214, 223-25, and Schlozman and Tierney, "More of the Same," pp. 357, 377.

12. U.S. Congress, House, Subcommittee on Fisheries and Wildlife Conservation and the Environment of the Committee on Merchant Marine and Fisheries, *Endangered Species Act: Hearings on Endangered Species Act Reauthorization— H.R. 1027*, March 14, 1985, 99th Cong., 1st. sess., Serial No. 99-10, pp. 6-10. See also Breaux's remarks, ibid.

13. See also Bud Ward and Jan Floyd, "Washington Lobby Groups . . . How They Rate," *Environmental Forum* 3 (April 1985), unpaged reprint distributed by NRDC, reporting the results of a 1985 survey of "environmental policy professionals." Environmental groups together placed above industry groups; the highest ranked among all groups were NRDC, NWF, the Conservation Foundation, EDF, and NAS. Among the qualities that contributed to high rankings were "technical knowledge, policy sophistication, timeliness, communication skills, ability to relate a particular interest to a broad national interest, ability to present information 'neutrally' and avoid 'posturing,' and willingness to stand by a position no matter how controversial it may be."

14. Harmon Ziegler and Michael Baer, *Lobbying: Interaction and Influence in American State Legislatures* (Belmont, Calif.: Wadsworth, 1969), p. 120.

15. The following text is based on interviews, NGO documents, and public records. These documents reveal a rich detail of interorganizational and interpersonal cooperation and conflict that can only be suggested here. See Elizabeth

Drew, *Senator* (New York: Simon and Schuster, 1979), chronicling ten days in the legislative life of Senator John C. Culver (D. Iowa), during which time he was shepherding the 1978 reauthorization of the Endangered Species Act through the Senate. See also Steven Lewis Yaffee, *Prohibitive Policy: Implementing the Endangered Species Act* (Cambridge, Mass.: MIT Press, 1982).

16. Testimony of Elizabeth Kaplan, representing Friends of the Earth, and of Tom Garrett, representing Defenders of Wildlife, U.S. Congress, House, Subcommittee on Fisheries and Wildlife Conservation and the Environment of the Committee on Merchant Marine and Fisheries, Hearings on Endangered Species Act Reauthorization–H.R. 10883, *Endangered Species–Part I*, Serial No. 95-39, 95th Cong., 2d sess., 1978, pp. 29-30.

17. Ibid., pp. 48-49.

18. Letter from Elizabeth Kaplan, Friends of the Earth, to Justas Bavarskis, *High Country News*, August 29, 1978.

19. Letter from Elvis J. Stahr, President, National Audubon Society, to Senator John C. Culver, July 17, 1978.

20. *Congressional Record*, July 18, 1978, p. S11034.

21. Letter from Madeleine Bemelmans, President, and Christine Stevens, Secretary, to "Humanitarians," July 27, 1978.

22. Letter from Kaplan to Bavarskis.

23. Letter from Senator John C. Culver to Elvis J. Stahr, September 5, 1978.

24. National Audubon Society, "Action Alert," July 29, 1978, and Environmental Study Conference, "House Floor Brief #2," ESC *Weekly Bulletin*, week of October 2, 1978, pp. 3-4.

25. Letter from Ann Graham, July 20, 1978.

26. Frank J. Graham, Jr., "The Folks Who Work on the Hill," *Audubon*, July 1980, p. 119.

27. Marion Edey, "Friends in Need: A Look at Some Crucial Campaigns," *Sierra*, September–October 1980, pp. 18-19.

28. For example, see Justas Bavarskis, "Debate Raises Questions about Truth in Lobbying," *High Country News*, July 28, 1978, p. 12, and Luther J. Carter, "Environmental Lobbyists Quarrel over Endangered Species Act," *Science* 201 (September 15, 1978): 997.

29. Letters from members received by National Audubon Society, dated September 2, 1978 and September 27, 1978.

30. Letter from Tom Garrett to Elvis Stahr, July 28, 1978. See also Carter, "Environmental Lobbyists," p. 997.

31. The language of the act was weakened, but in practice, whether this would result in more or less protection for particular endangered species was to depend on implementation.

32. New York *Times*, June 2, 1982, p. A8; *Not Man Apart*, November 1982, p. 3. See numerous issues of the *Endangered Species Act Reauthorization Bulletin*, especially No. 9 (October 26, 1982) and No. 10 (April 6, 1983).

33. See Council on Environmental Quality, *Environmental Quality – The Third Annual Report of the Council on Environmental Quality* (Washington, D.C.: Government Printing Office, 1972), pp. 221-67, for a review of the first three years of NEPA implementation.

34. Council on Environmental Quality, *Environmental Impact Statements: An Analysis of Six Years' Experience by Seventy Federal Agencies*, March 1976, pp. 18, 21.

35. Council on Environmental Quality, *Environmental Quality 1984: The Fifteenth Annual Report of the Council on Environmental Quality* (Washington, D.C.: Government Printing Office), Table A-69, providing data for 1978-84.

36. Clough, N. K., P. C. Patton, and A. C. Christiansen, eds., *Arctic National Wildlife Refuge, Alaska, Coastal Plain Resource Assessment: Report and Recommendation to the Congress of the United States and Final Legislative Environmental Impact Statement*, 2 vols. (Washington, D.C.: U.S. Fish and Wildlife Service, U.S. Geological Survey, and Bureau of Land Management, 1987), Appendix: Public Comments and Responses. For assessments of NGO participation in the NEPA process, see Richard H. L. Andrews, *Environmental Policy and Administrative Change: Implementation of the National Environmental Policy Act* (Lexington, Mass.: D.C. Heath, 1976); Sally K. Fairfax, "A Disaster in the Environmental Movement," *Science* 199 (February 17, 1978): 743-48; and subsequent debate, *Science* 202 (December 8, 1978): 1034-40.

37. Monitor meeting of February 11, 1980.

38. Jay D. Hair, "National Fish and Wildlife Policy, State-Federal Relationships," draft (11-28-79 JDH), National Fish and Wildlife Policy, *State-Federal Relationships* November 28, 1979.

39. Council on Environmental Quality "Comments of the Council on Environmental Quality on Draft National Wildlife Policy, State-Federal Relationships Section," February 7, 1980.

40. Robert L. Herbst, "A National Fish and Wildlife Policy," in *Transactions of the Forty-fifth North American Wildlife and Natural Resources Conference* (Washington, D.C.: Wildlife Management Institute, 1980), pp. 52, 53.

41. *Federal Register* 45 (May 2, 1980): 29542-43, and 45 (September 24, 1980): 63363.

42. Remarks of IAFWA president Larry R. Gale at the association's business meeting of September 15, 1981. International Association of Fish and Wildlife Agencies, *Proceedings of the Seventy-first Convention*, Washington, D.C., September 13-16, 1981, p. 69.

43. International Association of Fish and Wildlife Agencies (IAFWA), minutes of Executive Committee, October 10, 1981, and IAFWA, report of joint meeting of the Legislative and States' Rights committees to the Executive Committee, December 10, 1981, in IAFWA, *Proceedings of the Seventy-first Convention*, pp. 231, 241-48.

44. IAFWA minutes of Executive Committee, March 28, 1982, in IAFWA,

Proceedings of the Seventy-second Convention, Washington, D.C., September 19-22, 1982, pp. 211-12.

45. *Federal Register* 47 (October 15, 1982): 46147-50.

46. *Federal Register* 48 (March 18, 1983): 11642-45.

47. The project, "American Attitudes, Knowledge, and Behaviors toward Wildlife and Natural Habitats," was based on national surveys conducted in the fall of 1978. Selected findings are reported in Chapter 2 in the section "Patterns of Interaction."

48. Cited in Michael C. Lipske, "Washington Outlook: Who Can Speak for the Public?" *Defenders*, February 1978, p. 71.

49. Richard Starnes, "Starnes at Large—Hunting's Newest Powderkeg," *Outdoor Life*, May 1978, p. 11.

50. Lipske, "Washington Outlook," p. 71; Starnes, "Hunting's Newest Powderkeg," p. 11.

51. Richard Starnes, "Starnes at Large—Exploding the Anti-Hunting Myth," *Outdoor Life*, April 1980, p. 16.

52. Stephen R. Kellert, *Phase I: Public Attitudes toward Critical Wildlife and Natural Habitat Issues*, U.S. Fish and Wildlife Service, October 15, 1979, Tables 48-49, pp. 111-12.

53. Yaffee, *Prohibitive Policy*, pp. 134, 137, and Chapters 5 and 7, passim.

54. The import ban was finally lifted in 1981, but kangaroos remain "threatened" species under the Endangered Species Act. Greenpeace and the International Wildlife Coalition are currently mounting public education campaigns to limit the demand for kangaroo leather and other products. New York *Times*, January 16, 1987, p. A20. See also George Reiger, "Kangaroo Imperialism," *Field and Stream*, February 1984, pp. 38-43.

55. NRDC *Newsline*, February-March 1987, p. 4; *EDF Letter*, March 1987, p. 1. See also Michael Weber, "TEDS: Salvation for Sea Turtles?" *Defenders*, January-February 1987, pp. 8-13.

56. NRDC *Newsline*, February-March 1987, p. 4.

57. New York *Times*, March 29, 1987, p. 24, sec. 4; Michael J. Bean, "Congressmen vs. Sea Turtles," New York *Times*, June 29, 1987, p. A17.

58. Lawrence Susskind and Gerard McMahon, "The Theory and Practice of Negotiated Rulemaking," *Yale Journal on Regulation* 3 (1985): 133-65.

59. See "TRAFFIC (USA) Watches World Wildlife Trade," *Focus* 1 (Spring 1979): 1, and the quarterly bulletin *TRAFFIC (USA)*, published by World Wildlife Fund-U.S.

60. *EDF Letter*, July-August 1979, p. 3.

61. Sam Iker, "The Crackdown on Animal Smuggling," *National Wildlife*, October-November 1979, pp. 33-39; Edward R. Riccuiti, "Shady Dealings," *Audubon*, January 1982, pp. 26-29; and Sam Iker, "The Great American Snake Sting," *National Wildlife*, February-March 1982, pp. 13-15.

62. U.S. Department of the Interior, news release, "'Know Before You Go!' are Watchwords of New Brochure for Travelers from Fish and Wildlife Service, World Wildlife Fund-US," September 29, 1986; World Wildlife Fund, *Annual Report 1986*, pp. 35–36.

63. U.S. Congress, Senate, Committee on Environment and Public Works, *National Fish and Wildlife Foundation Act: Report to Accompany H.R. 2809*, October 19, 1983, Rept. 98-272, p. 2. The foundation was created by PL 98-244.

64. National Fish and Wildlife Foundation, news release, February 10, 1987.

65. Lynn A. Greenwalt, "A Federal Agency Perspective," *Nature Conservancy News*, March–April 1981, p. 18.

66. U.S. General Accounting Office (GAO), *Federal Land Acquisition and Management Practices*, September 11, 1981, CED-81-135, p. 26; see also Philip C. Metzger, "Public-Private Partnerships for Land Conservation," in *Transactions of the Forty-eighth North American Wildlife and Natural Resources Conference* (Washington, D.C.: Wildlife Management Institute, 1983), pp. 423-32, and Steven L. Yaffee, "Using Non-Profit Organizations to Manage Public Lands," in ibid., pp. 413-22.

67. GAO, *Federal Land Acquisition*, p. 27.

68. The GAO made no effort, however, to calculate the net gain, if any, considering tax expenditures through the charitable donation of lands to qualifying NGOs.

69. GAO, *Federal Land Acquisition*, p. 30. See also Granville Corporation, *Study of Land and Water Conservation Fund Financial Assistance Alternatives* (Washington, D.C.: Division of State Programs, Heritage Conservation and Recreation Service, U.S. Department of the Interior, 1981, pp. 36-38, offering an overlapping set of advantages of NGO cooperation.

70. U.S. Department of the Interior, news release, March 14, 1984.

71. Brattleboro *Reformer*, January 29, 1987, p. 18, and U.S. Department of the Interior, news release, March 31, 1987.

72. New York *Times*, August 29, 1986, p. D18.

73. U.S. Department of State and U.S. Department of the Interior, *Conserving International Wildlife Resources: The United States Response*, report to Congress by the Secretary of State and the Secretary of the Interior, December 1984, p. 2. See also Council on Environmental Quality, *Environmental Quality 1985: The Sixteenth Annual Report of the Council on Environmental Quality* (Washington, D.C.: Government Printing Office), Chapter 12, "The Emerging Role of Voluntary Organizations in International Environmental Issues."

74. Letter to the author from Alan Levitt, Chief, Current Information, U.S. Fish and Wildlife Service, October 5, 1983.

75. Robert A. Jones, "Businesses Move to Save Wildlife," Los Angeles *Times*, January 24, 1983, p. 1.

76. Susskind and McMahon, "Theory and Practice of Negotiated Rulemaking," p. 134.

77. See, generally, Michael J. Bean, *The Evolution of National Wildlife Law*, rev. ed. (New York: Praeger, 1983); Lettie McSpadden Wenner, *The Environmental Decade in Court* (Bloomington: Indiana University Press, 1982), and David M. Trubek, "Environmental Defense I: Introduction to Interest Group Advocacy," and Trubek and William J. Gillen, "Environmental Defense II: Examining the Limits of Interest Group Advocacy," in *Public Interest Law: An Economic and Institutional Analysis*, Burton A. Weisbrod, study director, in collaboration with Joel. F. Handler and Neil K. Komesar, (Berkeley: University of California Press, 1978), pp. 151–94; 195–217.

78. P.L. 93–205, Sec. 11 (g).

79. Data Processing Service *v.* Camp, 397 U.S. 150 (1970). See Council on Environmental Quality, *Environmental Quality 1971: The Second Annual Report of the Council on Environmental Quality* (Washington, D.C.: Government Printing Office, 1971), p. 167.

80. 405 U.S. 727 (1972). The Mineral King case is of interest as well for the dissent of Justice William O. Douglas, who argued for a simplification of the standing question by fashioning "a federal rule that allowed environmental issues to be litigated before federal agencies or federal courts in the name of the inanimate object about to be despoiled, defaced, or invaded by roads and bulldozers and where injury is the subject of public outrage." See Christopher D. Stone, *Should Trees Have Standing? Toward Legal Rights for Natural Objects* (Los Altos, Calif.: William Kaufmann, 1974). In U.S. *v.* Students Challenging Regulatory Agency Procedures (SCRAP), the court indicated that a weak claim to injury was sufficient. The organization sought to restrain railroads from collecting a surcharge on scrap metal freight because its members, who enjoyed outdoor recreation, would be harmed by reductions in the quality of natural environments if recycling was discouraged and more natural resources were thereby consumed. See Karen Orren, "Standing to Sue: Interest Group Conflict in the Federal Courts," *American Political Science Review*, 70 (1976): 738.

81. Lettie McSpadden Wenner, "Interest Group Litigation and Environmental Policy," *Policy Studies Journal* 11 (1983): 671–83.

82. Berry, *Lobbying for the People*, p. 214. Among Schlozman and Tierney's sample of 24 public interest groups, litigation had been employed by 79 percent and was the twelfth most common strategy. "More of the Same," Table 4, p. 377.

83. Charles J. Goetz and Gordon Brady, "Environmental Policy Formation and the Tax Treatment of Citizen Interest Groups," *Law and Contemporary Problems* 39 (1975): 225.

84. Robert J. Golton, "Mediation: A 'Sell-out' for Conservation Advocates? or a Bargain?" *Transactions of the Forty-fifth North American Wildlife and Natural Resources Conference*, p. 83.

85. Trubek and Gillen, "Environmental Defense II," p. 216.

86. Lettie McSpadden Wenner, "Judicial Oversight of Environmental Deregulation," in *Environmental Policy in the 1980s: Reagan's New Agenda*, edited by Norman J. Vig and Michael E. Kraft (Washington, D.C.: Congressional Quarterly Press, 1984), p. 181.

87. These issues are discussed in Peter Steinhart, "Talking it Over," *Audubon*, January 1984, pp. 8–13. See also Lawrence Susskind and Alan Weinstein, "Towards a Theory of Environmental Dispute Resolution," *Boston College Environmental Affairs Law Review* 9 (1980–81), and Gail Bingham, *Resolving Environmental Disputes: A Decade of Experience* (Washington, D.C.: Conservation Foundation, 1986), pp. 65–67.

88. Quoted in Steinhart, "Talking it Over," p. 10.

89. Bingham, *Resolving Environmental Disputes*, especially Chapter 4.

90. See also Berry, *Lobbying for the People*, pp. 231–37.

91. See, for example, Common Cause, *Who's Minding the Store? A Common Cause Guide to Top Officials at the Department of the Interior* (Washington, D.C.: Common Cause, 1981); Friends of the Earth et al., *Ronald Reagan and the American Environment: An Indictment, Alternate Budget Proposal, and Citizen's Guide to Action* (San Francisco: Friends of the Earth, 1982); Robert Cahn, ed., *An Environmental Agenda for the Future* (Washington, D.C.: Agenda Press, 1985); and Defenders of Wildlife, *Saving Endangered Species: A Report and Plan for Action*, May 1984 and subsequent annual reports.

92. Kevin Kasowski, "Showdown on the Hunting Ground," *Outdoor America*, Winter 1986, p. 9; Steven Greenhouse, "Bardot Sells Her Memories to Aid Animals," New York *Times*, June 19, 1987, p. A11. Bardot raised $500,000 for a new animal protection foundation to be named for her. "As she sought to move from the stage to her seat, she was nearly stampeded by 15 television crews from 14 countries." Ibid.

93. On press coverage of these events, see Carrol J. Glynn and Albert R. Tims, "Environmental and Natural Resource Issues: Press Sensationalism," *Transactions of the Forty-fifth North American Wildlife and Natural Resources Conference*, pp. 99–109.

94. *Audubon*, May 1980, p. 136.

95. New York *Times*, June 7, 1982, p. All. On nature films, see Peter Steinhart, "Wildlife Films: End of an Era?" *National Wildlife*, December–January 1980, pp. 37–45. The growth in wildlife films, especially for television, can be ascribed in part to an FCC ruling that at least one hour of early evening broadcast time be reserved for nonnetwork programming. Educational programming was exempted. "This precipitated a rush of syndicated wildlife shows to fill the 'prime access time' openings." Ibid., p. 38.

96. Roger Tory Peterson, *Field Guide to the Birds East of the Rockies*, 4th ed. (Boston: Houghton Mifflin, 1980).

97. Statement of Alden Meyer, Executive Director of LCV, November 7, 1986.

98. Federal Election Commission, *FEC Reports on Financial Activity, 1983–1984, Final Report: Party and Non-Party Political Committees*, vol. 1, summary tables; vol. 4, Non-Party PACS, detailed tables (Washington, D.C.: Federal Election Commission, 1985). See Ronald Brownstein, "On Paper, Conservative PACs Were Tigers in 1984—But Look Again," *National Journal*, June 29, 1984, pp. 1504–9; M. Margaret Conway, "PACs and Congressional Elections in the 1980s," in *Interest Group Politics*, 2nd ed., edited by Allan J. Cigler and Burdett A. Loomis (Washington, D.C.: Congressional Quarterly Press, 1986), pp. 70–90; Jeffrey M. Berry, *The Interest Group Society* (Boston: Little, Brown and Company, 1984), pp. 156–81.

99. The federation reported that while two-thirds of its members voted for Reagan, 69 percent of the associate (national) members surveyed said that Watt's policies were "too extreme in promoting development." New York *Times*, July 15, 1981, p. A14.

100. New York *Times*, February 2, 1982, p. A13.

101. Friends of the Earth, et. al, *Ronald Reagan and the American Environment*, p. 6. See also New York *Times*, April 1, 1982, p. A23.

102. Philip Shabecoff, "Memo: Meese and the Environmentalists," New York *Times*, February 5, 1982, p. A14.

103. Philip Shabecoff, "Watt and Foes are Best of Enemies," New York *Times*, November 11, 1981, p. A22.

104. Quoted in Mary McGrory, "Unhorsing Watt," Brattleboro *Reformer*, July 13, 1981, p. 4.

105. See Edward Skloot, "Enterprise and Commerce in Nonprofit Organizations," in *The Nonprofit Sector: A Research Handbook*, edited by Walter W. Powell (New Haven: Yale University Press, 1987), pp. 380–93.

106. *Nature Conservancy News*, December 1986–January 1987, p. 30; *Focus*, May–June 1986, p. 7; *Humane Society News*, Summer 1986, p. 3; WLFA *Update*, March 1986, p. 4.

107. WLFA *Update*, September 1985; December 1985; June 1986, p. 3; December 1986; March 1987.

108. Myron Levin, "Cereal Maker Helps Park Service Out of Its Crunch," Los Angeles *Times*, April 23, 1986 (Valley ed.), p. II: 6. Another variation is the proprietary organization that, but for its tax status, might be taken for an NGO. For instance, Jim Morris Environmental T-Shirts donate 10 percent of profits to environmental groups. The shirts, which themselves carry environmental messages, are supported by recommendations for environmental advocacy, preprinted postcards addressed to various public officials on issues such as tropical deforestation and wildlife trade, and lists of environmental groups worthy of support. Letter from Jim Morris T-Shirts, March 10, 1987.

109. See, for example, Kerry B. Livengood, "Value of Big Game from Markets for Hunting Leases," *Land Economics* 59 (1983): 287–91. For examples of proprietary conservation efforts, see Council on Environmental Quality, *Environ-*

mental Quality 1984, Chapter 9, "Special Report: The Public Benefits of Private Conservation," pp. 363–429.

110. New York *Times*, March 1, 1981, p. 41, and Mark Wexler, "Yankee Don't Go Home," *National Wildlife*, June–July 1981, pp. 4–11.

111. See James A. Tober, *Who Owns the Wildlife? The Political Economy of Conservation in Nineteenth-Century America* (Westport, Conn.: Greenwood, 1981.

112. U.S. Department of the Interior, news release, "Duck Stamp Isn't Just a Stamp Anymore; New Provisions Allow Image on Retail Products, Fish and Wildlife Service Announces," September 17, 1985.

113. U.S. Department of the Interior, Fish and Wildlife Service, *Potential Funding Sources to Implement the Fish and Wildlife Conservation Act of 1980*, Biological Report 85(5), March 1985.

114. Estelle James argues that government may be viewed as a giant, multi-purpose nonprofit organization, the donors to which have no control over the disposition of their monies and, as a result, have (in addition to the free-rider problem) little incentive to donate in the absence of such arrangements. "How Nonprofits Grow: A Model," *Journal of Policy Analysis and Management* 2 (Spring 1983): 355–56.

115. U.S. Department of the Interior, news release, "Secretary Clark Urges Americans to 'Buy a Duck Stamp—Save Wetlands for Wildlife'," March 21, 1984.

116. Los Angeles *Times*, December 29, 1983, p. 3.

117. *Endangered Species Technical Bulletin* 7 (November 1982): 4–5, and 8 (April 1983): 5–6; Susan Cerulean and Whit Fosburgh, "State Nongame Wildlife Programs," in *Audubon Wildlife Report 1986*, pp. 631–56; and Susan Q. Stranahan, "Many Happy Returns For Wildlife," *National Wildlife*, April–May 1987, pp. 50–51.

118. This possibility was suggested by Stephen R. Kellert.

119. Henry Hansmann, "The Role of Nonprofit Enterprise," *Yale Law Journal* 89 (April 1980): 840–43.

120. The analogy with a business is occasionally made, as in the following:

If Defenders were a business, at work for dollar profits instead of victories for a cause, you as our members would be the stockholders. Having bought a share you would look for a return on your investment. You should do no less in our case. The dividends paid by Defenders, however, are in the form of the progress we have made in fighting for wildlife. We do everything in our power to keep our costs down, to make the dollar count, to be cost-effective in pursuing our goals. There will be no price-earnings ratio, but if you feel deeply that there is splendor in the wild howl of an Arctic wolf or in the shuddering wing of a butterfly, then we are your kind of company. You have equity.

Defenders of Wildlife, *Annual Report*, 1978, p. 1.

121. Burton A. Weisbrod, "Toward a Theory of the Voluntary Nonprofit Sector in a Three-Sector Economy," in *The Voluntary Nonprofit Sector: An Eco-*

nomic Analysis, edited by Burton A. Weisbrod (Lexington, Mass.: Lexington Books, Heath, 1977), pp. 51-76.

122. Hansmann, "Role of Nonprofit Enterprise," pp. 843-45. The effectiveness of this explanation is questioned in Susan Rose-Ackerman and Estelle James, "The Nonprofit Enterprise in Market Economics," Yale University, Program on Non-Profit Organizations, Working Paper No. 95, July 1985, pp. 11-14. In "Consumer Perceptions of Nonprofit Enterprise," *Yale Law Journal* 90 (1981): 1623-38, Steven E. Permut demonstrates that consumers are not reliably able to distinguish nonprofit from proprietary organizations.

123. See, for example, Martin Feldstein and Charles Clotfelter, "Tax Incentives and Charitable Contributions in the United States," *Journal of Public Economics* 5 (1976): 1-26.

124. National Wildlife Federation, *Conservation Report*, February 1, 1980.

125. This wording arose in 1934 amendments to the Internal Revenue Code. U.S. Congress, Senate, Subcommittee on Intergovernmental Relations of the Committee on Governmental Affairs, *Congress and Pressure Groups: Lobbying in A Modern Democracy*, June 1986, 99th Cong., 2d sess., S. Prt 99-161, pp. 9-10.

126. Charles J. Goetz and Gordon Brady, "Environmental Policy Formation." See also Mortimer M. Caplin and Richard E. Timbie, "Legislative Activities of Public Charities," *Law and Contemporary Problems* 39 (Autumn 1975): 183-210.

127. In 1963 David Brower remarked that the "Sierra Club is deductible but willing to explore at some risk into the never-never land of undefined undeductability so as to do in the public interest what John Muir founded it to do." Although the IRS action gained the club much notoriety and many new members, large donations fell off. Several years later, the organization deeply in debt, Brower was forced out. Stephen Fox, *John Muir and His Legacy: The American Conservation Movement* (Boston: Little, Brown, 1981), pp. 280, 319-22.

128. Quoted in Caplin and Timbie, "Legislative Activities," p. 200.

129. Frank J. Graham, Jr., "The Folks Who Work on the Hill," *Audubon*, July 1980, pp. 118-19; "Memorandum: Lobbying by Tax-Exempt Organizations," prepared by the American Association for the Advancement of Science legal counsel, January 21, 1977.

130. *Federal Register* 51 (November 5, 1986): 40211; Los Angeles *Times*, January 1, 1987, p. 1; New York *Times*, January 11, 1987, p. 22, sec. 1; New York *Times*, May 19, 1987, p. D2.

131. Henry Hansmann, "The Rationale for Exempting Nonprofit Organizations from the Corporate Income Tax," *Yale Law Journal* 91 (1981): 54-100.

132. Weisbrod, "Toward a Theory of the Voluntary Sector"; Dennis R. Young, "Entrepreneurship and the Behavior of Nonprofit Organizations," in *Nonprofit Firms in a Three Sector Economy*, edited by Michelle J. White. *COUPE Papers on Public Economics*, vol. 6 (Washington, D.C.: Urban Institute, 1981), pp. 135-62; and John G. Simon, "Charity and Dynasty under the Federal Tax System," *Probate Lawyer* 5 (1978).

6

Wildlife and the
Public Interest

Organizations have heretofore been viewed primarily in isolation, as they set their agendas, lobby, sue, grow, and change. The limited discussion of the wildlife industry as a whole has focused on boundaries and structure. This chapter represents a shift to industry performance, examining the relationships between organizations and the resources that flow among them. Nonprofit organizations in the wildlife industry work, at least nominally, toward goals that can be measured only outside of organizational boundaries—such as public knowledge, ecosystem diversity, or condor numbers. Internal indicators such as financial health, growth, and member satisfaction, even if they mark a dying organization, are at best imperfect and perhaps misleading proxies for organizational success. An organization may fade because it has transferred portions of its operations to other organizations or because it cannot survive despite the best efforts of those in control; again, it may thrive but make little progress toward nominal goals. The fates of particular organizations may owe as much to chance as to strategic behavior or entrepreneurial talent.[1]

In pursuit of their nominal goals, organizations may cooperate and compete with other organizations whose goals coincide, overlap, or conflict with their own. But organizations have unique life histories and constituencies that combine to produce behaviors directed toward a variety of other goals. Furthermore, although their actions are generally taken in the name of the organizations, and organizations constrain some actions and promote others, it is individuals who develop and execute strategies, and they do so to meet both personal and organizational needs.

Even if neither organizational nor personal goals compromise nominal organizational goals, numerous other obstacles slow progress toward them. Limited knowledge, risk, and uncertainty place a wedge between actions and outcomes. This wedge may be technical, arising from an incomplete understanding of cause and effect, or it may be institutional, arising from externalities and synergies thrown by the actions of one organization onto others. More information, other things equal, is better than less information, but collecting it is costly, and the very structure of the inquiry will constrain the outcome. Furthermore, new information as often highlights what is not known, and it may increase uncertainty by challenging value structures and decision processes.[2]

The actions that are appropriate for an individual organization depend on the actions and potential actions of other organizations and individuals. Each organization's knowledge of such actions is necessarily imperfect, but even were the knowledge complete, other market imperfections would prevent the achievement of efficient organizational resource use. An NGO may bear training costs for a staff member who then moves to another job and may or may not support the goals of the training organization while there. Much of this movement occurs between rather than within a sector, as staff members move from NGO to congressional committee to agency to the proprietary sector. Such costs may offset one another from the organizational point of view, but even if certain organizations consistently subsidize training for the industry, the cross-fertilization may offer a synergistic boost to industry output at some higher level of aggregation. Another spillover occurs as the successes of one organization, resulting from its own commitment of resources, increase the legitimacy or fund-raising success of associated organizations. Such impacts, of course, may be negative as well as positive. An additional effect may result from public confusion over organizational identities. NGOs must distinguish themselves to receive credit for their own actions and to avoid criticism for the unpopular actions of others.

For organizations working at cross-purposes, the efficiency question is different, because these groups deliberately impose costs on other groups as they seek goals that speak to distinct visions of efficiency and equity. Such groups may find themselves in a "prisoner's dilemma" where each is compelled to choose a course of action resulting in an outcome that, on balance, no group prefers—in other words, the resources consumed in the process outweigh the expected gains from participation, but refusal to participate risks even greater losses. The growth of environmental mediation and negotiated rule making suggests that some advocacy may be so characterized. But these approaches address discrete interactions rather than the more protracted conflicts that characterize the evolution of social values; it is considerably more difficult to assess the performance of the system in this latter regard.

Actions may thus be four steps from nominal organizational goals, first, as they are compromised by incomplete information; second, as they mix with personal goals; third, as they mix with other organizational goals; and fourth, as they mix with the actions of other organizations and individuals. This chapter constitutes a broad exploration of the relationships among organizational actions, the performance of the industry, and the conduct of public policy.

ORGANIZATIONS AND ENVIRONMENTS

Strategies pursued by individual actors may serve personal, organizational, or issue area goals. Some individuals encountered in this study demonstrate a fundamental allegiance to the nonprofit, especially public interest, sector; others have strong attachments to the wildlife, or more broadly, conservation, industry. Their career paths take them back and forth across sectors, depending on opportunities for advancement, rewards of power, congeniality of the work environment, income, freedom, or the environmental views of elected officials. Another group adheres to professional boundaries, practicing law, for example, in the public or private sector, in or out of the wildlife industry.[3]

The careers of forty-six professional staff members of the private, nonprofit, and government sectors of the wildlife industry were tracked between 1980 and 1986. Ten of this number, or 24 percent, held the same—or essentially the same—position during this period. Eight of the ten are on NGO staffs, one in Congress, and one in private law practice representing the same NGO client. Eleven individuals left the industry during this six-year period, four of them attorneys who have gone into private practice (who in some cases have continued to do pro bono or fee work on environmental issues). Of the remaining twenty-five, eleven have changed sectors one or more times.

Five of these have moved from government to NGO positions and six have moved in the reverse direction. The remaining fourteen have changed positions within the same sector; six of these have moved between government organizations, as for example from FWS to the House Merchant Marine Committee.[4] This considerable mobility of individuals between groups and sectors within the industry is strong support for the existence of an issue network attending to the broad, diffuse wildlife policy arena. Indeed, it is difficult, as Heclo remarks, to locate precisely the boundary separating network from environment.[5]

Perhaps the most dramatic transitions follow federal elections. Jimmy Carter, who enjoyed the uncertain but hopeful support of the environmental—and more broadly, the public interest—community during his 1976 campaign, upon election drew widely on environmental and public interest NGOs for more than 50 major appointments throughout his administration.[6] As a result the public interest sector was uniquely represented in the Carter administration, but the leadership and expertise of the nonprofit sector was depleted. David Brower of FOE reflected on the resulting circumstance in 1980.

Well, I do like the access we have received because some of the leaders of the environmental movement are part of the Carter administration. But, while I like the access, I don't like the absence of those people as leaders of the environmental organizations from which they were taken. These groups have suffered rather uniformly from the lack of leadership, as well as from a slight softness on the part of others who were bucking for jobs in the Carter administration and didn't want to sound unreasonable.[7]

Another NGO spokesman was distressed that his former colleagues "bend over backwards too much trying to appear reasonable, and lose sight of their mandate. They forget that they are political appointees of an Administration that was elected on an environmentalist platform."[8] Rupert Cutler, Assistant Secretary of Agriculture for Natural Resources and Environment, reflected on his experience: "I used to be in their shoes. I know how the game is played. Interest groups by definition have to take strong and doctrinaire positions. Privately, they will say you are doing pretty well, but publicly they will kick your ass."[9] Appointees, whatever they may expect of themselves or others expect of them, cannot ignore the context in which they find themselves once in government. Not only are they constrained by regulations and agendas already in place, but as they view the issues through new organizational lenses, they often alter their positions. Secretaries of the Interior may develop into better friends of the environmental community than expected, and legislators who find themselves heading environmental committees may discover compelling reasons to advocate strong positions on issues that previously had not captured their interest.

Not only did the 1976 shift from the nonprofit to the government sector offer appointees new perspectives on old problems, but for many young advocates it was an important step in career growth and political education. One former lobbyist remarked from her perspective within the State Department that "I didn't realize how little I knew." She recalled that she had often taken positions without careful investigation and could attribute some of her successes to "lucky guesses." She had seen the "feds" as enemies rather than as useful allies in achieving organizational goals. She saw later, as never before, the importance of good information and of answers to the "whys" that decision makers must ask to protect themselves and to be accountable to their superiors and constituencies. Although she was glad to be on the inside where she could directly guide and influence policy, she expected that she could achieve her goals more effectively were there others on the outside who were fully familiar with the issues and articulately pressing for more radical positions than she herself could maintain within the department. This would enable her to justify her positions against pressures from consumption-oriented constituencies on the other side. The problem is that "there are no NGOs beating on us."

The degree of satisfaction of the environmental community with Jimmy Carter's administration ebbed and flowed over his four years in office. By primary season those NGOs that were actively electioneering were favoring Jerry Brown or Edward Kennedy over Carter.[10] But from the perspective of the business community, Carter had opened his administration to "public interest lawyers, consumerists, civil rights workers and especially environmental advocates," who had turned the administration "into a government of intolerant zealots, almost religious in the intensity of their beliefs."[11] The 1980 election of Ronald Reagan reversed the flow, sending environmentalists out from the federal government and replacing them with "intolerant zealots" of a different stripe. Of those who left the Carter administration, only a few went directly back to the public interest sector. Their reasons varied from concern about living on a public interest salary, to changed perceptions of the appropriate strategies for environmental politics, to changed personal politics.[12] But several NGOs were able to gain substantial staff strength following the 1980 election. The Wilderness Society made the most aggressive moves, bringing on former senator Gaylord Nelson as chairman, former representative Joseph Fisher as director of the new Economic and Policy Analysis Department, and former Interior secretary Cecil Andrus as corporate consultant.[13]

The mobility of individuals within the wildlife and environmental issue areas suggests the limitations of a narrow view of nonprofit organizations, illustrating instead the coherence of a larger set of structures. The wildlife industry consists of a complex and interconnected set of niches scattered among organizations and institutions that moderate the behavior of those who occupy the niches at any time. Individual decisions are made at the margin, given the existing institutional matrix. One NGO advocate, asked in 1977 whether he felt he could accomplish more for the environment in his new Interior Department position, responded, "It's not accurate to say you're inside or outside the government. You're part of it by the simple act of trying to make it work."[14]

It should not be concluded from the foregoing discussion, emphasizing resource mobility and the interdependence of organizations in several sectors, that the distribution of resources among organizations and sectors is of little consequence—that resources presently captured by the nonprofit sector might just as well relocate within the Interior Department or that the same resources could be equally productive scattered here and there, were the nonprofit form unavailable. While decisions at the margin, made individually for idiosyncratic reasons, may have little consequence for the industry as a whole, the cumulative effect of such voluntary sorting creates an environment that presents individuals with choices. The resulting pattern is not merely a chance event. But to determine the efficiency of the present distribution is problematic. We cannot merely ask whether free resources exist that could be packaged as a new organization or whether resources presently lodged within certain organizations might be better situated within the boundaries of others. Organizational evolution has led to the establishment of organizational niches. The existence of an organization defines the niche that it occupies. The organization can enhance its own viability by controlling the resources constituting that niche, even at the cost of effectiveness in achieving nominal goals.

Existing organizations clearly have an interest in controlling the evolution of the industry. They may create, support, or otherwise aid groups that complement or cooperate but do not threaten them. This is not to suggest that such strategies are primarily defensive, although their effect may be to co-opt organizational resources and thereby preempt niches in organizational space. The World Wildlife Fund (WWF) was created in 1961 with the support of the international conservation community primarily to channel funds to other groups and projects rather than to develop and implement its own agenda. The movement of WWF–US toward more aggressive fund raising, creation of an active membership, and a clearer policy direction in the 1980s suggests possible conflicts, particularly in the domestic arena. Russell E. Train, chairman and former president of the organization, in an effort to clarify the possible confusion among prospective donors who receive what appear to be similar solicitations from a variety of organizations, addressed the issue in a 1982 essay. Noting the differences among groups in "purpose, program and style," Train argued that forcing diverse groups into a single mold would save on administrative and fund-raising costs, "but I believe we would lose far more in terms of real strength. The organization that tries to be all things to all people may end up appealing to none at all!" He singled out WWF–US as a "united fund" for international conservation, helping to coordinate activity in the industry by providing regular funding for some organizations and by joining in cooperative ventures with others.[15]

These cooperative ventures have led to a number of permanent alliances. In 1979 WWF–US created TRAFFIC (USA)—Trade Records Analysis of Flora and Fauna in Commerce—the second of what has become a network of ten organizations worldwide, to monitor wildlife trade, provide information to the public and governments about illegal or threatening trade, and promote enforcement of trade restrictions. The African Wildlife Foundation (formerly the African Wildlife Leadership Foundation, of which Train was a founding trustee in 1958 and president from that date until 1969) has agreed with WWF–US to a closer working relationship "that is only common sense," in which WWF–US will raise funds for wildlife conservation in Africa and AWF will coordinate and manage a jointly agreed upon program. "Frequently I am asked," Train reported in announcing the agreement, "'Why don't all you environmental groups get together and stop duplicating each other's work?' Well, now we are doing just that!"[16] In another move, RARE, Inc., a conservation education organization focusing on Latin America and the Caribbean, moved to WWF–US headquarters in Washington and became a WWF–US affiliate, serving as the fund's educational arm in Latin America in exchange for basic financial support.[17]

In 1985 WWF–US joined forces with the Conservation Foundation, a nonprofit research and policy institute that Train headed from 1965 to 1969. Although the organizations retain their separate legal identities, they share an integrated administration, board of directors, and development staff. The Conservation Foundation, primarily interested in domestic policy, is developing a stronger international focus to support the work of WWF–US. William K. Reilly, for eleven years president of the Conservation Foundation, now heads the combined organizations, while Train has moved from WWF–US president to chairman of the joint board of trustees.[18] This strong affiliation has also brought RESOLVE, Center for Environmental Conflict Resolution, into the WWF–US family. RESOLVE, founded in 1977 with substantial corporate support and initially chaired by Train, was absorbed by the Conservation Foundation in 1981.

It might be tempting to view particularly this last change as the opening wedge of a major shake-up, in which mergers and collapses, brought about by efforts to rationalize the industry in tighter times, will produce a leaner, more efficient structure. There is, of course, considerable logic to the alliance. Train notes that "the nature of the skills required to further conservation goals has broadened. . . . We need the kind of specialists in water resources, urban planning, land economics, and pollution control that make up The Conservation Foundation." Reilly, observing the growing overlap between the two organizations, suggested that if "we didn't affiliate, we probably would move into each other's programs with resulting duplication and competition."[19] Despite the logic, however, these changes appear less the result of inexorable forces than of idiosyncratic and personal considerations.

At the same time, there has been clear change in the industry, resulting in part from the forces that have shaped the recent history of the World Wildlife Fund. Symbolic of this change is the turnover in top management that has occurred since 1984 in virtually all of the major public interest groups in the industry: Audubon (NAS), Defenders, Sierra Club, Wilderness Society, Greenpeace, Friends of the Earth (FOE), and the Environmental Defense Fund (EDF). The management of multimillion-dollar enterprises in a highly competitive environment seemed to require business acumen perhaps more than passion for environmental values. The Sierra Club's Michael McCloskey observed that "environmental leaders have become victims of their own success. . . . I spent most of last year developing a budget and finally realized I did not want to be in this movement to crunch numbers."[20] The job description for McCloskey's successor, developed with the assistance of an executive search firm, sought a person who "will have an outstanding financial background, and [will] have achieved the position of CEO or have been groomed as the second in command. . . . Prior experience with an environmental organization is not required. . . . An advanced degree is highly desirable with a concentration in management or finance."[21] The prospective changes in leadership orientation prompted the Los Angeles *Times* to ask, "Will the Harvard or Stanford MBA replace the climbing boot and ice ax as the leadership symbol of the nation's major environmental groups?"[22] Ultimately, however, the vacancies were filled from within the environmental community, although in no case from within the organization.

The result of these changes, combined with the broadening of purpose noted in Chapter 2, is a certain homogenization among the major organizations—in structure, scope, politics, fund raising, and general style. As organizations share personnel, as they strive to appeal to a short list of foundation and corporate donors, as they seek a legitimate place of influence in the policy network, and as they observe one another and work together in the public policy arena, they have become increasingly similar. Survival in the competitive world of the public interest group offers little incentive to elect the high-risk, untried path.[23] At the same time, the common path offers no guarantee of organizational survival. Despite growing memberships and budgets, many organizations are feeling the budgetary pinch. Audubon, for example, announced substantial program cutbacks in the face of a prospective fiscal 1988 operating deficit of $2.5 million.[24]

On the other hand, this central tendency opens space on both ends of the ideological spectrum for NGOs that appeal to constituencies represented marginally or not at all by the major groups—particularly groups that address single-issue concerns with the studied passion that has become anathema to their mainstream colleagues. These groups may have narrow professional or geographic constituencies that can be organized at a relatively low cost. A new set of outspoken antihunting groups has arisen to join a few established groups in seeking to limit the influence of hunters in directing wildlife management. Competition is fierce among these groups as they seek to carve out a territory in this rapidly growing issue area. Although this competition rarely escalates to the level of direct attack by one group against another, examples may be found. (Recall the NGO attacks against Audubon during the 1978 reauthorization of the Endangered Species Act.) The Committee to Abolish Sport Hunting (CASH), in a recent solicitation seeking to raise $50,000 "to defeat hunting," observed that it is "a paltry sum considering that Mobilization for Animals wasted $350,000 on a series of useless rallies."

While the major established NGOs have become increasingly similar in purpose and scope, and while they compete broadly for organizational resources, they also cooperate on numerous issues and generally respect a division of labor that emerges or is strategically created. In describing the agenda-setting processes in their own organizations, many staff members interviewed for this study referred to existing commitments of other organizations as important determinants of their own courses of action. The public representation of this division is important to NGOs that seek to create distinctions among groups for fund-raising purposes. The division is of course always subject to change. As detailed in Chapter 5, the League of Conservation Voters (LCV), created and supported by the industry as its political action committee, has been joined by the PACs of Environmental Action, Sierra Club, and Friends of the Earth (FOE).

The informal and formal coalition-based cooperation among organizations has been frequently noted. NGOs cooperatively prepare, or sign on to one another's, congressional testimony; present joint press conferences; and sponsor common research efforts. These alliances extend beyond the environmental and even beyond the nonprofit realm. Their broader connections facilitate traditional applications of influence, as when proharvest wildlife NGOs join union groups to support fur trapping or when energy NGOs combine with the solar industry to support government funding for alternative energy programs. Additionally, they may reflect expansions of traditional interest jurisdictions, as when Greenpeace extends its purview over the marine environment to include nuclear testing, NRDC creates an alliance with Soviet scientists to implement a nuclear test monitoring system, or WWF, on the occasion of its 25th anniversary, initiates a new dialogue with the major religious leaders of the world.[25]

But much of the evolution of the industry is reflected in the unfolding of new structures that permit interorganizational cooperation, combining the strengths of several organizational types. The dominant characteristic of these new forms is the potential they demonstrate for the growing role of the private, even profit-making, sectors. Among those efforts already noted are Clean Sites, Inc., the industry-sponsored, Conservation Foundation initiated, nonprofit to finance clean-up of hazardous waste sites; the Fish and Wildlife Foundation, chartered to encourage public donations to projects supported but not funded by the U.S. Fish and Wildlife Service (FWS); state income tax check-offs, created to channel public donations to state nongame wildlife programs that receive only limited funding through traditional state sources; negotiated rule making, devised to reduce costs and encourage the legitimation of government regulation by bringing together interested parties from all realms of organizational life to negotiate proposed rules; the Buyer Beware program, created by World Wildlife Fund's TRAFFIC (USA) in cooperation with FWS and with the support of the Fish and Wildlife Foundation and the American Society of Travel Agents to educate the U.S. traveling public about wildlife trade regulations; and the Senate Interior Appropriation Committee's matching grants, requiring that contributed funds be located to free governmental appropriations for certain wildlife and natural resources programs. It is not accidental that these hybrid organizations, falling between the customarily divided efforts of the governmental, proprietary, and nonprofit sectors, have arisen at this time in the history of the environmental movement and this time in the political and economic life of the nation.

LEGITIMACY AND PARTICIPATION

Naturally, organizations and individuals with power in the policy arena wish to preserve that power and justify its preservation in terms of a desirable vision of the policy process. Those without power observe the failures of the current process and argue for the improved efficiency and fairness that would follow modifications to the process. This debate occurs implicitly as constituencies vie for the attention of policy makers, and it occurs explicitly as legislatures, agencies, and courts debate the merits of formal changes in the decision-making structure.

A critical ingredient in the creation and maintenance of access is information. This is demonstrated in the case studies, supported in the literature, and validated by informants to this study. Four levels of information may be discerned: descriptive statics (How many snail darters exist, and where are they?); descriptive dynamics (What are the implications for the snail darter if the Tellico Dam is completed? of transplanting the species to another tributary of the river? How does the species relate to other species that may also be objects of policy?); social dynamics (What are the human implications of the alternative snail darter outcomes in terms of settlement patterns, income distribution, recreation opportunities, energy supply?); and values and opinions (What preferences do people have about the snail darter? What values do they hold regarding natural environments and alternative social processes for making resource decisions?).

One might wish to argue that, while the categories of social dynamics and opinion admit to partisan analysis and honest differences, the categories of descriptive statistics and descriptive dynamics might properly be relegated to scientists and managers. However, these divisions are not independent, nor are the questions that properly lie within each division agreed upon. There is, for example, no uniform view among taxonomists as to the correct definition of species to be counted, nor among ecologists as to the proper unit of analysis. Furthermore, the information actually collected, systematized, and disseminated is but a fraction of all possible information. The choices made by collectors, organizers, and disseminators depend on past agendas and the momentum they generate, on current funding sources, on bureaucratic and institutional requirements and constraints, and on perceptions of current problems and individual preferences. At the same time organizations, individually, and society, collectively, determine the quantity of information gathering as well as the mix among information types. It is clear that information generally is in short supply.[26] Numerous environmental and wildlife policies are embarked upon out of a commitment to action or in support of certain values, limited information notwithstanding. And the actions taken are often modified as knowledge is acquired.

An NGO may be in a unique position to provide, collect, or disseminate information and opinions. It may promote the collection of certain kinds of information directly through grant making or in-house research and indirectly through political action leading to inquiry by the public or proprietary sectors. NGOs may take these actions as competitive strategies to gain influence in a policy process that values information and analysis. They may even arise to fill a niche in the information environment. We have remarked earlier on the creation of TRAFFIC (USA) and on the upgrading of the scientific and analytical capabilities of numerous NGOs in the wildlife arena. An NGO is often most effective, in terms of immediate goals, when it joins decision makers on their own terms, on technical grounds, even with their own data, as for example by proposing a revised condor recovery plan or by offering an interpretation of the status of the bobcat population. Legislation typically speaks to evidence customarily regarded as objective; although the Endangered Species Act allows that the values of the wildlife to be protected are esthetic, educational, historical, and recreational as well as scientific, it is scientific and commercial data that provide the basis for protection of species. Thus the criteria are clearly stated, and competing interests, although they obviously represent underlying values and opinions, cannot as easily be charged with partisan analysis.[27]

Cross-cutting this information hierarchy is a hierarchy of risk and uncertainty. Constituences may have more or less confidence in the accuracy of shared information. They may also, of course, have misplaced confidence, discovering after the fact that shared information widely accepted as correct and on which policy has been based, is incorrect. The policy debate is complicated by the incomplete knowledge that participants have about the magnitude of risks, particularly those that threaten health and safety. Even were knowledge complete, risk preferences might differ. For small risks, frequently repeated and with nominal payoffs, the expected outcome might be a widely acceptable basis on which to establish policy. For risks involving the small likelihood of large, involuntary, and negative outcomes, broad policy agreement is less likely. Furthermore, the extensive opportunities for participation in policy making encourage a competition among contrasting notions of risk.[28] In the matter of endangered species, some would demand near-perfect assurance that the consequences of risking an extinction are very small and would accept little chance that an error might be made. Others would be reluctant to sacrifice a valuable program that places a species at risk unless the species could be shown with some certainty to have a large value. Although determining the magnitude and likelihood of such risks appears to be more or less susceptible to objective measurement, within the limits of available knowledge, the analysis of those risks is clearly not best regarded as primarily a technical problem.[29] More information, however, may reduce the number of cases subject to dispute.

Finally, there are differences along the dimensions of space and time. Even if constituencies share facts and risk preferences, they may differ with respect to distributional concerns related to geography, social and economic class, and generation. How widely will the net be cast, and whose values will be given weight in the analysis? To what extent should U.S. wildlife policy accommodate the wildlife values of other nations? Constituencies also may not share a common willingness to trade present against future costs and benefits. Indeed, the very criteria by which one might assess intergenerational trade-offs are in dispute.

Debates over the Endangered Species Act regularly raise these differences concerning information, risk, and time preference. During the 1978 reauthorization hearings, which led to the first substantive amendment limiting the categorical protection for endangered species, Charles Warren, then chairman of the Council on Environmental Quality (CEQ), advised that "if we err, let's err on the side of preserving species, because there is so much that is not known about their value, not only to human beings, but to the entire world community."[30] A representative from the Upper Colorado River Commission noted that "it appears ridiculous to the point of perversity, and completely unreasonable to believe that the human race—especially Americans—would permit a system to exist under which a snail darter in Tennessee becomes more important than the enhancement of man's welfare."[31] But, as EDF's Michael J. Bean made clear, the act ought not to be characterized as pitting the interests of man against the interests of other species. Rather, our present interests are "pitted against our own future interests."[32] This only begs the question of how to weigh present against future interests. The future human benefits are largely unknown, but this state of affairs does not necessarily recommend preservation. W. Samuel Tucker, Jr., of Florida Light and Power Company argued that "risks work both ways, and the opportunities lost in a project abandoned solely because of a perceived threat to some species or its habitat, especially when there are no practical alternatives, also create risks which must be assumed by society."[33]

How do we collectively assess these risks? One approach is to look to congressional intent. Although many analysts have argued the merits of a representative legislature as an expression of the public interest, fewer have suggested that Congress, as presently constituted, offers the ideal format.[34] The first objection is that Congress as a whole doesn't necessarily mean what it says. At a fundamental level, most legislators do not care about most issues. Presumably some measure of balance is achieved over the longer term through a succession of actions, each engaging a small number of legislators on behalf of passionate interests. But even when most legislators care, the outcome may correspond not to a compromise in the public interest but to a hodge-podge of individual elements that, in sum, do not satisfy any standard of the public interest. This problem is aggravated by piecemeal amendments to existing legislation. The Endangered Species Act of 1973 was amended in 1976, 1977, 1978, 1979, 1980, and 1982 and "has been tinkered with to the point it is no surprise that a number of unwanted byproducts and implications that weren't adequately foreseen when adjustments were made have arisen."[35] Had Congress deliberately and forthrightly inserted the prohibitive passages of the Endangered Species Act as a clear expression of the public interest, it does not follow, as Steven Yaffee observes, that "prohibitive policy is *meant* to be implemented prohibitively" nor that "prohibitive policy *is* implemented prohibitively."[36] Legislators understand implementation and account for it in the legislative process. In this instance, however, little notice was taken in Congress of the prohibitive Section 7 until several court cases compelled more detailed attention.[37]

Furthermore, legislators may not all have the same conception of their representational responsibilities. They may seek to transmit the preferences of their constituents, or they may speak to the interests of their constituents, expressed or implied. Or instead they may work from a personal agenda that is merely tolerated by constituents. In seeking higher office, they may address the perceived needs of broader constituencies. One recent analysis suggests that the broad environmental legislation of the 1970s resulted not from congressional responsiveness to organized environmental interests but to the competitive efforts of several leading legislators to place themselves in the vanguard of the nascent environmental movement. The result was more stringent legislation than these legislators preferred and more than could have been achieved by environmental groups through the normal application of influence.[38]

The alleged weaknesses of a legislative approach perhaps recommend an administrative approach based on policy analysis. But the policy process does not function according to the analyst's model, in which a problem is identified, alternative solutions proposed, necessary data amassed, solutions compared with respect to a set of criteria, and the optimal solution identified and implemented. Nor are institutions necessarily in place to facilitate that kind of analysis. Efforts to rationalize the policy structure are sometimes successful and sometimes not. While the independent Environmental Protection Agency (EPA) and the Commerce Department's National Oceanographic and Atmospheric Administration were created in 1970 on the recommendation of President Nixon's Advisory Council on Executive Organization, a department of natural resources, a version of which has been recommended by four presidents, has yet to materialize. Nor has Congress established a joint committee on the environment, despite joint resolutions to do so.[39] Contrary to the analyst's view, problems continue to be identified as the policy process plays itself out. Risk and uncertainty are pervasive, and a universal evaluative scale does not exist. The competition among NGOs for places in the policy process based on critical information and analytical expertise is thus transformed into a competition among perspectives, opinions, and values that should be accorded legitimacy. Two criteria often identified by groups, to establish their own legitimacy and to detract from that of their opposition, are scientific objectivity and accountability.

Scientific reasoning is seen to stand above partisan analysis or emotionalism. In wildlife management, "scientific" has come to be associated with scientific game management.[40] Sport hunters, historically linked to the rise of scientific game management, are threatened by the broadening of the policy debate to include nongame wildlife and plants, insofar as managing for these species compromises harvested populations. Although antihunting NGOs are widely regarded as having great influence, few large groups are, as a matter of explicit policy, opposed to all hunting. Many groups, however, oppose particular hunting technologies, such as the leg-hold trap, or the harvest of particular species, such as whales. This confusion forces such groups into defensive postures with respect to the issue of hunting itself, and it derails the policy debate from more manageable and immediate issues of resource allocation.[41] The Fur Takers of America, in a statement submitted during the 1978 Endangered Species Act reauthorization hearings and in reference to the bobcat, questioned the

legitimacy of Defenders of Wildlife's efforts. They have basically pursued a negative attack on established wildlife management throughout their existence and continue to do so as a tax exempt "humanitarian" group. . . . We seek impartial, knowledgeable wildlife professionals as administrators, not protectionist zealots.[42]

Safari Club International found the Interior Department to be

under the thumb of persons who are opposed to the scientific management of wildlife, including regulated sports hunting. The Department is the handmaiden of the few but vocal and wealthy so-called "preservationists" who look upon hunting as immoral and who would prefer to have the surplus population of a species die the painful and wasteful death of starvation rather than be usefully taken and consumed by Americans in pursuit of their traditional heritage of sport hunting.[43]

But the large populations of certain game animals that must be spared a "painful and wasteful death" exist, at least in part, as the result of past management practices.[44] Present policies are creatures of past policy structures and the historic legitimation of interests.

Symbolic of the threat perceived by sportsmen was the inclusion of sporting among the list of activities (others are commercial, scientific, and educational) that, according to the Endangered Species Act, may contribute to the endangerment of species. During the 1981–82 hearings, the Wildlife Legislative Fund of America (WLFA) sought to delete sporting as a listed cause. James Glass, WLFA president, testified as follows in the Senate:

Senator Chafee. Suppose we made that "illegal sport hunting is a cause of endangerment?"

Mr. Glass. Well, once again, you are saying that sportsmen perform illegal acts. I don't agree with that. There are many people who hunt who violate the law and should be prosecuted, but I do not believe we should put the word "sport hunting" in there.

Senator Chafee. How about "illegal hunting?"

Mr. Glass. I would just like to encourage that we not use the word hunting in there.[45]

Randy Bowman, WLFA director of federal relations, testified as follows in the House:

Mr. Breaux. Maybe I am missing something. I just do not see where sport hunting is a big deal. When I shoot a duck, I am not helping to increase the population. It does have an effect on the population. It decreases it. That is what I am trying to do.

Mr. Bowman. I would not argue with that. . . .

Mr. Breaux. Do you object to overutilization for commercial or scientific or educational purposes being looked at in determining whether a species is endangered or threatened as a result of one of those factors?

Mr. Bowman. No. We did not feel that sport hunting was a cause of endangerment. Poaching, maybe.[46]

The 1982 amendments removed "sporting" and inserted "recreational" overutilization as a cause of endangerment.

The condor and bobcat cases each raised the question of legitimate participation in policy making. Under what circumstances can new constituencies challenge the existing decision-making structure? In the bobcat case, Congress reaffirmed the conventional wisdom of state wildlife managers by asserting that population estimates as such were not required to establish the impact of export on the wild population. At the same time, the controversy changed the ways in which states managed the species, assuring increased protection. In the condor case, opponents of the captive breeding plan suggested, implicitly at least, that the controversy centered not only on technical questions but on questions of value that might legitimately be resolved by an expression of public preference.

In several states the role of the public in wildlife management has manifested itself in regard to the management of game populations. In Vermont control over the state's deer herd was closely held until 1979 by the legislature, which opposed the antlerless hunting season that the state fish and game department would implement in the name of scientific games management. In 1988 the legislature has asserted a renewed interest in control. In November 1983 Maine voters were asked to determine the future of the state's moose season, recently opened after 35 years of full protection for the species. Opponents of the hunt, organized as SMOOSA (Save Maine's Only Official State Animal), lamented the complete absence of sport in shooting the unwary creatures. Hunters and wildlife managers argued that the state's 20,000 moose approach the carrying capacity of their habitat and that a regulated hunt is an efficient way to manage the population. The animals supply meat for the freezer and revenues from license sales for the state; they pose significant hazards to unwary drivers. The Sportsmen's Alliance of Maine spent $400,000 to defeat the referendum, which it viewed as a threat to scientific management and the control exercised by fish and game departments. If the public at large were to take over the state's moose population, it would set a precedent "whereby more wildlife would become subject to management by guess and by golly than by professionals who are trained to husband the resource in the public interest." Opponents argued for a different vision of the public interest. The hunt was upheld by a two-to-one margin.[47]

Economic interest groups, while the extent of their power may be questioned, are clearly accountable to the industries that support them. Public interest groups, on the other hand, may find themselves on the defensive with respect to accountability. Their constituencies are broad and ill defined, and their members may not have a direct economic interest in organizational achievements. The weakness of this link is not lost on industry groups. A spokesman for the National Coal Council, critical of environmental groups supporting strong stripmining regulations, remarked that they "don't have the grass roots backing that one would believe from reading the newspapers, especially in the Northeast. They don't have a constituency. Their decisions on strategies and issues are made by a group of young people who don't have to answer to anybody."[48] Observations such as this, although usually with a less critical undertone, were offered by several congressional staff people in the course of the present study. The generalization is narrowly true for many organizations; a small number of relatively young staff members do have considerable flexibility in setting short-term organizational agendas and designing strategies. But except for the rare organization that depends only on endowment income or is funded out of the pockets of volunteers and staff members, the groups' survival depends on a constant flow of resources, which suggests at least a modest accountability to some constituency. Furthermore, the political success of organizations, at least in Congress, is related, if imperfectly, to the constituency that lobbyists bring to the Hill. Legislators may misjudge public sentiment, and they may take personal but unpopular stands on some issues, but they cannot survive in the long run if they consistently ignore voter preferences on salient issues.

Legitimacy does not require that an organization enroll as members or supporters all, most, or even any individuals who would benefit were the organization to achieve its goals. In fact, the public goods nature of those goals guarantees at best limited success in this regard. NGOs obviously represent latent interests much broader than their own memberships. Public opinion surveys, ranging from national issues polls to specialized and detailed studies on environmental issues, show strong and consistent support for a wide range of goals pursued by public interest environmental organizations.[49] Groups make use of the findings from such polls to legitimize their involvement in the policy process. The Reagan administration's misreading of this public support figures significantly in its failure to bring about the thorough revision of federal environmental policy described by the President's transition team and promoted by its partisans in and out of government.[50]

But limited accountability may be turned from a liability to an asset, for if the public interest NGO is accountable to no one, it is not captured by any clientele or constituency. An NRDC solicitation quotes U.S. District Judge Charles Richey in testimony before the Senate Judiciary Committee: "Everytime I see somebody . . . like the NRDC come into my court, I say 'Thank God' because I know I am going to have competent counsel . . . that does not represent any governmental or proprietary interest." Indeed, it is the limited accountability of governmental and proprietary interests to the broader public that speaks for open government and citizen participation. Other organized interests, although they are accountable to identifiable constituencies, are accountable only to those constituencies. Arguments for financial assistance to public interest participation in environmental decision making are predicated on a balancing of interests made necessary by the inside track of the wealthy and well connected.

Economic interests represent before the policy process values that emerge from the marketplace, whereas public interest groups represent values that the marketplace obscures. Such groups patrol the boundaries that separate the proprietary, voluntary, and government sectors in an effort to allocate activities to their appropriate realms. There is, of course, no uniform opinion as to the proper allocation. Perspectives move in and out of fashion in response to changes in technology and changes in the abundance and distribution of resources; they also move in response to the evolving views of resource management and government that are presented by managers, politicians, and scholars. The arguments against a pure market allocation of natural environments are well known.[51] Less well known, but increasingly promoted, are the arguments against a pure governmental allocation of natural environments.[52] The new resource economics, articulating free market solutions to problems of allocating environmental resources, rests on the alleged widespread failure of government control and on the efficiency of voluntary exchange among private owners.[53]

Thus NGOs do not merely serve to fill in pieces of the analyst's puzzle by arguing for particular shadow prices for nonmarketed amenities or debating discount rates in the interest of future generations. What, after all, is in the interest of future generations—natural resources in place, or dams and highways? There is, of course, no way to know. Indeed, as Mark Sagoff has argued, what future generations want will depend on what they are taught to want and what is available. "There are few decisions favorable to our wishes that cannot be justified by a likely story about future preferences."[54] Edward O. Wilson has argued similarly that, while we owe our remote descendants nothing, we owe ourselves everything in planning for them. "If human existence has any verifiable meaning, it is that our passions and toil are enabling mechanisms to continue that existence unbroken, unsullied, and progressively secure. It is for ourselves, and not for them or any abstract morality that we think into the distant future."[55] NGOs enter into a process that concerns not the anticipation of future demands but the creation of those very demands.[56]

It is for this reason that NGOs care so much about educational programs that seek to convey knowledge and perspectives on wildlife, on natural resources generally, and on the policy process itself. And it is for this reason that the evolution of ideas and values is so important. James Q. Wilson remarked that insofar as an agency can influence policy "its choices will be importantly shaped by what its executives learned in college a decade or two earlier."[57] In the wildlife arena, the childhood experiences of its executives may prove more telling. Prospective NGO members select groups with which to affiliate, and the search for support influences the strategies and structure of the organization, but groups educate members to prefer their own styles and substance.

The increased involvement of nonprofit organizations and increased public participation in the policy process cannot be denied, but the impact of that participation is greatly debated. At least five positions can be discerned. The first three fundamentally accept a pluralistic view of policymaking in which the outcomes correspond to expressions of interest, some of which are better organized, more articulate, in control of more resources—in short, more powerful—than others. The interests of bureaucrats, the interests of legislators, and the interests of business are among those presumed to enjoy disproportionate influence. The interests of the poor, the interests of diffuse constituencies, and the interests of the public, broadly speaking, are among those presumed to suffer from underrepresentation. Enhanced participation, whether through public interest groups, grass-roots community organizations, or agency-sponsored participatory mechanisms, is presumed to redress the balance. The three positions can be distinguished according to the efficacy of participation in this regard. The first holds that participation has been extended too far, forcing agencies into incorrect and hastily conceived decisions under pressure from vigilant constituencies and preventing Congress from taking decisive action in the public interest. Participation absorbs valuable resources that not only may fail to return better decisions but may lead to even worse decisions.[58] In the wildlife arena such claims frequently arise when managers are confronted by nonhunting constituencies over strategies for harvest or for the removal of exotic species that threaten native ecosystems. Participation is seen to limit the implementation of what are regarded as purely technical solutions to wildlife management problems. While it is often true that such participation delays implementation, it is also true that mutually agreeable solutions can be negotiated, solutions that accomplish the management goals and protect the interests of newly legitimized constituencies. The efforts to discourage bison from wandering out of Yellowstone National Park and onto state lands, where they are subject to harvest, and the removal of burros from the Grand Canyon by Friends of Animals in lieu of their destruction by the National Park Service, provide examples.[59]

A second position is that participation has not been, and perhaps cannot be, extended far enough. The dominance of business interests in a capitalist system cannot but fail to repress unorganized interests and noncommercial values. Although the forward movement of the 1960s and 1970s represents significant progress, the backsliding of the 1980s must be reversed by aggressive expansion of participation.[60] But it seems clear that business interests have been compromised by public interest legislation and that a business response has been elicited.[61]

A third position is that participation is effective, that a proper balance has been achieved, and that changes in the process emerge to meet the needs of an evolving society.[62] Measuring the impact of participation in the wildlife issue area presents difficult problems, as should by now be evident. Even if groups appear to exercise power by getting what they want over the objections of other groups, they may be fundamentally limited in what they can achieve by the agenda control that others maintain, or they may be limited in what they want by a "false consciousness" inherent in the power structure.[63] Even if full participation is genuinely possible, the measurement of power and influence can be made at different times and places, leading to different assessments. Organized interests, through both formal and informal processes, sift through potential agenda items and contribute to the evolution of solutions that may or may not be implemented. They engage in research and education, the impact of which may be at considerable remove from the activities themselves. Influence will be improperly measured if only the final legislative, regulatory, or judicial outcome is examined.[64] Every advocate can identify successes even in the face of what appear to be contradictory events.[65] On the other hand, groups may minimize public perception of the power they hold, to emphasize the extent to which their policies derive legitimacy from broad public support. This view particularly, but all three views to some extent, evaluates participation with reference to the final policy outcome: Does participation move us closer to or farther from where we want to be? This comparison presumes an independent method of identifying and ranking outcomes. If such a method exists and the outcome is all that matters, participation may be discarded altogether.

Thus the fourth position. This view recognizes that participation may be of some value but holds that emphasis on the paradigm of participation misstates the nature of the policy problems that face us. It fosters an adversarial relationship at the expense of productive problem solving and turns technical issues into political ones.[66] Public preferences and values can be administratively determined through analytical techniques such as surveys and quasi-market experiments.[67] Where actual markets would function efficiently and without compromising other important values, allocation of wildlife might be entrusted to voluntary exchange.

Participation can be resurrected if its contribution is not limited to problem solving in a narrow sense. Participation may be viewed as a necessary, if costly, antidote to the skewing of the policy process by corporate and bureaucratic powers. But public demands are created out of the participatory process itself and cannot be fully discerned through abstract analysis. In a related way, participation may be valued in and of itself for the legitimacy it conveys to the outcome of the policy process. Furthermore, a preference for participation in decision making is confirmed by historical experience, by the persistence of such participatory mechanisms as the jury trial, and by survey research.[68]

Finally, interest groups do not merely transmit member preferences so that the political marketplace can properly aggregate them. Rather, they represent a fundamentally different order of input. Hazel Henderson writes of the new perspectives that NGOs bring to the decision-making process and of the "higher" needs that participation meets for individuals. Institutional structures are designed to screen out information that is unwanted or irrelevant to the narrow tasks at hand; they overreward analysis and discourage synthesis. The delays, disruptions, and costs that appear in a short-run analysis of public participation are, in a longer view, liberating and valuable.[69]

Most broadly speaking, the process of legitimizing participation consists of vesting rights through a partitioning of claims to the policy arena. These partitions do not represent mutually exclusive divisions; instead they fall across one another and by now are deep in places with potentially conflicting rights. Such claims, once legitimized, are not always exercised, and some fall into disuse, but in general, the more rights we invest, the more interests must be satisfied at every turn. This surely risks a kind of decision-making grid-lock, of which critics of participation have complained, but the failure to accommodate new rights limits policy outcomes to combinations sanctioned by interests legitimized at a particular moment in history.

The vitality of the wildlife issue area as portrayed here, regularly accommodating newly articulated interests as it has, should cast into doubt the wisdom of such limitations.

NOTES

1. Herbert Kaufman, *Time, Chance, and Organizations: Natural Selection in a Perilous Environment* (Chatham, N.J.: Chatham House, 1985).

2. Hazel Henderson, *Creating Alternative Futures: The End of Economics* (New York: Berkley, 1978), p. 294.

3. On the match between individuals and organizational settings, see Dennis R. Young, "Entrepreneurship and the Behavior of Nonprofit Organizations," in *Nonprofit Firms in a Three Sector Economy*, edited by Michelle J. White. *COUPE Papers on Public Economics*, vol 6. (Washington, D.C.: Urban Institute, 1981), pp. 135–62.

4. On the training and other characteristics of public interest lobbyists, see Jeffrey M. Berry, *Lobbying for the People: The Political Behavior of Public Interest Groups* (Princeton, N.J.: Princeton University Press, 1977), pp. 84–96; for an analysis of data suggesting less mobility among lobbyists than revealed in the present study, see Robert H. Salisbury, "Washington Lobbyists: A Collective Portrait," in *Interest Group Politics*, 2d ed., edited by Allan J. Cigler and Burdett A. Loomis (Washington, D.C.: Congressional Quarterly Press, 1986), pp. 146–61.

5. Hugh Heclo, "Issue Networks and the Executive Establishment," in *The New American Political System*, edited by Anthony King (Washington, D.C.: American Enterprise Institute, 1978), p. 102.

6. Linda E. Demkovich, "From Public Interest Advocates to Administration Defenders," *National Journal*, November 25, 1978, p. 1892.

7. *Citizen Participation*, July–August 1980, p. 6.

8. Rafe Pomerance of Friends of the Earth, quoted in Dick Kirschten, "Environmentalists Tell Carter Thanks but No Thanks," *National Journal*, June 23, 1979, p. 1038.

9. Ibid., p. 1039. Cutler worked for NWF and the Wilderness Society before joining the Agriculture Department. He moved from the Carter administration, to NAS, and to Environment/Population Balance, an NGO concerned with the environmental consequences of population growth in the United States. In February 1988 he became president of Defenders of Wildlife.

10. For an early, critical view of Carter's environmental policy, see Michael Frome, "Carter & Friends: Tarnished Halos," *Defenders*, June 1979, pp. 166–68.

11. Quoted in Kirschten, "Environmentalists Tell Carter," p. 1037.

12. See James W. Singer, "That Old Public Interest Movement Gang Moves Into New—and Private—Fields," *National Journal*, February 14, 1981, p. 269.

13. According to *Living Wilderness* in 1981, Nelson, former governor of Wisconsin and three-term senator, known as the father of Earth Day 1970 and as a

champion of numerous environmentalist causes, "brings to The Society and to the larger conservation community a level of experience, stature, credibility and intellectual creativity never previously attained." Fisher was president of Resources for the Future prior to his six-year term as a Virginia congressman and "is uniquely equipped to establish the first economic department in an activist conservation organization." Spring, pp. 32–35. Andrus, "perhaps the greatest Secretary of the Interior in our nation's history," will "help us develop a much-needed dialogue with the corporate community." Summer, p. 43.

14. Remarks of Joe B. Browder, quoted in Michael C. Lipske, "Washington Outlook—Administration Brings Cheer to Conservationists, *Defenders*, June 1977, p. 213.

15. Russell E. Train, "Going About Our Job—United With Others," *Focus*, Spring 1982, p. 2.

16. *Focus*, July 1983, p. 1; World Wildlife Fund-U.S. (WWF–US), *Annual Report 1983*, p. 2.

17. *Focus*, July 1983, p. 2. RARE, Inc. was fully absorbed by WWF–US in 1985. *Focus*, November–December 1985, p. 4.

18. WWF–US, *Annual Report 1985*, pp. 3–4.

19. Conservation Foundation, *CF Letter*, September–October 1985, p. 7.

20. Robert A. Jones, "Environmental Movement—Wholesale Changes at Top," Los Angeles *Times*, December 27, 1984, p. I: 3.

21. Cited in Grant P. Thompson, "New Faces, New Opportunities," *Environment* 27 (May 1985): 9.

22. "New Generation of Leaders," editorial in Los Angeles *Times*, January 3, 1985, p. II: 4.

23. See Paul J. DiMaggio and Walter W. Powell, "The Iron Cage Revisited: Institutional Isomorphism and Collective Rationality in Organizational Fields," *American Sociological Review* 48 (April 1983): 147–60.

24. Brattleboro *Reformer*, July 18, 1987, p. 7; *Audubon Activist*, July–August 1987, p. 10. See also Peter Borrelli, "Environmentalism at the Crossroads," *Amicus Journal*, Summer 1987, pp. 24–37.

25. New York *Times*, September 30, 1986, p. A36; Lis Harris, "Brother Sun, Sister Moon," *New Yorker*, April 27, 1987, pp. 80–101.

26. See Sally K. Fairfax, "Environmental Assessment: Gains and Challenges," in *Transactions of the Forty-sixth North American Wildlife and Natural Resources Conference* (Washington, D.C.: Wildlife Management Institute, 1981), pp. 27–34.

27. President Reagan's Executive Order 12291, mandating economic impact analysis of proposed federal regulations, was applied to the listing of endangered species under the Endangered Species Act. This slowed the listing process dramatically and limited the role of scientific decision making. The 1982 amendments to the act constrained agency discretion in this regard. See *Endangered Species Reauthorization Bulletin*, no. 9 (October 26, 1982).

28. The technical basis for regulation is debated more intensively in the United States than in Britain, France, or West Germany. Sheila Jasanoff, *Risk Management and Political Culture: A Comparative Study of Science in the Policy Context*, Social Research Perspectives, Occasional Reports on Current Topics No. 12 (New York: Russell Sage Foundation, 1986), p. 5.

29. Ibid., Chapters 8 and 9.

30. U.S. Congress, House, Subcommittee on Fisheries and Wildlife Conservation and the Environment of the Committee on Merchant Marine and Fisheries, *Endangered Species: Part 1, Hearings on Endangered Species Oversight*, May 24, 25, June 1, 15, 16, 20, 23, and 28, 1978, 95th Cong., 2d sess., Serial No. 95-39, p. 495.

31. U.S. Congress, Senate, Subcommittee on Resources Protection of the Committee on Environment and Public Works, *Amending the Endangered Species Act of 1973, Hearings on S. 2899*, April 13 and 14, 1978, 95th Cong., 2d. sess., Serial No. 95-H60, p. 149.

32. U.S. Congress, House, *Endangered Species: Part 1*, Serial No. 95-39, p. 556.

33. U.S. Congress, Senate, *Amending the Endangered Species Act*, Serial No. 95-H60, pp. 174-75.

34. "It is equally plausible to identify the public interest with whatever legislation Congress passes and the President signs, after reasonable debate and consideration." Mark Sagoff, "On the Preservation of Species," *Columbia Journal of Environmental Law* 7 (1980), p. 66. See also Edwin T. Haefele, *Representative Government and Environmental Management* (Baltimore: Johns Hopkins University Press, 1973): "There is a need to force environmental issues into partisan politics at every level of government" (p. 60), and John Jackson, "People or Ducks? Who Decides?" In *Economic Analysis of Environmental Problems*, edited by Edwin S. Mills (New York: Columbia University Press, 1975): "The best way to insure adequate consideration of the legitimate interests associated with decisions in the public sector is by a multipurpose legislative type body which has jurisdiction and control over the various functional agencies or departments and whose members are elected from equal-sized districts throughout the area affected by the decisions" (p. 389).

35. Remarks of Patrick Parenteau, Vice-President for Resource Conservation, National Wildlife Federation, to U.S. Congress, Senate, Subcommittee on Environmental Pollution of the Committee on Environment and Public Works, *Endangered Species Act Oversight, Hearings*, December 8 and 10, 1981, 97th Cong., 1st sess., Serial No. 97-H34, p. 53.

36. Steven Lewis Yaffee, *Prohibitive Policy: Implementing the Endangered Species Act* (Cambridge, Mass.: MIT Press, 1982), p. 5.

37. Section 7 attracted little attention in Congress at the time of passage and was initially ignored by the agencies. As the full measure of its power was worked by the courts on the agencies, Congress responded quickly, expanding two sen-

tences of the 1973 act into ten pages of statutory language, including detailed procedures for implementation and exemption. See Michael J. Bean, *The Evolution of National Wildlife Law*, rev. ed. (New York: Praeger, 1983), pp. 355-73.

38. E. Donald Elliott, Bruce A. Ackerman, and John C. Millian, "Toward a Theory of Statutory Evolution: The Federalization of Environmental Law," *Journal of Law, Economics, and Organization* 1 (1985): 313-40. See also David M. Trubeck and William J. Gillen, who remark that the "initial successes of the environmental movement in securing passage of laws like NEPA were not the result of normal group politics. Rather, these laws emerged from a period in which mass attention had been drawn to environmental concerns through the media and the activity of politicians and policy entrepreneurs who worked from relatively narrow organizational bases." "Environmental Defense II: Examining the Limits of Interest Group Advocacy," in *Public Interest Law: An Economic and Institutional Analysis*, Burton A. Weisbrod, study director, in collaboration with Joel F. Handler and Neil K. Komesar (Berkeley: University of California Press, 1978), p. 216. On concepts of representation, see Dorthea M. Bradley and Helen M. Ingram, "Science vs. the Grass Roots: Representation in the Bureau of Land Management," *Natural Resources Journal* 26 (Summer 1986): 493-518.

39. Council on Environmental Quality, *Environmental Quality 1970: The First Annual Report of the Council on Environmental Quality* (Washington, D.C.: Government Printing Office, 1970), pp. 19-28; Council on Environmental Quality, *Environmental Quality 1971, The Second Annual Report of the Council on Environmental Quality* (Washington, D.C.: Government Printing Office, 1971), pp. 4-8. On the proposal to rationalize the management of natural resources through the creation of a new cabinet department, see *Science* 203 (March 16, 1979): 1097, and 204 (June 1, 1979): 924. Congress did however create the Environmental Study Conference in 1975, providing members with information and analyses of legislative issues.

40. The seminal work is Aldo Leopold, *Game Management* (New York: Scribner's, 1933).

41. The Society for Animal Protective Legislation, for example, has "not taken a position against killing if it is done painlessly and does not deplete populations or species. For example, we do not criticize the instant death of an animal caused by a well-aimed rifle bullet, but we strongly object to capturing that same animal in a leghold trap because of the fear and pain inflicted." Christine Stevens, "Statement for a Debate on State-Provincial Management Rights and Responsibilities vs. Federal Rights and Responsibilities," annual meeting of the International Association of Fish and Wildlife Agencies, West Yellowstone, Montana, September 11, 1979. Reprinted in Greta Nilsson et al., *Facts About Furs*, 3rd ed. (Washington, D.C.: Animal Welfare Institute, 1980), pp. 205-08.

42. Statement of Major L. Boddicker, Western Region Representative, Conservation Committee, in U.S. Congress, House, *Endangered Species: Part 2*, 1978, Serial No. 95-40, p. 1224.

43. Statement of Dr. Carroll Mann, President, Safari Club International, in U.S. Congress, Senate, Subcommittee on Resources Protection of the Committee on Environment and Public Works, *Amending the Endangered Species Act of 1973*, April 13 and 14, 1978, Serial No. 95-H60, p. 287. Senator Jesse Helms, who introduced Dr. Mann, a fellow North Carolinian, to the subcommittee, inserted Mann's testimony in the *Congressional Record*: "It is unfortunate that too often we hear from only the extremist elements of the environmental lobby. Frankly, at least up until now, they have done a much better job of advocating their viewpoint in the media and before the Congress." But under Mann's leadership, he said, the club "has been turned from a largely social organization into a highly effective group expressing the concerns and viewpoints of hunters and sportsmen everywhere." 1978, S5710, daily edition.

44. See, for example, Bill Clark, "How Hunters Upset the Natural Balance," New York *Times*, March 23, 1980, Section 5, p. 2.

45. U.S. Congress, Senate, Subcommittee on Environmental Pollution, *Endangered Species Act Oversight*, pp. 47-48.

46. U.S. Congress, House, Subcommittee on Fisheries and Wildlife Conservation and the Environment of the Committee on Merchant Marine and Fisheries. *Endangered Species Act: Hearings on Endangered Species Act Reauthorization and Oversight*, February 22, March 8, 1982, 97th Cong., 2nd. sess., Serial No. 97-32, p. 74.

47. Wildlife Management Institute, *Outdoor News Bulletin* 37 (July 15, 1983); Nelson Bryant, "Maine Will Vote on Moose," New York *Times*, October 3, 1983, p. 8, sec. 5; Brattleboro *Reformer*, November 9, 1983, p. 1.

48. Remarks of William E. Hynan, quoted in Arthur J. Magida, "Environment Report: Movement Undaunted by Economic, Energy Crises," *National Journal*, January 17, 1976, p. 62. Similarly, Ronald Reagan suggested that James Watt was the victim, not of rank and file environmentalists, but of professionals who misrepresent the public interest to further their careers. New York *Times*, March 30, 1983, p. A14.

49. See Robert Cameron Mitchell, "Public Opinion and Environmental Politics in the 1970s and 1980s," in *Environmental Policy in the 1980s: Reagan's New Agenda*, edited by Norman J. Vig and Michael E. Kraft (Washington, D.C.: Congressional Quarterly Press, 1984), pp. 51-74.

50. Henry C. Kenski and Helen M. Ingram, "The Reagan Administration and Environmental Regulation: The Constraint of the Political Market," in *Controversies in Environmental Policy*, edited by Sheldon Kamieniecki, Robert O'Brien, and Michael Clark (Albany: State University of New York Press, 1986), pp. 275-98.

51. See, for example, John V. Krutilla, "Conservation Reconsidered," *American Economic Review* 47 (1967): 777-96, and Anthony C. Fisher, *Resource and Environmental Economics* (Cambridge: Cambridge University Press, 1981), especially Chapter 5.

52. See, for example, Charles Wolf, Jr., "A Theory of Non-Market Failure," *The Public Interest*, no. 55 (Spring 1979): 114–33.

53. Richard L. Stroup and John A. Baden, *Natural Resources: Bureaucratic Myths and Environmental Management*, Pacific Studies in Public Policy (Cambridge, Mass.: Ballinger, 1983). For the case of wildlife, see Robert J. Smith, "Resolving the Tragedy of the Commons by Creating Private Property Rights in Wildlife," *Cato Journal* 1 (Fall 1981): 439–68. The arguments raised by Smith and others are reminiscent of the nineteenth-century debates over property rights in wildlife. See James A. Tober, *Who Owns the Wildlife? The Political Economy of Conservation in Nineteenth-Century America* (Westport, Conn.: Greenwood, 1981), Chapter 4.

54. Mark Sagoff, "We Have Met the Enemy and He Is Us, or Conflict and Contradiction in Environmental Law," *Environmental Law* 12 (1982): 295–96.

55. Edward O. Wilson, *Biophilia* (Cambridge, Mass.: Harvard University Press, 1984), p. 121.

56. However, on the projection of future wildlife values, see Edward E. Langenau, Jr., "Anticipating Wildlife Values of Tomorrow," in *Valuing Wildlife: Economic and Social Perspectives*, edited by Daniel J. Decker and Gary R. Goff (Boulder, Colo.: Westview, 1987), pp. 309–17. See also Bill Devall, "The Deep Ecology Movement," *Natural Resources Journal* 20 (April 1980): 299–322, and Lester W. Milbrath, *Environmentalists: Vanguard for a New Society* (Albany: State University of New York Press, 1984).

57. James Q. Wilson, "The Politics of Regulation," in *The Politics of Regulation*, edited by James Q. Wilson (New York: Basic Books, 1980), p. 393.

58. See D. Stephen Cupps, "Emerging Problems of Citizen Participation," *Public Administration Review* 37 (September–October 1977): 478–87; and Susan M. Schectman, "The 'Bambi Syndrome': How NEPA's Public Participation in Wildlife Management Is Hurting the Environment," *Environmental Law* 8 (1978): 611–43.

59. New York *Times*, February 13, 1986, p. A18; December 14, 1986, p. 36; Molly Ivins, "Wild Burros Plucked Out of Grand Canyon," New York *Times*, July 30, 1980, p. A12.

60. See Charles E. Lindblom, *The Policy-Making Process*, 2nd ed. (Englewood Cliffs, N.J.: Prentice-Hall, 1980), Chapter 9, and Mark E. Kann, "Environmental Democracy in the United States," in *Controversies in Environmental Policy*, p. 269.

61. David Vogel, "The Power of Business in America: A Re-Appraisal," *British Journal of Political Science* 13 (1983): 19–43; David Vogel, "The New Political Science of Corporate Power," *Public Interest*, no. 87 (Spring 1987): 63–79; Philip Shabecoff, "Big Business on the Offensive," New York *Times Magazine*, December 4, 1979, pp. 134ff.

62. Paul J. Culhane, "Natural Resources Policy: Procedural Change and Substantive Environmentalism," in *Nationalizing Government*, edited by Theodore

Lowi (New York: Sage, 1977), pp. 201–62; Paul J. Culhane, *Public Lands Politics: Interest Group Influence on the Forest Service and the Bureau of Land Management* (Baltimore: Johns Hopkins University Press, 1981), and Daniel A. Mazmanian and Jeanne Nienaber, *Can Organizations Change? Environmental Protection, Citizen Participation, and the Corps of Engineers* (Washington, D.C.: Brookings Institution, 1979).

63. See Graham K. Wilson, *Interest Groups in the United States* (New York: Oxford University Press, 1981), pp. 5–15.

64. W. Douglas Costain and Anne N. Costain, "Interest Groups as Policy Aggregators in the Legislative Process," *Polity* 14 (Winter 1981): 249–72; and Joel F. Handler, *Social Movements and the Legal System: A Theory of Law Reform and Social Change* (New York: Academic Press, 1978), pp. 34–41.

65. See Berry, *Lobbying for the People*, p. 280.

66. Sally K. Fairfax, "A Disaster in the Environmental Movement," *Science* 199 (February 17, 1978): 743–48; and Sally K. Fairfax and Barbara T. Andrews, "Debate Within and Debate Without: NEPA and the Redefinition of the 'Prudent Man' Rule," *Natural Resources Journal* 19 (July 1979): 505–35.

67. For example, see David S. Brookshire, Larry S. Eubanks, and Alan Randall, "Estimating Option Prices and Existence Values for Wildlife Resources," *Land Economics* 59 (1983): 1–15, and John R. Stoll and Lee Ann Johnson, "Concepts of Value, Nonmarket Valuation, and the Case of the Whooping Crane," Natural Resources Work Group, Natural Resources Working Paper Series, Department of Agricultural Economics, Texas A & M University, 1984.

68. Milbrath, *Environmentalists*, pp. 35–36.

69. Henderson, *Creating Alternative Futures*, p. 393.

Conclusion

A return to the condor case study provides a useful framework for concluding remarks. What has been accomplished after fifty years of concern, seven years of hands-on involvement, and the expenditure of millions of dollars? For one thing, we don't know if we have saved the species. The birds may or may not continue to breed in captivity; if they do, they may or may not survive release; if they survive release, they may or may not reestablish themselves as a viable wild population. Some of these uncertainties may be reduced through further research, experimentation on Andean condors, expanded habitat preservation, and aggressive work toward understanding and reducing mortality in the wild. The resolution of other uncertainties depends pretty much on the luck of the draw.

Even if we do save the species, in that it is one day restored as a viable population in some portion of its historic natural range, we do not know whether we have done it efficiently, that is, with the least amount of society's resources. Some will say that earlier captive breeding experiments, for example at the time of the San Diego Zoo's efforts in the 1950s, would have saved millions of dollars, many years, and much unpleasantness. Others will say that the species would have recovered on its own had we not handled the birds and reduced their numbers through capture, especially if some earlier attention had been paid to providing safer habitat.

Even if we save the species, and even if it turns out that we have saved it efficiently, what exactly will we have saved? The population of the future will differ from that of the past, not only in its narrower genetic variability but in its behavior, which will not initially represent the learned traditions of wild birds. To what extent is it correct to say that it is even the same species? Does it foster the same human values?

Finally, if we save the condor, if we determine that we have done it efficiently, and if we agree that it is the same or an equivalent species, we still do not know whether this is a worthy accomplishment. There are, as of January 1988, 369 U.S. species listed as endangered under the 1973 act, 263 of which have approved recovery plans. There are in addition 48 species proposed for listing and thousands more that might be eligible were there adequate data and sufficient resources at the Office of Endangered Species to cope with the regulatory burden of considering them. And this is in the United States alone; worldwide, the problem of endangered species is orders of magnitude more severe. The budget for the federal endangered species program is approximately $30 million per year, which must cover all administrative costs as well as research and recovery programs. The federal share of the condor recovery (excluding $3.5 million spent to acquire the Hudson ranch) was about $1.0 million in 1986, roughly 20 percent of the total research budget of the endangered species program. The expenditures on this program by the Audubon Society, the State of California, the U.S. Forest Service, the Bureau of Land Management, the two zoos, and other cooperators together add nearly as much.

So why the condor and not these other species? Policy analysis would call for a systematic comparison of all possible species, ranked according to the expected benefits from the expenditure of resources for protection. Dollars would then be spent for the species that promise the greatest return. Such an analysis would not be limited to endangered species. The condor, the Nashville crayfish, and the Alabama leatherflower would have to hold their own against the white-tailed deer, the wild mustang, and the harp seal. It is not at all clear how the condor would fare in such a comparison.

But why focus on species at all, rather than, for example, on habitat? There is a bureaucratic answer to this in the language of the Endangered Species Act, providing for the identification of endangered and threatened species and their recovery. There is also a legal and economic answer, in that governments can legally protect endangered species on private lands, but they cannot easily protect private lands themselves without acquiring them, all or in part. The species approach is thus perhaps cheaper or less intrusive. There is also a political answer, in that the public can identify with and take interest in individual species with certain characteristics—cute and cuddly, or symbolic, or majestic, or beautiful. Preservation monies may be available if raised in the names of particular species that would not be available for habitat protection or some other environmental purpose. There is, finally, an ecological answer, in that certain highly visible species that attract public attention may also be keystone species important not only in maintaining ecological stability but in requiring wide expanses of habitat the protection of which benefits numerous other species and the environment at large.[1] In this regard, for example, the very expensive programs to restore the Atlantic salmon to northeastern river systems may be viewed not as wildlife policy but as clean water policy.

But these answers are not entirely satisfying. First, in the case of the condor at least, not much will be lost ecologically if the condor becomes extinct; and anything that would be lost may be lost in any event while the species is in captivity. Second, if the goal is the preservation of diversity, and even if this is interpreted to mean preservation of as many currently existing species as possible, this goal can perhaps be accomplished more efficiently by focusing on needed habitat diversity rather than on individual species. But an even more serious challenge to the species approach recognizes extinction as a natural process. The vast majority of the species that have ever existed on earth are extinct. What conservationists might wish to conserve in this view is not the particular set of life forms now existing but the capacity of the biosphere to support future evolution and speciation.[2] In this broader picture the condor, as a single, rare, ecologically insignificant species, hardly merits attention.

What if, on the other hand, the rescue efforts fail and the condor joins the ranks of the extinct? Is all lost? Not likely, for it may be rational to design and implement policies even where uncertainty predicts a chance—even a large chance—of failure. A single case of failure after the fact does not necessarily indicate ill-conceived policy; all cases taken together may nonetheless produce the expected outcome. Furthermore, saving the species may be largely incidental. What is important, some argue, is the scientific knowledge, the increased understanding of public policy making, and the public education that occur. But this raises the same question again: Is it better to expend limited resources learning with the condor or learning with some other species or in some other way?

Finally, we can ask not about the benefits of saving or trying to save the condor but about the costs of failing to make the effort. It is one thing to accept the unknowing extinction of species, but it is quite another for society to knowingly forego an opportunity to prevent that same extinction, which is a much more painful decision. In addition, once we have made a commitment to save a species, the recovery effort—especially in the case of the condor and a few other highly visible species—takes on additional importance, symbolizing our collective willingness to address the consequences of human impact on the biosphere. Abandonment of the effort suggests a certain futility that might threaten the integrity of other environmental policies.

The rhetorical questions continue. How much of society's resources are we willing to devote to any or all of these matters? At one level we can ask whether, of a given $30 million budget for the federal endangered species program, more should be devoted to the condor and less to the whooping crane. At another level we can ask whether, of a given $400 million budget for FWS, more should be devoted to listing and preservation of individual species and less to acquiring wildlife refuge lands or building federal fish hatcheries. Of a $4 billion budget for the Department of the Interior, should more be devoted to wildlife and less to firefighting in the national parks or regulating all-terrain vehicles on Western desert lands? Of a $1 trillion federal budget, should more be devoted to the Interior Department and less to strategic defense initiatives or food stamps? Of the $4 trillion economy, should more be allocated to the federal government and less to the state and local governments or the private sector? And furthermore, how does this allocation affect the total value of the resources to be divided and ultimately available to the condor? Decisions are being made simultaneously on all of these levels, and similar simultaneous processes are at work within state and local governments and nonprofit organizations.

These questions were phrased as if all parties were striving to serve the public interest. But of course they are not necessarily doing so.[3] Individuals and organizations pursue personal and organizational goals that may have little in common with the public interest. Individuals seek power and prestige, promotion and prominence. Organizations seek survival, growth, and influence. The results of these actions are consonant with the public interest to varying degrees. Alternatively, while individuals and groups may work in good faith toward the public interest, they may hold conflicting visions of it. Thus, while some actors in the system strive harmoniously toward common goals, others work at cross-purposes, sometimes out of conflict over strategies but at other times out of conflict over values.

Thus there are two sets of reasons why we might have cause to suspect the merits of existing policy responses to the condor or, for that matter, to other wildlife concerns. First, the system is too complex to produce the planners' outcomes, and second, even if such outcomes could conceptually be produced, individuals and organizations are not always responding to incentives that support their production.

It may appear that we are inevitably at some remove from "good policy" and that widespread public participation, decentralized decision making, and a robust nonprofit sector have taken us there. But the complexity of the issues and the deeply held constituency values do not recommend obvious alternatives. Wildlife policies unfold gradually, through the institutionalized interplay of organizations and interests, as illustrated by the history of our relationship with the California condor. These interests, and the values they reflect, could not otherwise have been anticipated. We are left with a participatory decision-making process reflecting a yeasty mix of perspectives and positions—a process that itself evolves in response to the unfolding of interests and issues.

Central to this study is the fact that wildlife is not merely any resource. Participatory claims derive strength not only from the participatory traditions of the nation but from a history of special caring for wildlife and from public involvement in its management. Although the focus of this study has been on organizations, it has been made clear throughout that organizations consist of individuals—individuals with passions, interests, and deeply held beliefs—individuals with idiosyncrasies, with single-minded devotion to their vision of right and justice, often without regard for the usual calculus of self-interest.

The preface to this book highlighted two features of the study: its industrywide orientation and its nonprofit focus. As to the first, it was suggested that, despite its complexity, the industry view would reveal critical aspects of the wildlife issue-area that a narrower view would obscure. Policy toward wildlife resources is severely constrained by laws, values, and preferences as old as the nation. These constraints are selectively relaxed and tightened in response to new information, technological change, and patterns of supply and demand. Constituencies are caught up in this evolution, protecting their legitimacy and influence as well as their substantive interests. Within the broad industry context, organizational resources flow rather freely; a narrow focus misses these dynamics. Thus, in the industry setting, performance can be viewed more broadly than in terms of the efficiency of a single organization.

The second feature of this study is its emphasis on nonprofit organizations. It is clear that nonprofits are important in the wildlife issue area. They control and mobilize substantial resources that have important implications for the allocation of rights to wildlife and ultimate patterns of interactions with wildlife. While most of the resources employed within the nonprofit sector would find employment in other sectors were the nonprofit form unavailable, there would be efficiency losses and distributional changes as a result.

The nonprofit form adds a dimension to the realm of organizational choice. This additional degree of freedom increases the efficiency of resource use; by permitting individuals more latitude in creating organizational settings that increase their productivity, a closer match is permitted between resources and roles. The contribution that this diversity makes to static efficiency is offset, to some extent, by the stalemate in collective decision making that may result from the proliferation of legitimate constituencies and the resources that are consumed by their interaction.

The more important claims for nonprofit organizations lie in the realm of dynamic rather than static efficiency. Nonprofit organizations, and especially interest groups, tend to be more flexible than government agencies that are bound by statutory, budgetary, and political constraints. Nonprofit organizations may undertake tasks that governments are prohibited from undertaking and that proprietary firms cannot justify. This role is especially important in the international arena, where the institutional framework is weak.

Nonprofits mediate between the corporate and government worlds, on the one hand, and the public, on the other hand, interpreting and translating activities into language meaningful to their constituents, actual and potential. Selective interpretation may, of course, serve the narrower goals of organizations and individuals rather than a latent public interest (to the extent that such an interest can be said to exist prior to its elicitation in a particular form). The critical element of this dynamic component is the role that nonprofits play in articulating competing values and visions of the future. They facilitate orderly transitions to those futures. Within the realm of wildlife policy, the transitions from unlimited harvest to game management and from game management to more comprehensive views of rights and responsibilities toward wildlife have been facilitated, if not actually created, by a large and energetic nonprofit sector.

NOTES

1. Michael E. Soulé, "Opinion: Scarce Resources and Endangered Species," *Endangered Species Technical Bulletin Reprint* 4 (December 1986–January 1987): 5.

2. Alan Randall, "Human Preferences, Economics, and the Preservation of Species," in *The Preservation of Species: The Value of Biological Diversity*, edited by Bryan G. Norton (Princeton, N.J.: Princeton University Press, 1986), pp. 86–89.

3. Steven Kelman, "Public Choice and the Public Spirit," *Public Interest* 87 (Spring 1987): 80–94.

Selected Bibliography

Akey, Denise, ed. *Encyclopedia of Associations—1986.* 20th ed. Detroit: Gale Research, 1985.

Allen, Durward L. *Our Wildlife Legacy.* Rev. ed. New York: Funk & Wagnalls, 1962.

Allen, Jeremiah. "Anti-Sealing as an Industry." *Journal of Political Economy* 87 (1979): 423-28.

Andrews, Richard H. L. *Environmental Policy and Administrative Change: Implementation of the National Environmental Policy Act.* Lexington, Mass.: Lexington, D. C. Heath, 1976.

Bean, Michael J. *The Evolution of National Wildlife Law.* Rev. ed. New York: Praeger, 1983.

Berry, Jeffrey M. *Lobbying for the People: The Political Behavior of Public Interest Groups.* Princeton, N.J.: Princeton University Press, 1977.

——— . "On the Origins of Public Interest Groups: A Test of Two Theories." *Polity* 10 (Spring 1978): 379-97.

——— . *The Interest Group Society.* Boston: Little, Brown, 1984.

Bingham, Gail. *Resolving Environmental Disputes: A Decade of Experience.* Washington, D.C.: Conservation Foundation, 1986.

Borrelli, Peter. "Environmentalism at the Crossroads." *Amicus Journal*, Summer 1987, pp. 24-37.

Bradley, Dorthea M., and Helen M. Ingram. "Science vs. the Grass Roots: Representation in the Bureau of Land Management." *Natural Resources Journal* 26 (Summer 1986): 493-518.

Brookshire, David S., Larry S. Eubanks, and Alan Randall. "Estimating Option Prices and Existence Values for Wildlife Resources." *Land Economics* 59 (1983): 1-15.

Brower, Kenneth. "The Naked Vulture and the Thinking Ape." *Atlantic*, October 1983, pp. 70–88.

Brownstein, Ronald. "On Paper, Conservative PACs Were Tigers in 1984—But Look Again." *National Journal*, June 29, 1984, pp. 1504-9.

Burke, Tom. "Friends of the Earth and the Conservation of Resources." In *Pressure Groups in the Global System: The Transnational Relations of Issue-Oriented Non-Government Organizations*, edited by Peter Willetts. New York: St. Martin's, 1982.

Cahn, Robert, ed. *An Environmental Agenda for the Future*. Washington, D.C.: Agenda Press, 1985.

Caplin, Mortimer M., and Richard E. Timbie. "Legislative Activities of Public Charities." *Law and Contemporary Problems* 39 (Autumn 1975): 183–210.

Carter, Luther J. "Environmental Lobbyists Quarrel over Endangered Species Act." *Science* 201 (September 15, 1978): 997.

———. "Environmentalists Seek New Strategies." *Science* 208 (May 2, 1980): 477-78.

Cerulean, Susan, and Whit Fosburgh. "State Nongame Programs." In *Audubon Wildlife Report 1986*, edited by Roger DiSilvestro, New York: National Audubon Society, 1986, pp. 631-56.

Chaimov, Gregory A., and James E. Durr. "*Defenders of Wildlife Inc. v. Endangered Species Scientific Authority*: The Court as Biologist." *Environmental Law* 12 (1982): 773-810.

Chandler, William J. "Migratory Bird Protection and Management." In *Audubon Wildlife Report 1986*, edited by Roger DiSilvestro, New York: National Audubon Society, 1986, pp. 236-40.

Cigler, Allan J., and Burdett A. Loomis, eds. *Interest Group Politics*. 2nd ed. Washington, D.C.: Congressional Quarterly Press, 1986.

Close, Arthur C., John P. Gregg, and Regina Germain, eds. *Washington Representatives—1986*. Washington, D.C.: Columbus Books, 1986.

Clough, N. K., P. C. Patton, and A. C. Christiansen, eds. *Arctic National Wildlife Refuge, Alaska, Coastal Plain Resource Assessment: Report and Recommendation to the Congress of the United States and Final Legislative Environmental Impact Statement*. 2 vols. Washington, D.C.: U.S. Fish and Wildlife Service, U.S. Geological Survey, and Bureau of Land Management, 1987.

Cobb, Roger W., and Charles D. Elder. *Participation in American Politics: The Dynamics of Agenda-Building*. 2nd ed. Baltimore: Johns Hopkins University Press, 1983.

Common Cause. *Who's Minding the Store? A Common Cause Guide to Top Officials at the Department of the Interior*. Washington, D.C.: Common Cause, 1981.

Conway, M. Margaret. "PACs and Congressional Elections in the 1980s." In *Interest Group Politics*, 2d. ed., edited by Allan J. Cigler and Burdett A. Loomis. Washington, D.C.: Congressional Quarterly Press, 1986, pp. 70-90.

Cooper, Toby. "Blow by Blow: Calling the Punches in Washington's Battle of the Bowhead." *Defenders*, February 1978, pp. 58-61.

Cooperrider, Allen Y. "BLM's Desert Bighorn Sheep Program." In *Transactions of the Fifty-first North American Wildlife and Natural Resources Conference*. Washington, D.C.: Wildlife Management Institute, 1986, pp. 45-51.

Costain, W. Douglas, and Anne N. Costain. "Interest Groups as Policy Aggregators in the Legislative Press." *Polity* 14 (Winter 1981): 249-72.

Council on Environmental Quality. *Environmental Quality: The Annual Report of the Council on Environmental Quality*, 1970-85. Washington, D.C.: Government Printing Office, 1970-1987.

————. *Environmental Impact Statements: An Analysis of Six Years' Experience by Seventy Federal Agencies*. Washington, DC, March 1976.

————. *Public Opinion on Environmental Issues: Results of a National Public Opinion Survey*. Washington, D.C.: Government Printing Office, 1980.

———— and U.S. Department of State. *The Global 2000 Report to the President: Entering the Twenty-first Century*. 2 vols. Washington, D.C.: Government Printing Office, 1980.

Crawford, Mark. "The Last Days of the Wild Condor?" *Science* 229 (August 30, 1985): 844-45.

Culhane, Paul J. "Natural Resources Policy: Procedural Change and Substantive Environmentalism." In *Nationalizing Government*, edited by Theodore Lowi. New York: Sage, 1977, pp. 201-62.

————. *Public Lands Politics: Interest Group Influence on the Forest Service and the Bureau of Land Management*. Baltimore: published for Resources for the Future by Johns Hopkins University Press, 1981.

Cupps, D. Stephen. "Emerging Problems of Citizen Participation." *Public Administration Review* 37 (September-October 1977): 478-87.

Defenders of Wildlife. *Saving Endangered Species*. Annual, 1984-86.

Demkovich, Linda E. "From Public Interest Advocates to Administration Defenders." *National Journal*, November 25, 1978, pp. 1892-98.

Devall, Bill. "The Deep Ecology Movement." *Natural Resources Journal* 20 (April 1980): 299-322.

DiMaggio, Paul J., and Walter W. Powell. "The Iron Cage Revisited: Institutional Isomorphism and Collective Rationality in Organizational Fields." *American Sociological Review* 48 (April 1983): 147-60.

Drew, Elizabeth. *Senator*. New York: Simon and Schuster, 1979.

Elliott, E. Donald, Bruce A. Ackerman, and John C. Millian. "Toward a Theory of Statutory Evolution: The Federalization of Environmental Law." *Journal of Law, Economics, and Organization* 1 (1985): 313-40.

Erlich, Paul, and Anne Erlich. *Extinction: The Causes and Consequences of the Disappearance of Species*. New York: Random House, 1981.

Fairfax, Sally K. "A Disaster in the Environmental Movement." *Science* 199 (February 17, 1978): 743–48.

———. "Environmental Assessment: Gains and Challenges." In *Transactions of the Forty-sixth North American Wildlife and Natural Resources Conference*. Washington, D.C.: Wildlife Management Institute, 1981, pp. 27–34.

——— and Barbara T. Andrews. "Debate Within and Debate Without: NEPA and the Redefinition of the 'Prudent Man' Rule." *Natural Resources Journal* 19 (July 1979): 505–35.

Feldstein, Martin, and Charles Clotfelter. "Tax Incentives and Charitable Contributions in the United States." *Journal of Public Economics* 5 (1976): 1–26.

Fisher, Anthony C. *Resource and Environmental Economics*. Cambridge: Cambridge University Press, 1981.

Fleming, Donald. "Roots of the New Conservation Movement." In *Perspectives in American History*, vol. 6, edited by Donald Fleming and Bernard Bailyn, pp. 7–91. Cambridge, Mass.: Charles Warren Center for Studies in American History, Harvard University, 1972.

Forsythe, David P. "Humanizing American Foreign Policy: Non-Profit Lobbying and Human Rights." Program on Non-Profit Organizations, Yale University, Working Paper No. 12, 1980.

——— and Susan Welch. "Citizen Support for Non-Profit Public Interest Groups." Program on Non-Profit Organizations, Yale University, Working Paper No. 35, n.d.

Foster, Charles H. W. "Counsel for the Concerned." In *Law and the Environment*, edited by Malcolm F. Baldwin and James K. Page. New York: Walker, 1970, pp. 277–88.

Fox, Stephen. *John Muir and His Legacy: The American Conservation Movement*. Boston: Little, Brown, 1981.

Friends of the Earth et al. *Ronald Reagan and the American Environment: An Indictment, Alternate Budget Proposal, and Citizen's Guide to Action*. San Francisco: Friends of the Earth, 1982.

Frome, Michael. "Carter & Friends: Tarnished Halos." *Defenders*, June 1979, pp. 166–68.

Fuller, Doug. "American Ginseng: Harvest and Export, 1982–1984." *Traffic (USA)*, June 1986, p. 7.

Gilbert, Bil. "The Nature Conservancy Game." *Sports Illustrated*, October 20, 1986, pp. 86–100.

Gluesing, Ernest A., S. Douglas Miller, and Richard M. Mitchell. "Management of the North American Bobcat: Information Needs for Nondetriment Findings." In *Transactions of the Fifty-first North American Wildlife and*

Natural Resources Conference, Washington, D.C.: Wildlife Management Institute, 1986, pp. 183-192.

Glynn, Carroll J., and Albert R. Tims. "Environmental and Natural Resource Issues: Press Sensationalism." In *Transactions of the Forty-fifth North American Wildlife and Natural Resources Conference*. Washington, D.C.: Wildlife Management Institute, 1980, pp. 99-109.

Goetz, Charles J., and Gordon Brady. "Environmental Policy Formation and the Tax Treatment of Citizen Interest Groups." *Law and Contemporary Problems* 39 (1975): 211-31.

Golton, Robert J. "Mediation: A 'Sell-out' for Conservation Advocates? or a Bargain?" In *Transactions of the Forty-fifth North American Wildlife and Natural Resources Conference*. Washington, D.C.: Wildlife Management Institute, 1980, pp. 83-89.

Graham, Frank J., Jr. "A New Hand in the Wildlife Business." *Audubon*, May 1979, pp. 94-113.

———. "The Folks Who Work on the Hill," *Audubon*, July 1980, pp. 108-19.

Granville Corporation. *Study of Land and Water Conservation Fund Financial Assistance Alternative*. Washington, D.C.: Division of State Programs, Heritage Conservation and Recreation Service, U.S. Department of the Interior, 1981.

Greenwalt, Lynn A. "A Federal Agency Perspective." *Nature Conservancy News*, March-April 1981, pp. 18-21.

Haefele, Edwin T. *Representative Government and Environmental Management*. Baltimore: Johns Hopkins University Press, 1973.

Handler, Joel F. *Social Movements and the Legal System: A Theory of Law Reform and Social Change*. New York: Academic Press, 1978.

———, Betsy Ginsberg, and Arthur Snow. "The Public Interest Law Industry." In *Public Interest Law: An Economic and Institutional Analysis*, Burton A. Weisbrod, study director, in collaboration with Joel F. Handler and Neil K. Komesar. Berkeley: University of California Press, 1978, pp. 42-79.

Hansmann, Henry. "The Role of Nonprofit Enterprise." *Yale Law Journal* 89 (April 1980): 835-902.

———. "The Rationale for Exempting Nonprofit Organizations from the Corporate Income Tax." *Yale Law Journal* 91 (1981): 54-100.

Harris, Lis. "Brother Sun, Sister Moon." *New Yorker*, April 27, 1987, pp. 87-101.

Heard, Jamie. "Washington Pressures/Friends of the Earth Give Environmental Interests an Activist Voice." *National Journal*, August 8, 1970, pp. 1711-19.

Heclo, Hugh. "Issue Networks and the Executive Establishment." In *The New American Political System*, edited by Anthony King. Washington, D.C.: American Enterprise Institute, 1978, pp. 87-124.

Henderson, Hazel. *Creating Alternative Futures: The End of Economics.* New York: Berkley, 1978.

Herbst, Robert L. "A National Fish and Wildlife Policy." In *Transactions of the Forty-fifth North American Wildlife and Natural Resources Conference.* Washington, D.C., Wildlife Management Institute, 1980, pp. 51-55.

Hodgkinson, Virginia Ann, and Murray S. Weitzman. *Dimensions of the Independent Sector: A Statistical Profile.* 2nd ed. Washington, D.C.: Independent Sector, 1986.

Holden, Constance. "Condor Flap in California." *Science* 209 (August 8, 1980): 670-72.

Iker, Sam. "The Crackdown on Animal Smuggling." *National Wildlife*, October-November 1979, pp. 33-39.

————. "The Great American Snake Sting and Other Tales of Intrigue." *National Wildlife*, February-March 1982, pp. 13-15.

Jackson, John. "'People or Ducks?' Who Decides?" In *Economic Analysis of Environmental Problems*, edited by Edwin S. Mills. New York: Columbia University Press, 1975, pp. 351-94.

James, Estelle, "How Nonprofits Grow: A Model." *Journal of Policy Analysis and Management* 2 (Spring 1983): 350-65.

Jasanoff, Sheila. *Risk Management and Political Culture: A Comparative Study of Science in the Policy Context.* Social Research Perspectives, Occasional Reports on Current Topics No. 12. New York: Russell Sage Foundation, 1986.

Jenkins, J. Craig. "Nonprofit Organizations and Policy Advocacy." In *The Nonprofit Sector: A Research Handbook*, edited by Walter W. Powell. New Haven, Conn.: Yale University Press, 1987, pp. 296-318.

Jenkins, Robert E. "Habitat Preservation by Private Organizations." In Council on Environmental Quality, *Wildlife and America: Contributions to an Understanding of American Wildlife and Its Conservation*, edited by Howard P. Brokaw. Washington, D.C.: Government Printing Office, 1978, pp. 413-27.

Johnson, William Weber. "California Condor: Embroiled in a Flap Not of Its Making." *Smithsonian*, December 1985, pp. 73-80.

Jorgenson, Amanda. "Biologists Express Concern for Huge Trade in Bullfrogs." *Traffic (USA)*, April 1985, pp. 25-26.

Kahn, E. J. "The Indigenists." *New Yorker*, August 31, 1981, pp. 60-77.

Kann, Mark E. "Environmental Democracy in the United States." In *Controversies in Environmental Policy*, edited by Sheldon Kamieniecki, Robert O'Brien, and Michael Clarke. Albany: State University of New York Press, 1986, pp. 252-74.

Kasowski, Kevin. "Showdown on the Hunting Ground." *Outdoor America*, Winter 1986, pp. 8-34.

Kaufman, Herbert. *Time, Chance, and Organizations: Natural Selection in a Perilous Environment.* Chatham, N.J.: Chatham House, 1985.

Kellert, Stephen R. *Phase I: Public Attitudes toward Critical Wildlife and Natural Habitat Issues.* U.S. Fish and Wildlife Service, October 15, 1979.

———. *Phase II: Activities of the American Public Relating to Animals.* U.S. Fish and Wildlife Service, April 1980.

———. and Joyce K. Berry. *Phase III: Knowledge, Affection and Basic Attitudes toward Animals in American Society.* U.S. Fish and Wildlife Service, 1980.

Kelman, Steven. "'Public Choice' and Public Spirit." *Public Interest* 87 (Spring 1987): 80–94.

Kenski, Henry C., and Helen M. Ingram. "The Reagan Administration and Environmental Regulation: The Constraint of the Political Market." In *Controversies in Environmental Policy*, edited by Seldon Kamieniecki, Robert O'Brien, and Michael Clark. Albany: State University of New York Press, 1986, pp. 275–98.

King, F. Wayne. "Preservation of Genetic Diversity." In *Sustaining Tomorrow: A Strategy for World Conservation and Development*, edited by Francis R. Thibodeau and Hermann H. Field. Hanover, N.H.: published for Tufts University by University Press of New England, 1984, pp. 41–55.

Kirschten, Dick. "Environmentalists Tell Carter Thanks but No Thanks." *National Journal*, June 23, 1979, pp. 1036–39.

Krutilla, John V. "Conservation Reconsidered." *American Economic Review* 47 (1967): 777–96.

Langeneau, Edward E., Jr. "Anticipating Wildlife Values of Tomorrow." In *Valuing Wildlife: Economic and Social Perspectives*, edited by Daniel J. Decker and Gary R. Goff. Boulder, Colo.: Westview, 1987, pp. 309–17.

Leopold, Aldo. *Game Management.* New York: Scribner's, 1933.

Lewin, Roger. "Damage to Tropical Forests, or Why Were There So Many Kinds of Animals?" *Science* 234 (October 10, 1986): 149–50.

Leyland, R. C. "Last Flight of the Condor." *Whole Life Monthly*, July 1986, p. 30.

Lindblom, Charles E. *The Policy-making Process.* 2nd ed., Englewood Cliffs, N.J.: Prentice-Hall, 1980.

Lipske, Michael C. "Washington Outlook—Administration Brings Cheer to Conservationists." *Defenders*, June 1977, pp. 213–14.

———. "Washington Outlook: Who Can Speak for the Public?" *Defenders*, February 1978, pp. 70–71.

Livengood, Kerry B. "Value of Big Game from Markets for Hunting Leases." *Land Economics* 59 (1983): 287–91.

Loomis, Burdett A., and Allan J. Cigler. "Introduction: The Changing Nature of Interest Group Politics." In *Interest Group Politics*, 2d. ed., edited by Cigler and Loomis. Washington, D.C.: Congressional Quarterly Press, 1986, pp. 1–26.

Lowe, Philip, and Jane Goyder. *Environmental Groups in Politics*. London: Allen & Unwin, 1983.

Luoma, Jon R. "Forests Are Dying but Is Acid Rain to Blame?" *Audubon*, March 1987, pp. 37–51.

Lyster, Simon. *International Wildlife Law: An Analysis of International Treaties Concerned with the Conservation of Wildlife*. Research Centre for International Law, University of Cambridge, with International Union for the Conservation of Nature and Natural Resources. Cambridge: Grotius, 1985.

McFarland, Andrew S. *Public Interest Lobbies: Decision Making on Energy*. Washington, D.C.: American Enterprise Institute, 1978.

––––––. *Common Cause: Lobbying in the Public Interest*. Chatham, N.J.: Chatham House, 1984.

McNulty, Faith. "The Last Days of the Condor." *Audubon*, March 1978, pp. 53–87, and May 1978, pp. 78–100.

Magida, Arthur J. "Environment Report: Movement Undaunted by Economic, Energy Crises." *National Journal*, January 17, 1976, pp. 61–68.

Matthiessen, Peter. *Wildlife in America*. New York: Viking, 1959.

Mazmanian, Daniel A., and Jeanne Nienaber. *Can Organizations Change? Environmental Protection, Citizen Participation, and the Corps of Engineers*. Washington, D.C.: Brookings Institution, 1979.

Merchant, Ginger. "Thwarting the Effort to 'Unlist' Bobcats." *Defenders*, April 1979, pp. 119–20.

––––––. "Defenders and Bobcats Win Appeals Court Decision." *Defenders*, June 1981, pp. 46–47.

Metzger, Philip C. "Public-Private Partnerships for Land Conservation." In *Transactions of the Forty-eighth North American Wildlife and Natural Resources Conference*. Washington, D.C.: Wildlife Management Institute, 1983, pp. 423–32.

Milbrath, Lester W. *Environmentalists: Vanguard for a New Society*. Albany: State University of New York Press, 1984.

Mitchell, Robert Cameron. "National Environmental Lobbies and the Apparent Illogic of Collective Action." In *Collective Decision Making: Applications from Public Choice Theory*, edited by Clifford S. Russell. Baltimore: Johns Hopkins University Press, 1979, pp. 87–136.

––––––. "Public Opinion and Environmental Politics in the 1970s and 1980s." In *Environmental Policy in the 1980s: Reagan's New Agenda*, edited by Norman J. Vig and Michael E. Kraft. Washington, D.C.: Congressional Quarterly Press, 1984, pp. 51–74.

––––––. "From Conservation to Environmental Movement: The Development of the Modern Environmental Lobbies." Resources for the Future, Discussion Paper QE85-12, June 1985.

—— and J. Clarence Davies, III. "The United States Environmental Movement and Its Political Context: An Overview." Resources for the Future Discussion Paper D-32, May 1978.

Moe, Terry M. *The Organization of Interests: Incentives and the Internal Dynamics of Political Interest Groups.* Chicago: University of Chicago Press, 1980.

Myers, Norman. *A Wealth of Wild Species: Storehouse for Human Welfare.* Boulder, Colo.: Westview, 1983.

National Audubon Society. *Audubon Wildlife Report.* New York: National Audubon Society, 1985, 1986.

National Wildlife Federation. *Conservation Directory: List of Organizations, Agencies, and Officials Concerned with Natural Resource Use and Management.* Washington, D.C.: National Wildlife Federation, annual.

Nilsson, Greta. *The Endangered Species Handbook.* Washington, D.C.: Animal Welfare Institute, 1983.

—— et al. *Facts about Furs.* 3rd ed. Washington, D.C.: Animal Welfare Institute, 1980.

Nugent, John Peer. "Is the California Condor Worth Saving?" *National Wildlife,* August–September 1981, pp. 25–29.

Oldfield, Margery L. *The Value of Conserving Genetic Resources.* U.S. Department of the Interior, National Park Service. Washington, D.C.: Government Printing Office, 1984.

Olson, Mancur. *The Logic of Collective Action.* Cambridge, Mass.: Harvard University Press, 1965.

Orren, Karen. "Standing to Sue: Interest Group Conflict in the Federal Courts." *American Political Science Review* 70 (1976): 723–41.

Permut, Steven E. "Consumer Perceptions of Nonprofit Enterprise." *Yale Law Journal* 90 (1981): 1623–38.

Peterson, Roger Tory. *Field Guide to the Birds East of the Rockies,* 4th ed. Boston: Houghton Mifflin, 1980.

Phillips, David, and Hugh Nash, eds. *The Condor Question: Captive or Forever Free?* San Francisco: Friends of the Earth, 1981.

Prescott-Allen, Christine, and Robert Prescott-Allen. *The First Resource: Wild Species in the North American Economy.* New Haven: Yale University Press, 1986.

Randall, Alan. "Human Preferences, Economics, and the Preservation of Species." In *The Preservation of Species: The Value of Biological Diversity,* edited by Bryan G. Norton. Princeton, N.J.: Princeton University Press, 1986, pp. 79–109.

Raup, David M. "Biological Extinction in Earth History." *Science* 231 (March 28, 1986): 1528–33.

Reiger, George. "Kangaroo Imperialism." *Field and Stream,* February 1984, pp. 38–43.

Reiger, John F. *American Sportsmen and the Origins of Conservation.* New York: Winchester, 1975.

Riccuiti, Edward R. "Shady Dealings." *Audubon*, January 1982, pp. 26-29.

Ricklefs, Robert E., ed. *Report of the Advisory Panel on the California Condor.* Audubon Conservation Report No. 6. New York: National Audubon Society, 1978.

Rose-Ackerman, Susan. "Charitable Giving and 'Excessive' Fundraising Costs." *Quarterly Journal of Economics* 97 (1982): 193-212.

—— and Estelle James. "The Nonprofit Enterprise in Market Economies." Yale University, Program on Non-Profit Organizations, Working Paper No. 95, July 1985.

Sagoff, Mark. "On the Preservation of Species." *Columbia Journal of Environmental Law* 7 (1980): 33-67.

—— . "We Have Met the Enemy and He Is Us, or Conflict and Contradiction in Environmental Law." *Environmental Law* 12 (1982): 283-315.

Salisbury, Robert H. "An Exchange Theory of Interest Groups." *Midwest Journal of Political Science* 13 (February 1969): 1-32.

—— . "Interest Representation: The Dominance of Institutions." *American Political Science Review* 78 (1984): 64-76.

—— . "Washington Lobbyists: A Collective Portrait." In *Interest Group Politics*, 2nd ed., edited by Allan J. Cigler and Burdett A. Loomis. Washington, D.C.: Congressional Quarterly Press, 1986, pp. 146-61.

Schectman, Susan M. "The 'Bambi Syndrome': How NEPA's Public Participation in Wildlife Management Is Hurting the Environment." *Environmental Law* 8 (1978): 611-43.

Scherer, Frederic. *Industrial Market Structure and Economic Performance.* 2nd ed. Chicago: Rand McNally, 1980.

Schlozman, Kay Lehman, "What Accent the Heavenly Chorus? Political Equality and the American Pressure System." *Journal of Politics* 46 (1984): 1006-32.

—— and John T. Tierney. "More of the Same: Washington Pressure Group Activity in a Decade of Change." *Journal of Politics* 45 (1983): 351-77.

Sierra Club. *Report of the Sierra Club California Condor Advisory Committee,* August 1980.

Sills, David L. "The Environmental Movement and Its Critics." *Human Ecology* 3 (1975): 1-41.

Simon, John G. "Charity and Dynasty under the Federal Tax System." *Probate Lawyer* 5 (1978).

Singer, James W. "That Old Public Interest Movement Gang Moves into New— and Private—Fields." *National Journal*, February 14, 1981, pp. 269-73.

Skloot, Edward. "Enterprise and Commerce in Nonprofit Organizations." In *The Nonprofit Sector: A Research Handbook*, edited by Walter W. Powell. New Haven: Yale University Press, 1987, pp. 380-93.

Smith, Robert J. "Resolving the Tragedy of the Commons by Creating Private Property Rights in Wildlife." *Cato Journal* 1 (Fall 1981): 439-68.

Smith, V. Kerry. "The Green Lobby." *American Political Science Review* 79 (1985): 133-47.

Soulé, Michael E. "Opinion: Scarce Resources and Endangered Species." *Endangered Species Technical Bulletin Reprint* 4 (December 1986-January 1987): 5.

Stahr, Elvis J., and Charles H. Callison. "The Role of Private Organizations." In Council on Environmental Quality, *Wildlife and America: Contributions to an Understanding of American Wildlife and Conservation*, edited by Howard P. Brokaw. Washington, D.C.: Government Printing Office, 1978, pp. 498-511.

Stanfield, Rochelle L. "Environmental Lobby's Changing of the Guard is Part of Movement's Evolution." *National Journal*, June 8, 1985, pp. 1350-53.

――――. "Tilting on Development." *National Journal*, February 7, 1987, pp. 313-18.

Starnes, Richard. "Starnes at Large: Hunting's Newest Powderkeg." *Outdoor Life*, May 1978, pp. 11-18.

――――. "Starnes at Large: Exploding the Anti-Hunting Myth." *Outdoor Life*, April 1980, pp. 10-16.

Steinhart, Peter. "Wildlife Films: End of an Era?" *National Wildlife*, December-January 1980, pp. 37-45.

――――. "Talking It Over." *Audubon*, January 1984, pp. 8-13.

――――. "Abundance." *Audubon*, January 1987, pp. 8-11.

Stokey, Edith, and Richard Zeckhauser. *A Primer for Policy Analysis.* New York: Norton, 1978.

Stoll, John R., and Lee Ann Johnson. "Concepts of Value, Nonmarket Valuation, and the Case of the Whooping Crane." Natural Resources Work Group, Natural Resources Working Paper Series. Department of Agricultural Economics, Texas A & M University, 1984.

Stone, Christopher D. *Should Trees Have Standing? Toward Legal Rights for Natural Objects.* Los Altos, Calif.: William Kaufmann, 1974.

Stranahan, Susan Q. "Many Happy Returns for Wildlife." *National Wildlife*, April-May 1987, pp. 50-51.

Stroup, Richard L., and John A. Baden. *Natural Resources: Bureaucratic Myths and Environmental Management.* Pacific Studies in Public Policy. Cambridge, Mass.: Ballinger, 1983.

Susskind, Lawrence, and Alan Weinstein. "Towards a Theory of Environmental Dispute Resolution." *Boston College Environmental Affairs Law Review* 9 (1980-81): 311-57.

Susskind, Lawrence, and Gerard McMahon. "The Theory and Practice of Negotiated Rulemaking." *Yale Journal on Regulation* 3 (1985): 133-65.

Thompson, Grant P. "New Faces, New Opportunities." *Environment* 27 (May 1985): 6–30.

Tober, James A. *Who Owns the Wildlife? The Political Economy of Conservation in Nineteenth-Century America.* Westport, Conn.: Greenwood, 1981.

Trefethen, James. *Crusade for Wildlife: Highlights in Conservation Progress.* Harrisburg, Pa.: Stackpole Company and Boone and Crockett Club, 1961.

Troy, Kathryn. *Annual Survey of Corporate Contributions, 1984 Edition.* New York: Conference Board, 1984.

Trubek, David M. "Environmental Defense I: Introduction to Interest Group Advocacy." In *Public Interest Law: An Economic and Institutional Analysis*, Burton A. Weisbrod, study director, in collaboration with Joel F. Handler and Neil K. Komesar, Berkeley: University of California Press, 1978, pp. 151–94.

————— and William J. Gillen. "Environmental Defense II: Examining the Limits of Interest Group Advocacy." In *Public Interest Law: An Economic and Institutional Analysis*, Burton A. Weisbrod, study director, in collaboration with Joel F. Handler and Neil K. Komesar, Berkeley: University of California Press, 1978, pp. 195–217.

Truman, David B. *The Governmental Process.* 2nd ed. New York: Knopf, 1971.

Tucker, William. *Progress and Privilege: America in the Age of Environmentalism.* Garden City, N.Y.: Anchor Press, Doubleday, 1982.

U.S. Congress. Senate. Subcommittee on Governmental Affairs. *Congress and Pressure Groups: Lobbying in a Modern Democracy.* Report prepared by the Congressional Research Service, June 1986. 99th Cong., 2d sess., S. Prt. 99–161.

U.S. Department of the Interior. Fish and Wildlife Service. *Recommendations for Implementing the California Condor Contingency Plan.* 1979.

—————. *Final Environmental Assessment: Conservation of the California Condor by Trapping and Captive Propagation.* December 1979.

—————. *California Condor Recovery Plan.* U.S. Fish and Wildlife Service in Cooperation with the Recovery Team, January 1980.

—————. *Draft Environmental Assessment: Conservation of the California Condor by Trapping and Captive Propagation*, 1981.

—————. *California Condor Recovery Plan.* Portland, Oreg.: U.S. Fish and Wildlife Service, July 31, 1984.

—————. *Potential Funding Sources to Implement the Fish and Wildlife Conservation Act of 1980.* Biological Report 85 (5), March 1985.

—————. *Restoring America's Wildlife, 1937–1987: The First 50 Years of the Federal Aid in Wildlife Restoration (Pittman-Robertson) Act.* Washington, D.C.: Government Printing Office, 1987.

————— and U.S. Department of Commerce. Bureau of the Census. *1980 National Survey of Fishing, Hunting, and Wildlife-associated Recreation.* Washington, D.C.: Government Printing Office, 1982.

U.S. Department of State. *Draft Environmental Impact Statement concerning the Convention on the Conservation of Migratory Species of Wild Animals Proposed by the Federal Republic of Germany.* Vol. 2, Appendixes.

———. and U.S. Department of the Interior. *Conserving International Wildlife Resources: The United States Response.* Report to Congress by the Secretary of State and the Secretary of the Interior, December 1984.

U.S. General Accounting Office. *Federal Land Acquisition and Management Practices.* September 11, 1981. CED-81-135.

Useem, Michael. "Corporate Philanthropy." In *The Nonprofit Sector: A Research Handbook*, edited by Walter W. Powell. New Haven, Conn.: Yale University Press, 1987, pp. 340-59.

Vogel, David. "The Power of Business in America: A Re-Appraisal." *British Journal of Political Science* 13 (1983): 19-43.

———. "The New Political Science of Corporate Power." *Public Interest*, no. 87 (Spring 1987): 63-79.

Walker, Jack L. "The Origins and Maintenance of Interest Groups in America." *American Political Science Review* 77 (1983): 390-406.

Ward, Bud, and Jan Floyd. "Washington Lobby Groups . . . How They Rate." *Environmental Forum*, 3 (April 1985), unpaged reprint.

Weber, Michael. "TEDs: Salvation for Sea Turtles?" *Defenders*, January–February 1987, pp. 8-13.

Weisbrod, Burton A. "Toward a Theory of the Voluntary Nonprofit Sector in a Three-Sector Economy." In *The Voluntary Nonprofit Sector: An Economic Analysis*, edited by Burton A. Weisbrod. Lexington, Mass.: Lexington Books, Heath, 1977, pp. 51-76.

Wenner, Lettie McSpadden. *The Environmental Decade in Court.* Bloomington: Indiana University Press, 1982.

———. "Interest Group Litigation and Environmental Policy." *Policy Studies Journal* 11 (1983): 671-83.

———. "Judicial Oversight of Environmental Deregulation." In *Environmental Policy in the 1980s: Reagan's New Agenda*, edited by Norman J. Vig and Michael E. Kraft. Washington, D.C.: Congressional Quarterly Press, 1984, pp. 181-99.

Wilbur, Sanford R. *The California Condor, 1966-1976: A Look at Its Past and Future.* U.S. Fish and Wildlife Service, North American Fauna No. 72. Washington, D.C.: Government Printing Office, 1978.

Williams, Ted. "The Fur Still Flies." *Audubon*, January 1984, pp. 28-31.

Wilson, Edward O. *Biophilia.* Cambridge, Mass.: Harvard University Press, 1984.

Wilson, Graham K. *Interest Groups in the United States.* New York: Oxford University Press, 1981.

Wilson, James Q. "The Politics of Regulation." In *The Politics of Regulation*, edited by James Q. Wilson. New York: Basic Books, 1980, pp. 357-94.

Wolf, Charles, Jr. "A Theory of Non-Market Failure." *Public Interest*, no. 55 (Spring 1979): 114–33.

Wood, Peter. "Business-Suited Saviors of Nation's Vanishing Wilds." *Smithsonian*, December 1978, pp. 77–84.

Yaffee, Steven Lewis. *Prohibitive Policy: Implementing the Endangered Species Act*. Cambridge, Mass.: MIT Press, 1982.

——— . "Using Non-Profit Organizations to Manage Public Lands." In *Transactions of the Forty-eighth North American Wildlife and Natural Resources Conference*. Washington, D.C.: Wildlife Management Institute, 1983, pp. 413–22.

Yancey, Richard K. "Implications of International Conventions on Management of Living Resources." In *Transactions of the Forty-fifth North American Wildlife and Natural Resources Conference*. Washington, D.C.: Wildlife Management Institute, 1980, pp. 38–43.

Young, Dennis R. "Entrepreneurship and the Behavior of Nonprofit Organizations." In *Nonprofit Firms in a Three Sector Economy*, edited by Michelle J. White. *COUPE Papers on Public Economics*, vol. 6. Washington, D.C.: Urban Institute, 1981, pp. 135–62.

Ziegler, Harmon, and Michael Baer. *Lobbying: Interaction and Influence in American State Legislatures*. Belmont, Calif.: Wadsworth, 1969.

Index

About the Author

JAMES A. TOBER is a member of the faculty at Marlboro College, Marlboro, Vermont, where he has taught economics and environmental policy since 1973. In 1979–1980 and 1986–87 he held visiting appointments to the Program on Non-Profit Organizations, Institution for Social and Policy Studies, Yale University. Dr. Tober's previous publications include a related book, *Who Owns the Wildlife? The Political Economy of Conservation in Nineteenth-Century America* (Westport, Conn.: Greenwood, 1981). He holds a B.A. from the University of California at Berkeley and an M. Phil. and Ph.D. in economics from Yale University.